Developmental
MANAGEMENT

EUROPEAN STRATEGIC ALLIANCES

Developmental Management
General Editor: Ronnie Lessem

Foundations of Business
Ivan Alexander

Greening Business
John Davis

Ford on Management
*Henry Ford**

Integrative Management
Pauline Graham

Charting the Corporate Mind
*Charles Hampden-Turner**

Executive Leadership
Elliott Jaques and Stephen D. Clement

The Rise of NEC
Koji Kobayashi

Transcultural Management
Albert Koopman

Developmental Management
Ronnie Lessem

Total Quality Learning
Ronnie Lessem

Managing the Developing Organization
Bernard Lievegoed

Managing in the Information Society
Yoneji Masuda

The Great European Illusion
Alain Minc

Managing Your Self
Jagdish Parikh

Conceptual Toolmaking
Jerry Rhodes

Organizing Genius
Paul Thorne

European Strategic Alliances
Sabine Urban and Serge Vendemini

* *For copyright reasons this edition is not available in the USA*

Developmental MANAGEMENT

European Strategic Alliances

Co-operative Corporate Strategies in the New Europe

SABINE URBAN AND SERGE VENDEMINI

Translated by Roy Ingleton

WITH A FOREWORD BY RONNIE LESSEM

BLACKWELL Business

First published 1992

Blackwell Publishers
108 Cowley Road
Oxford OX4 1JF
UK

Three Cambridge Center
Cambridge, Massachusetts 02142
USA

British Library Cataloguing in Publication Data
A CIP catalogue record for this book is available from the British Library.

Library of Congress Cataloging in Publiction Data
Urban, Sabine M.–L.
European strategic alliances: cooperative corporate strategies in the new Europe / Sabine Urban and Serge Vendemini: translated by Roy Ingleton; with a foreword by Ronnie Lessem.
p. cm.—(Developmental management)
Includes index.
1. Strategic alliances (Business)—European Economic Community countries. 2. Europe 1992. I. Vendemini, Serge. II. Title.
III. Series.
HD4140.5.U73 1992
658′.044—dc20 91–35310 CIP
ISBN 0–631–186212 (alk. paper)

Typeset in 11 on 13pt Ehrhardt
by Hope Services (Abingdon) Ltd.
Printed in Great Britain by
T. J. Press Ltd., Padstow, Cornwall

This book is printed on acid-free paper

Contents

Foreword: European Strategic Alliances

by Ronnie Lessem

ICL buys half of Bell Atlantic Arm in Europe

ICL, the UK based computer company which is owned by Fujitsu of Japan, has bought a 50% share in the European computer service operation of Bell Atlantic, the US telephone company. ICL said that the purchase would strengthen its continental European operations and allow it to service computers provided by other manufacturers. The purchase follows ICL's acquisition, last year, of Nokia Data, the information systems arm of Nokjia of Finland.

The jointly held company, Bell Atlantic Customer Services International, will have its headquarters in London, though 60% of its sales come from continental Europe. The joint company will be headed by Mr Tom Vassiliades, chief executive officer of Bell Atlantic Business Systems, who said that his company would benefit from ICL's infrastructure and reputation in Europe. ICL operates in 18 European countries. Mr John Proctor, ICL's director of services, said that the purchase was part of the group's recognition that services and software had become a more attractive business than computer manufacturing.

This extract from the *Financial Times* of 26 July 1991, sketches the context for *European Strategic Alliances*. While mergers and acquisitions of the old, primal, acquisitive kind came in the 1980s and have, to a significant extent, gone in the 1990s, strategic alliances of the developmental variety are here to stay. Yet all too few people are aware of their full scope and significance. What Urban and Vendemini have done in this book is to delineate the nature and extent of 'co-operative corporate strategies' in a way which has never been done before. In so doing they have fundamentally, and indeed developmentally, transformed the subject matter of what has hitherto been termed, notably by Michael Porter[1] 'competitive strategy'.

As I indicated in my own book in this series, *Developmental*

Management,[2] when a company, an economy, or indeed a whole society, evolves from its entrepreneurial base towards a more 'scientifically' based approach to management it comes to focus less on competition and more on co-ordination. Competitive strategy, in effect, becomes co-operative strategy, for the company; and European bureaucracy begins to supplant national sovereignty, for the country. Realistically speaking, while Italy or Spain retains its sense of national identity, a pan-European identity emerges as a higher-order phenomenon.

In fact the developmental manager, in tune with the European times, has evolved to the point of understanding the value of competition through co-operation. For him or her it is 'co-operative strategy', rather than corporate or competitive strategy, that occupies pride of place. Why should this be? Why, indeed, should Urban and Vendemini's book be of such pathbreaking significance?

Developing in Phases

Bernard Lievegoed, the leading Dutch organizational psychologist, cites three major phases in the growth and development of any social organism.[3] For the firm, he identifies these stages as 'pioneering', 'scientific' and 'integrated'. For the individual, he cites respectively youth, adulthood and maturity: whereas youth is a time of exploration, and adulthood one of consolidation, maturity or midlife is a time for renewal.

Let us return to the case of ICL. In the early days some pioneering computer buffs got together and created a variety of technology-based enterprises. One competed with the other – to the death! In due course a phase of consolidation ensued during which these enterprises were brought together under a common ICL umbrella. This was the time of rationalization. Co-ordination supplanted competition as a guiding principle – but without ever precluding the workings of competition within the new phase.

The same process applies to the individual as to the organization. Having sown your wild oats in your youth, you seek to establish yourself, to consolidate your position, to mark out a place for yourself in society. The famous SWOT analysis, whereby you analyse your strengths and your weaknesses, your opportunities and threats, can at this stage be applied just as easily to yourself as to your organization.

This is a severely rational phase of development during which you concentrate your energies, focus your attention, get rid of the extraneous bits of your business and, in Tom Peters' terms, 'stick to the knitting'.[4] Corporate strategy, as a business discipline, allied with long-range planning, is born out of this rational attitude. The same goes for planning at the national level. In fact the very development of the nation state over the past few centuries exemplifies such a process of consolidation.

Interestingly enough, over the course of the past forty to fifty years, Western Europe has been gradually outgrowing this 'adult' phase of development. By way of contrast, the East European countries, thanks to perestroika, have been inclined simultaneously to return to their pioneering and parochial roots (as with the Serbs and the Croats in Yugoslavia), to consolidate as nation states (as in Czechoslovakia) and to co-operate (as in the states of the former Soviet Union). The developmental process is full of chaotic processes, bifurcations and dissipative structures along the evolutionary way.

Midlife, then, as a developmental stage for the individual, the corporation or the nation, involves simultaneously a linking back to roots – origination – and a joining of forces with bits of yourself which have hitherto been neglected – association. For example, Great Britain, originally formed out of a mixture of Celts from continental Europe, Danes and Vikings from the Nordic countries, Normans from France and Saxons from Germany, is now, hesitantly, forging new links with its original heritage. In linking back, moreover, it is also associating anew with its previously 'foreign' neighbours. The EC – and prospectively, as the French philosopher–businessman Alain Minc has indicated, Gorbachev's 'common European home' – is becoming the newly enlarged transnational association, supplanting the nation state.[5]

At an individual level, the process of renewal takes place when cultural, religious, attitudinal and behavioural aspects which have been neglected in earlier phases of the person's life become newly incorporated. This proccss of potential association, and even integration, is heralded by the proverbial midlife crisis. A successful resolution of such a crisis involves a process whereby the individual learns how to bring previously competing elements within the self, such as a technical versus a social orientation towards work, into co-operation with one another. If we return to the example of ICL–Fujitsu, we see that two previously competing companies, separated by huge expanses of land and ocean, are now co-operating. Moreover, this co-operative process is being extended in order to bring together different but associated products and markets.

It is within this context, reflected in the proliferating joint ventures of our day, that this book is set. The fact that one of its authors, Sabine Urban, is French, while the other, Serge Vendemini, is of Italian origin, is itself significant. Moreover, the fact that this first conceptually coherent and meticulously documented work on co-operative corporate strategies comes from Europe, where the world's first transnational community is taking shape, can be no surprise.

Towards A European Approach to Strategy

Corporate Strategy

Concepts of corporate and competitive strategy were originally, perhaps inevitably, developed in America, the veritable laboratory of management thinking, at least for the past seventy years. When I was at Harvard Business School, in the late 1960s, so called 'long-range planning' was in its infancy. Probably the first book on the subject, published by the associate editor of the *Harvard Business Review* in the 1950s, proclaimed that 'Planning symbolizes the purposefulness of modern management. Increasingly, the modern business manager wants to have a hand in moulding, rather than simply reacting to the future.'[6]

Interestingly, the conceptual foundations of corporate strategy were subsequently laid by Americans with a Germanic background, particularly by Peter Drucker, George Steiner and Igor Ansoff; and it became the ultra-rational managerial approach. Ansoff, the best known of the strategic thinkers in the 1960s and 1970s, stressed that the 'strategic problem is concerned with establishing an impedance match between the firm and its environment'.[7]

Competitive Strategy

In the 1980s, however, as America spearheaded the movement back to business basics, a more aggressive, Anglo-Saxon approach to strategy formulation emerged, with Michael Porter as the driving force behind it. 'The essence of formulating competitive strategy, he asserted, 'is relating a company to its environment. The key aspect of the firm's environment is the industry or industries in which it competes. The goal of competitive strategy is to attain a position in the industry where the company can best defend itself against these forces or influence them in its favour.'[8]

Whereas the Germanic-American rational approach to corporate strategy was less aggressively oriented than the more primal Anglo-Saxon approach to competitive strategy, both orientations separated the firm from its environment. In that respect both remained firmly attached to the classical, Newtonian world view, where subject (the firm) and object (the environment) are split apart.

Charting the Corporate Mind

The fundamental breakthrough in strategic thinking has come from Charles Hampden-Turner. The philosophical tradition on which Hampden-Turner draws is the existential.[9] Existentialism, which took strongest root in France and in the Nordic countries of Europe, focuses on the problematic character of the human (and hence managerial or corporate) situation, in which man or enterprise is continually confronted with diverse possibilities from which to choose, and based upon which he or it may project a future life or business.

The issue thus becomes one of individuating, in every concrete situation, the real possibilities offered to the manager or enterprise. Among the risks attached, the greatest is that of individual or organizational degradation – from a person into a thing, or from proactivity into reactivity – by virtue of alienation from the physical, social or economic reality in which the individual or enterprise is engaged. To the extent that the individual manager or organization engages with his environment, so he or it runs less of a risk of alienation, or degradation. The secret of success in this respect lies within the managerial capacity to resolve the dilemma of separation – between self and other, or between enterprise and environment – through integration. Such integration takes the form not of a SWOT analysis, or of the Boston Matrix, but the kind of circular, interactive process outlined in the figure.

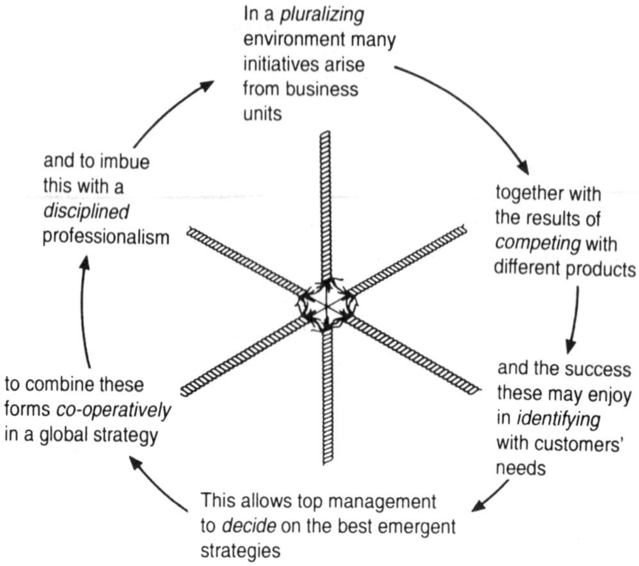

Figure F.1

Co-operative Corporate Strategies

Urban and Vendemini, seeking, like Hampden-Turner, an alternative to the suicidal rat-race of short-term competitive strategies, pursue their co-operative approach to the limit. Their strategic orientation 'is dominated by the conviction that co-operation is preferable to suicidal confrontation and that contemporary society must discover new types of human relations'. This is not some vague homage to an ideal of co-operative behaviour; nor do Urban and Vendemini merely put new wine into old strategic bottles. Their strategic orientation is set within the historic role that they see as Europe's own, leading the subcontinent towards a new and unique social organization, 'one in the tradition of the long European culture, both mercantile and humanist, both scientific and spiritual'.

The two authors start by laying out the political and economic scene within the European Community, setting '1992' in the context of increasing liberalization: 'Intra-European trading has been seen to be simplified and, at the same time, has seen a change in attitudes. It is presented as an opportunity not to be missed.' At the same time they highlight the extraordinary cultural diversity that Europe contains and the strategic challenges that such variety imposes on companies: 'Europe is not merely an economic community; it is also a cultural community which therefore has every chance of entering into fertile co-operative relations, based on middle-of-the-road management styles as compared to the two extremes – Japanese consensus and American aggression.'

Urban and Vendemini then specify three major forms of co-operation, which they term 'adaptive', 'functional' and 'co-ordinative'. With unprecedented thoroughness they assess the legal, technological, organizational and commercial aspects of each of these forms of co-operation. Furthermore, they assess the qualitative and quantitative nature and extent of such partnerships in Germany and Italy. For it is these two counries, each in its very different, culturally influenced way, that have made the most distinctive marks on the scene of strategic co-operation in Europe.

Conclusion

As Europe begins to reassert itself as a third force on the world stage, it is gradually becoming evident that such a force needs to make a qualitative as well as a quantitative impact. After all, the heart of European civilization lies within its richly diverse cultures, and in the artistic and scientific, political and economic forms that have emerged from them.

Accordingly, we shall be looking towards the European subcontinent for a profusion of richly diverse business forms, linked together co-operatively, as well as for a proliferation of new enterprises, vying against one another competitively. While Michael Porter and the conventional strategic wisdom will be very helpful in the latter, Hampden-Turner, and now Urban and Vendemini, will be more useful for the former.

Ronnie Lessem
London, 1992

Notes

1 M. Porter, *Competitive Strategy*, Macmillan, London, 1982.
2 R. Lessem, *Developmental Management*, Blackwell, Oxford, 1990.

EEC

3 B. Lievegoed, *Managing the Developing Organization*, Blackwell, Oxford, 1990.
4 T. Peters and R. Waterman, *In Search of Excellence*, Harper & Row, New York, 1982.
5 A. Minc, *The European Illusion*, Blackwell, Oxford, 1992.
6 D. Ewing (ed.), *Long Range Planning for Management*, Harper & Row, New York, 1958.
7 I. Ansoff, *Corporate Strategy*, McGraw Hill, New York, 1968.
8 Porter, *Competitive Strategy*.
9 C. Hampden-Turner, *Charting the Corporate Mind*, Blackwell, Oxford, 1990.

General Introduction

Exciting things are happening in Europe. Its shape is changing as freedom spreads, arousing interest and curiosity. In 1992 (a date which is not only symbolic for single market Europe but is also the 500th anniversary of the discovery of America by the Italian, Christopher Columbus) the world is discovering a new Europe. As a heading in the May/June 1989 issue of the *Harvard Business Review* put it, 'The old, inefficient, parochial Europe is giving way to an aggressive and integrated market place.'

This European renaissance did not just happen; on the contrary, it is the manifestation of a deliberately willed response to the industrial challenge posed at the close of the twentieth century, a period distinguished by the impressive growth in the power of Japan and the 'dragons' which surround it, posing a threat to the domination of the United States and the American dollar.

At the same time we are witnessing a real technological revolution which is forcing firms to incorporate changes and complexities into their development strategies and their management styles. They must adapt quickly, locate new reservoirs of business competence and sources of competitiveness; they must learn to combat fiercer forms of competition generated by a curious mixture of market forces and industrial policies, of natural selection and strategic manipulation.

Businesses are faced with great changes, fundamental transformations in the political landscape, in economic systems, in scientific and technical knowledge and in ethical values; more than this, they are faced with danger in the form of global economic war. Businesses must respond, must get organized; the strengths they possess must be consolidated – but what form should this consolidation take? Should they take over the competition or come to terms with their rivals? Attack in the hope of winning or seek friendly alliances? Increase their strength so as to be able to combat the enemy more efficiently or find a way to complement the activities of other companies in order to build enduring partnerships and increase mutual profitability?

Such are the central questions of the debate. This study aims to present a number of possible answers and the reasoning behind them. Its dominant theme is the conviction that collaboration is preferable to suicidal confrontation and that contemporary society must discover new types of human relations. An intensified quest for excellence (in the sense exemplified by Thomas Peters and Robert Waterman, authors of the 1982 best-seller *In Search of Excellence* which has become required bedside reading among the business community) would involve a cost in human terms which is difficult to calculate, approaching the 'pathology of excellence'.[1] In other words, we feel we can claim to have found that the pursuit of co-operative alliances as opposed to competitive dominance can be justified.

What does this mean? What does this concept of co-operative strategies imply?

First of all, we focus on co-operative agreements between enterprises, aimed at setting up activities in concert, in which the parties concerned operate on an equal footing, based on mutual respect for each other's individuality. Under the banner of a co-operative agreement we include such diverse arrangements as supply or distribution agreements, subcontracting, joint production, administration, engineering, research, etc. On the other hand, we exclude non-joint activities (such as hostile takeover bids and stock exchange 'raids') and those aimed at modifying the balance of power (portfolio investments resulting in a restructuring of share capital, the acquisition of disproportionate controlling interests, domination by asset holdings).

Whatever their purpose, inter-firm collaborative agreements assume a pooling of resources, whether human, technological, productive, informational or financial. This pooling of factors leads *de facto* to a mutual commitment (i.e. an 'alliance'), to the reciprocal dependence of the partners, counterbalanced by joint authority in decision-making methods, patterns of operation and the monitoring of the activities undertaken. The creation of a joint subsidiary in the form of a co-enterprise (or 50–50 joint venture) is the most tangible form this concerted organization could take.

In the second place, we contend that such co-operative agreements must have a strategic dimension. Not every contract for international purchasing, supply, sales or service will lead to the establishment of a co-operative situation. Transitory contractual relations are essentially dominated by anonymous market forces. Co-operative undertakings, on the other hand, are the expression of a more fundamental willingness to influence the decisive variables of company management. They are aimed, for example, at tempering the competitive environment (by organizing access to markets, by reducing the number of competitors, by bringing into play participatory channels of influence or decision-making) or at counterbalancing the relative strengths and weaknesses of the companies concerned (through quantitative increase in resources by pooling, sharing know-how, making common use of plant and equipment, risk-sharing, facilitating flexibility and saving adjustment time).

The aim of a properly implemented co-operative agreement is not to reduce creative initiatives but to co-ordinate them within a perspective of collective gain. The strategic concept of co-operation arises, in short, from the seldom admitted but keenly sought principle of 'organized competition'. The vigorous development and growing complexity of market phenomena and organizations effectively makes control of the economy solely by the laws of the market-place both inefficient (because they are overly concerned with the short term) and dangerous (because of the financial and social upheavals they produce).

Accordingly, the concepts of 'cut-throat' or 'pure and perfect' competition need to be modified, sobered down. This may be effected by national governments (the states) or by supranational bodies (the EC). It may also be effected by the players at the grass roots of economic development; in other words, by firms, who may decide, for example, to enter into strategic alliances. These inter-firm arrangements have an advantage over other types of controlled organization directed at state level in that they follow the principle of decentralized responsibility and are thus highly effective in adapting to change.

The formation of co-operative alliances, thus defined, is particularly relevant to contemporary Europe because the single market will destabilize the conditions under which European firms operate, as shown in part 1 of this book. The arrival of 1992 will be accompanied by a reorganization of markets – open markets and markets controlled at Community level – which will have the effect of imposing on firms new styles of growth and revitalized managerial skills.

Various possible responses are open to firms facing this challenge. One such response is to opt for the pursuit of co-operative strategies, and in part 2 we set out the reasons in favour of this choice. Here we present, on the basis of an analysis of effective practices (examined by means of investigation and interview), a conceptual model of collaborative alliances.

However sound these alliances may be, they will not necessarily enable firms to avoid the risks inherent in any undertaking. This is why part 3 is devoted to the conditions for the success of co-operative strategies. What measures must be taken to ensure the effectiveness of the alliance, or, in other words, to meet the expectations of one's partners? And what precautions should be taken to ensure that the legitimate interests of the parties concerned are protected?

Note

1 See the study by the Laboratoire du Changement Social, Université de Paris IX et Paris VII on behalf of MIRE (Mission Interministérielle de Recherche Expérimentale): Nicole Aubert and Vincent de Gaulejac, *Le Coût de l'excellence*, Seuil, Paris, 1991.

PART I

Management Methods for the New Europe

Introduction to Part I

Ever since the Berlin Wall toppled on 9 November 1989, Europe has been caught up in a kind of whirlwind. It has been difficult to determine the destabilizing effect of this force – or, on the other hand, the strength of its stimulus for creativity. The enthusiasm, emotion and ambitious speculation expressed by some are countered by the calculations and doubts of others.

The historic role of the subcontinent of Europe seems to be taking on a new dynamism. 'Europe 1992' could be described as a burst of energy on the part of twelve industrialized European nations in order to combat a relative decline manifested by such symptoms as:

- a fall in international market shares;
- an over-concentration of industrial production on products which provide low levels of added value;
- inadequate investment in production and creativity;
- low productivity;
- disquieting underemployment.

The causes of this dysfunction have been identified as follows:

- fragmented markets which hinder the various European national economies from specializing according to their respective comparative advantages;
- a system of controlled or regulated prices in many sectors;
- lack of market and company flexibility;
- protectionism, disguised to a greater or lesser degree, and various subventions which hamper the efficient allocation of resources.

Faced with what is doubtless a somewhat hasty, dogmatic diagnosis which can scarcely be termed reassuring, a response is being orchestrated by certain politicians, liberal economists and manufacturers, effectively supported by the media. The European Community authorities are being stirred into action; it is evident that the 'non-Europe' option is a costly one.[1]

It has been argued that a real, effective market is to be set up. International trade will increase the economic links among the Twelve, as will cross-company investments and a vast network of contractual alliances. There must be no more internal frontiers in Europe; it must become the focus of a new socio-political solidarity, coupled with a regenerated, powerful and aggressive industrial dynamism.

The logic of the process by which this new state of affairs comes into being deserves close examination, for it involves major adjustments, the immediate implications of which are not easy to accept. Ultimate success calls for short-term sacrifices in various areas, the relinquishing of vested interests, reorganization of every kind, recentring of activities and locations, new ways of thinking, new types of support; in other words, relations between public authorities and companies, and inter-company networks, are inexorably becoming both more co-operative and more complex.

One might also question the actual effectiveness of measures announced or already implemented with 1992 in prospect. In the social sciences, and especially in economics, it is indeed rare that a given effect results from a single cause, or that a process which has been set in motion brings only the desired and desirable results. If a dominant trend (in this case, economic liberalization) is to be followed because of its overall effectiveness, it is important nevertheless not to lose sight of the unintended, undesirable effects of its pursuit. The considerable risks engendered by the increased interpenetration of industrial economies, coupled with a spectacular acceleration in technological development, bear witness to the need for responses along the lines of *organizing competition* and *co-ordinating activities*.

The following chapters, then, set out first to explain how the technical and political steps taken to set up a single European market will impinge upon the remaining 'multiple' markets,[2] and secondly to lay bare the effects of these changes on company managements. Will they have to devise new strategies; to formulate 'Euro-strategies'?

Notes

1 See Commission of the European Communities, *Research on the Cost of Non-Europe*, 16 vols, Luxembourg, 1988, (the Cecchini Report); Alexis Jacquemin, *Economie industrielle européenne*, 2nd edn, Dunod, Paris, 1979.

2 This expression is taken from the title of the work published by the Observatoire des Statégies Industrielles, under the direction of Guy Crespy, 'Marché unique, marché multiple: strategies européennes des acteurs industriels', Economica, Paris, 1990.

I

Europe 1992: Reorganizing the Markets

Europe is so diverse and so changeable that it resists comprehension. In turn cradle of civilization and world war, centre of domination and conquest and arena of internal conflict, Europe is now dedicated to becoming a purposeful community. Having charted its evolution slowly but surely from six to nine to twelve, its significant move to twelve-plus with the addition of the former East Germany looks towards the future incorporation of the other European nations.

A step at a time, the European project for the end of the millennium takes shape. It expresses the weariness felt by Europeans for a past in which, according to the historian Fernand Braudel, 'Europe is both heaven and hell, a mixture of brilliant centuries and dark centuries. Throughout its history it has dominated and exploited the world, making use of both crime and inspired achievements.' The time has come to seek a more serene, a more convivial venture. Enrique Baron, President of the European Parliament, suggests that the 'abduction of the future' should lead Europe on to a new and unique social organization, one in the long tradition of European culture, both mercantile and humanist, both scientific and spiritual.[1] This underlines a willingness for commercial Europe to follow the lead of a social and democratic Europe, for the welfare of the people to take precedence over individual or national egoism. The route for collaboration on a European scale has been drawn.

The European Community is already making its presence felt in all the various spheres of social life: political, strategic, scientific, cultural, monetary and economic. But it does so using a variable geometry mechanism; the leading nations progress at differing speeds. The path is not an easy one.

Commerce would appear, by its very nature, to be the sector most easy to integrate. Like money, trading has a long tradition of internationalism. The common organization of production (the Common Agricultural Policy or the harmonization of standards, for example) follows the move to agree a common product policy in certain sectors, such as aerospace, armaments and semi-conductors. The apparatus being set up at Community level prescribes new methods of operation to be imposed on those participating in the economic and social life of all European regions as well as, beyond Europe, on our partners or competitors in the rest of the world.

The measures enacted with a view to 1992 and beyond represent a significant gamble. They are going to reshape the environment of businesses. To what extent will the apparatus adopted contravene the current rules of the game and result in the cards being re-dealt? The reply given in this chapter comes in two phases, which examine in turn the foreseeable effects of market mechanisms, which have their own logic, and the effects of Community regulations, designed to supplement the operation of these mechanisms.

Open Homogenized Markets

The Single European Act, which came into force on 1 July 1987 following ratification by all the European Community's member states, underlines the wish of those members to overcome the remaining elements of fragmentation within the European economic area.

Simplified decision-making procedures and an enhanced political commitment should lead to the effective realization of the common market, already strongly recommended in Article 2 of the 1957 Treaty of Rome which created the EEC. The initial 1957 mission has now become an absolute priority. The completely free circulation of all goods and services, of persons and capital is required by 1 January 1993. Liberalism is being set up triumphantly as a model.

In its wake, and as a direct result, the protectionist interventions of national governments stand condemned. Europe wants to be 'single', with its frontiers moved to the outer limits so as to protect a new common identity.

The Climate of Liberalism: Increased Competition and a Prevailing State of Flux

The markets have been declared open. They are there to be taken or retaken. All Europeans are in a position to compete; but they are not alone, protected by the walls of a fortress. Quite the contrary. Changes arouse interest and the external players will not remain mere spectators of this great 'internal' market, this highly promising, frontierless expanse of Europe.

The construction of the new Europe is now sufficiently advanced for it to be possible to describe what form this freely accessible expanse will take – and in part already has taken. Without embarking on a detailed analysis, we simply recall here the tenor of the principal technical measures put in place by the European Community as a preliminary to grasping what will stem from them.[2]

What is moving, or will move, freely

All movements that affect the markets are covered by the terms goods, services, people and capital. All goods and services should be able to move freely, without restriction.

The *free movement of goods* has been largely stimulated by the application of the provisions of the Treaty of Rome. Customs duties and quantitative restrictions have been eliminated but measures having similar effect remain. Moreover, technical obstacles (especially non-tariff barriers and fiscal barriers which entail checks at national frontiers and distort competition) remain in place.

With 1992 in prospect, what needs to be achieved is the definitive removal of remaining obstacles. The simplification of customs procedures, the computerization of statistical data and the drawing up of common policies, especially in the field of public health, are steps towards this target.

So far as customs are concerned, the preparatory work has concentrated on:

- the implementation of a common customs tariff;
- the adoption of a standard nomenclature listing all various types of goods circulating throughout EC territory;
- the definition of the customs value of goods;

- the concept of origin of goods (which complies with a distinct definition, depending on whether the importation is from a country which enjoys a preferential regime, or not).

As regards intra-Community trading, efforts have hitherto been concentrated on the simplification of customs controls and formalities (creation of a Community transit system and the introduction of a 'single administrative document'). They must now be addressed to the total elimination of internal frontiers, in particular through the computerization of administrative procedures.

In the field of health safeguards, the aims of the Community are equally ambitious, being directed at limiting veterinary and plant health checks on products. It is proposed that the products themselves be checked at their point of departure only, and that the assigned certificates be checked at the final destination only. This system presupposes the adoption of many common standards; this is no simple matter and progress in this area has been slow.

The general elimination of technical barriers constitutes the second aspect of free access to markets. It is probably also the most delicate aspect, for technical consraints on trade are numerous and widely practised. These barriers take the form of a huge variety of regulations, in the guise of measures aimed at safeguarding health or safety, which restrict access to national markets to local products and those imported in accordance with particular requirements covering, for example, the composition, shape, colour, presentation or labelling of those products. They tend to hamper the free movement of goods across the territory of the EC and protect national manufacturers. The struggle to eliminate these practices is proving difficult as considerable and conflicting vested interests are involved. The question is one of offering the consumer the widest possible choice of products (the principle accepted in the famous 1979 'Cassis de Dijon' ruling of the European Court of Justice) and, at the same time, protecting the user by requiring an acceptable level of safety and conserving a certain level of quality of the environment.

Agreement has been reached on the need to eliminate existing obstacles and to prevent the appearance of new ones. In pursuit of these ends, future legislation will make a clear distinction between those areas where European harmonization is called for (because it has been deemed essential from the point of view of health and safety) and those where the mutual recognition of national standards and rules will be sufficient (enabling specific industrial traditions and know-how to be respected).

'Technical' measures tend to be supplemented by intra-Community 'administrative' provisions, aimed at increasing the price of imports in a partisan manner. To compensate for the agreed prohibition on quantitative restrictions, manufacturers and their national lobbies have thought up measures having equivalent effect, namely, encumbering commercial transactions with additional costs in order to dissuade the purchasers of foreign products. All bureaucratic conditions devised to increase the required formalities (such as certificates of origin, certificates of quality, approvals, etc.), and frontier controls have the effect of slowing down the movement of goods, making it more costly and less appealing, if not impossible.

The agricultural foodstuffs sector has provided several notorious illustrative examples of quality disputes, including the 'purity of beer' imposed by the Germans under the provisions of the sixteenth-century Bavarian enactment; the definition of 'chocolate' which is not the same in the United Kingdom as it is in Belgium, the former accepting more vegetable fat in the composition of its chocolate than the latter; and the description of pasta, of necessity made with hard (durum) wheat flour as far as the Italians are concerned, whereas the Germans accept the manufacture of pasta with soft wheat. Many more could be cited. These quality disputes are invalid under the provisions of the Treaty of Rome (Article 36). The European Court of Justice's case law is strict with respect to the interpretation of these provisions. It also specifies that, from now on, it will be up to the importing member state to prove that any prohibitive measures employed are justified on health grounds.

The elimination of fiscal frontiers is the Community's term for the third panel of the triptych concerning the free movement of goods. This does not mean that national tax systems will be harmonized or consolidated by the end of 1992. Because of the uncompromising nature of each state's legislation and the real interests associated with it, the aim is limited to the removal of the more blatant differences which are likely to hamper the realization of the single market.

It is evident that, in Europe, the 'frontiers' are the boundaries which separate two or more sovereign states. The elimination of these frontiers must of necessity lead to the standardization of the law on either side of each frontier.

In the case of indirect taxation this means – putting oneself in the position of the taxpayer – that the rules of tax assessment and the rates of taxation must be consolidated in such a manner that no manufacturer or consumer has an advantage or is placed at a disadvantage because of the place where he or she lives, works or is a consumer. At the present time there are considerable differences across the twelve countries

- in the tax payment structures (proportion of direct and indirect taxation in the total);
- in the systems of VAT imposition (standard rate, reduced rate, higher rate, depending on the type of goods);
- in the levels of taxation imposed.

From the point of view of international competitiveness, these discrepancies are significant. In practice, the principle of VAT imposition currently used (i.e. payable in the country where the product is consumed and at the rate applicable in that country) actually benefits the economic agents of those states with a high level of indirect taxation as opposed to those with a high level of direct taxation. The manufacturing costs of the former (which pay a lower level of direct taxation) have every chance of being lower than the others. In other words, the disparities among national taxation structures are a major factor in distortions of competition.

It will not be an easy or rapid matter to put an end to these disparities. The stakes and social interests involved are enormous, both from the point of view of the taxpayer and from that of the states themselves (VAT currently represents more than 40 per cent of France's tax receipts as against 25 per cent in Germany and 15 per cent in the United Kingdom). It has therefore been accepted that the unifying logic according to which VAT would be imposed in the country in which the goods are produced with effect from 1993 will not be applied until later (the period of the delay has yet to be determined). No matter; the idea has been introduced and supported in the wake of the EC directive dated 17 May 1977 which deals with the generalization of the VAT system in each of the twelve member states. The progressive penetration of Community law into national legislations is rapidly increasing. There is no doubt that there is a positive Community vigour being directed at VAT harmonization.

The range of VAT rates will be reduced. At the moment it is very wide, ranging from zero (on certain foodstuffs in the UK and Denmark) to 36 per cent (higher rate in Italy) see figure 1.1. The

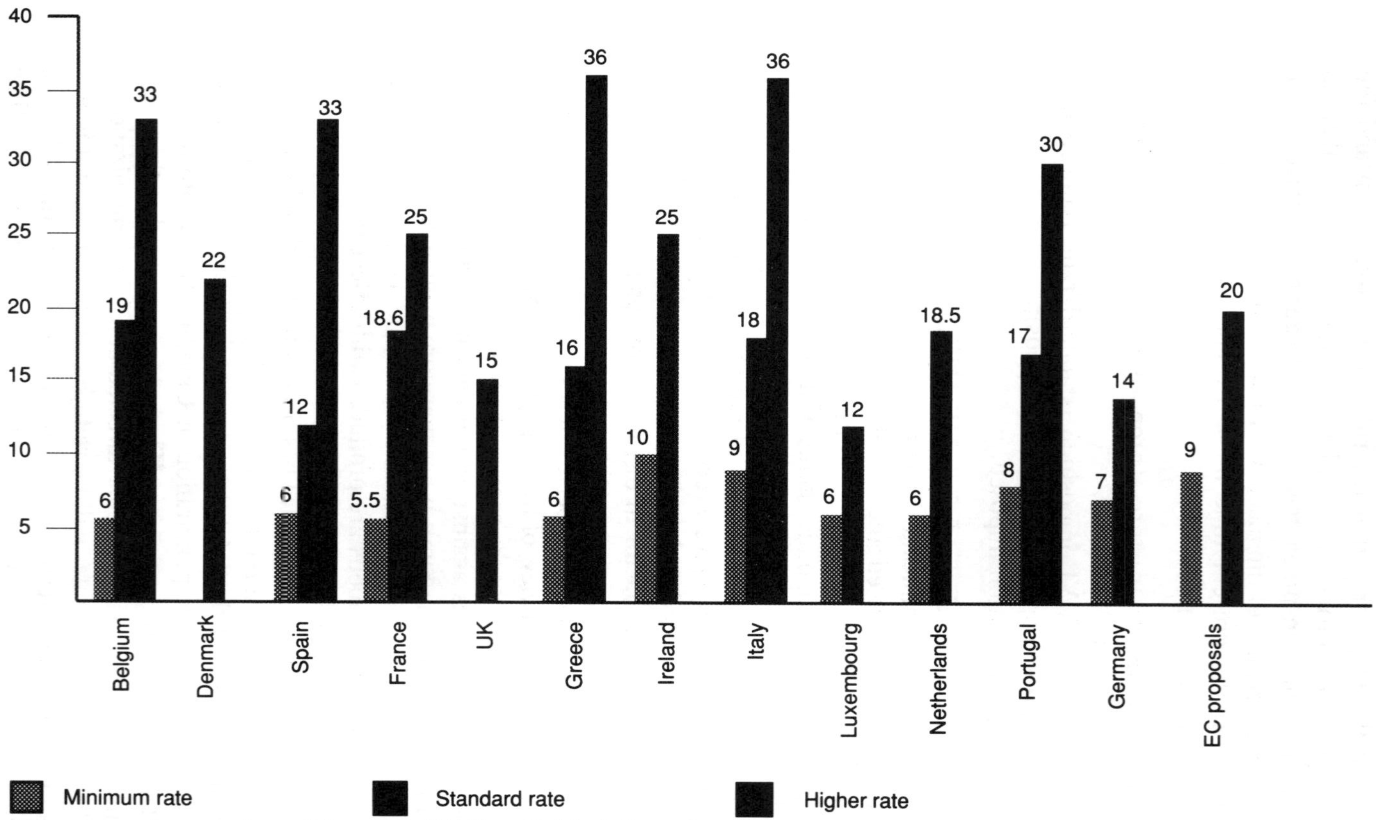

Figure 1.1 A comparison of the rates of VAT applied by EC member states at 1 January 1990
Source: Eurostat.

Brussels Commission proposes to 'harmonize' VAT rates (the stage prior to standardization) on the basis of a reduced rate for essential items (varying between 4 per cent and 9 per cent) and a standard rate for other goods, falling within a band of 14–20 per cent.

It stands to reason that the persistence of these disparities will not permit the immediate removal of frontier controls as desired by the principle of the single market, but the lifting of frontier controls will nevertheless be brought about progressively.

Major changes need to be made not merely at the territorial frontiers, but also in each state's budgetary policies. For good or ill, the states will have to adjust their fiscal systems to the European model. The countries which will have to make the greatest efforts to adapt are obviously those which deviate most from the Community's harmonization proposals: Belgium, France, Greece, Italy, Portugal and Spain. The systems of Germany and The Netherlands, on the other hand, already fall within the proposed limits. Their economies can therefore be smoothly prepared for integration into the single market without having to undergo the political tribulations and tensions which will inevitably be provoked in the other countries by required tax adjustment.

Apart from taxes on production (VAT), the Community is, of course, working towards the alignment of specific forms of indirect taxation applied to certain products (excise duties): tobacco, alcohol, wine, fuel and mineral oils. This too is a sensitive area, since fiscal power, like the right to mint money, remains an essential bastion of national sovereignty. Consumers, too, are sensitive to the rate of tax on (and therefore the prices of) these products which contribute to the quality of life. For the moment, the Commission is proposing a prudent policy of consolidation of the existing situation ('standstill') in order to avoid at least any expansion of the excise duty base, but the principle adopted is that of the general application of a single tax system per product over the whole of the Community, quoted in Ecus (19.5 Ecus for 1,000 cigarettes, 17 Ecus per hectolitre of beer, etc).

A single market naturally assumes that every person – both individuals and legal entities – from one of the Community countries may move around, settle, consume and work wherever he, she or it wishes within this area of Europe. In other words, it assumes the *free movement of persons*. The bringing into effect of the principle of a 'Citizens' Europe' and a 'Companies' Europe' will involve a great many innovations and changes in customs and practices.

The 'Citizens' Europe' (an expression made fashionable following the European Council meeting at Fontainebleau in 1984) has indeed a symbolic reality since the introduction of a European passport, but it has the particular aim of conferring the following specific rights on the Community citizen.

- Freedom of movement. The freedom to come and go is one of the fundamental rights of every democratic society. It also forms one of the requirements of international order. Every individual must be free to leave his or her country of origin and return there. However, paradoxically, no state is obliged (subject to any agreement to the contrary) to permit foreign nationals to enter its territory.

  The EC gives subjects of the member states rights of immigration in so far as they are wage-earning workers or suppliers of services (the European 'Economic' Community is concerned with 'economic factors'). The objective of giving all Community subjects a general and permanent right of residence in any one of the member states has yet to be achieved.
- The right of establishment: that is to say, the right of Europeans from anywhere in the Community to exercise their profession in any one of the twelve member states.

  This right effectively exists, without discrimination other than that which pertains to public offices – and even here openings occur. The mutual recognition of qualifications (a principle agreed by the Council in December 1988) is a notable one.
- The right to be a protected consumer over the whole of the Community territory.

  The interests of the EC consumer as a purchaser of agricultural products and potential victim of protectionist behaviour are protected. The Community has agreed to proscribe misleading advertisements and the damage caused by defective products, for which manufacturers will be held individually responsible. Recently fresh impetus has been given to finalizing the protection afforded to the European consumer, with relation in particular, to house-to-house canvassing, unfair clauses in contracts, package holidays, after-sale warranties and service, and the electronic transfer of funds, among other things. In short, the protected citizen is going to become increasingly demanding as a consumer.

The concept of the 'Companies' Europe' is aimed at recognizing the right of establishment and the freedom to provide services to industrial or commercial companies. The constitution of a single market presupposes that EC companies may operate everywhere within the EC under equal conditions of competition.

One of the more insidious factors contributing to the present distortions of competition is to be found in the disparity between the various national legal systems which apply to commercial firms. Harmonization in this field is trailing its feet. A common system of company mergers and acquisitions should logically follow in due course.

In the context of 'Companies Europe', the present lack of harmonization in direct taxation looms large.[3] The different rates imposed by each country (see table 1.1) constitute a factor which affects a company's choice of location. From this point of view, the twelve states are in direct competition with one another. In this area as in others, an increased 'European' awareness on the part of these states presupposes a reduction in their national egoisms.

It is obvious that the investment behaviour of companies and individual savers will prompt a movement towards harmonization on the European level because firms' investment choices are directly related to the rate of tax on profits together with the fiscal treatment of reserves, depreciation and appreciation, which in turn affect taxable profits. There is, therefore, a natural temptation for companies to set up in states with low tax pressure.

Moreover, corporation tax cannot be divorced from the tax on dividends or on interests on savings. Treatment which favours distribution of profits or the absence of double taxation is an encouragement for individuals to buy shares and receive dividends in the country of establishment. Under the pressure of open market forces, European states which exert a high direct tax pressure on companies will have to fall into line with states with low tax pressure, or see local investment and savings desert them. The operation of such 'market forces', widely supported by certain countries such as Great Britain and Luxembourg, is nevertheless opposed by other countries, including France, which wish to obtain a 'concerted harmonization' of tax systems, implying reciprocal concessions by each state, rather than a 'spontaneous harmonization' via the blunt instrument of the market. In short, a mean denominator is sought in the first case, whereas in the second there is a tendency to fit in with the lowest common denominator (taxation harmonization to the lowest level).

Table 1.1 Rates of corporate tax and withholding tax within the EC

Country	Corporate tax	Capital gains tax	Withholding tax	
			Dividends (non-treaty withholding tax rate)	Interest (non-treaty withholding tax rate)
	(%)	(%)	(%)	(%)
Belgium	43	21.5	25	25
Denmark	50	50	30	0
France	39 (undistributed)	15–42	25	45
	42 (distributed)			
West Germany	56 (50 from 1 January 1990; undistributed)	56 (50 from 1 January 1990)	25	0
	36 (distributed)	36 (distributed)	25	0
Greece	46	30	42–50	46
Republic of Ireland	43	36–60	0	35
Italy	36	36	32.4	12.5, 15, 30[a]
	16.2 (local tax)	15.2 (local tax)		
Luxembourg	34	34	15	0
Netherlands	35	35	25	0
	40 (on profits up to DFL250,000)			
Portugal	36.5	36.5	20, 25	20, 25[a]
Spain	35	35	20	20
United Kingdom	35	35	0	25

[a] The rate of withholding tax depends on the source of the interest.
Source: *Euro-business Review*, vol. 89, no. 4, p. 39.

The principle of free movement of services and capital complements the unrestricted right of establishment (through a subsidiary, branch, agency or joint venture) accorded to firms. Indeed, the right of establishment allows the partitioning of national markets to persist, since through the application of the national treatment rule, a company set up in a particular country is simply recognized as having the right to carry on business in the same way as a local firm. On the other hand, in the case of unrestricted provision of services, the provider of the services is not necessarily a resident of the country. Legal and fiscal frontiers are banned; supply and demand can be expressed and met throughout the economic community, fully open to competition. A British company can, then, buy and sell services in Italy or Germany, just as if it were set up in those countries, with virtually no restriction.

With effect from 1990 the free movement of services will be ratified and will cause radical changes in the conditions for capitalization in the financial, transport and telecommunication sectors.

Henceforth every financial product legally offered by a financial institution in a member state in which it has its registered office may be offered under the same conditions to the residents of the other member states. In order to clarify the debate, the Community has adopted a directive relating to the keeping of accounts (8 December 1986), a directive concerning the obligations regarding the publication of bank account documents (13 February 1989) and finally a directive concerning a bank's own funds (17 April 1989). Furthermore, in February 1988, the Commission submitted to the Council a draft directive on bank co-ordination, often described, in view of its essential character, as a veritable 'European banking law'.

Many banking operations have achieved mutual recognition among the member states. It will be possible for this to be extended to take account of continual financial innovations. The banking system used as a model for Europe's future is the German style of 'universal bank'.

Without overlooking prudential controls, aimed at ensuring that banks are solvent and at the protection of depositors, the new European economy will undoubtedly have the effect of stimulating inter-bank competition at the Community level. The substantial preparatory measures already being taken are evident. In those countries such as Spain, where numerous small or medium-sized banks coexist, a movement towards concentration has been set in motion in order to arrive at a limited number of establishments capable of operating on the European scale. Furthermore, real pan-European networks of banks and financial institutions are being created in order to provide customers with a wide range of services, densely spread over the whole of the European Community.

European harmonization in the field of insurance is no less important. The principles of responsibility, insurance requirements and the right of establishment of insurance companies are all becoming less national. A directive dated 22 June 1988 is aimed at accelerating the move towards the unrestricted provision of services but the absence of harmonized contract law (with profound differences existing between the Anglo-Saxon common law countries and the Roman law countries) still presents a major difficulty for the insurance sector. This is also a sector which (with the exceptions of the UK and The Netherlands), is traditionally subject to strict state control.

For these reasons the move towards liberalization in insurance is much slower than in banking. However, even in the current situation, greater restructuring initiatives (both national and trans-frontier) between insurance companies have been taken with a view to the single market. In July 1990 the European Commission adopted a draft directive authorizing insurance companies established in the EC to offer non-life policies and to open branches in any EC country. This development is combined with the recent tendency to form conglomerates linking banks and insurance companies.

The financial services field is becoming more and more open. The bringing together of laws on securities, together with the improved integration of European stock markets, have contributed towards this. But the decisive step was the abolition of controls on the international transfer of funds; in other words, the definitive freeing of the movement of capital. Two directives have given this a strong boost: that of 17 November 1982 and that of 24 June 1988. The first of these abolished controls on long-term commercial borrowing (five years or more), security transactions (whether negotiated on the stock exchanges or not) and foreign issues (shares or bonds) made by companies in a member state on the capital markets of another member state.

The second extended the principle of freedom to all capital movements, in particular short-term borrowing, current account and deposit operations, investment in short-term securities (on the money markets), personal loans and the import and export of methods of payment.

Transport services are also going to see a relaxing of national regulations. Of course, there is still no question of a common transport policy; but, bit by bit, significant progress has been made towards the liberalization of the provision of services and the elimination of those factors which pervent competition. Progress up to now has been variable, depending on the type of transport (land, air, sea) and on the member states. But though progress is slow, advances are being made. Europe-wide competition is being propounded, specified. The Europeanization of methods of transport is becoming a reality.

The significant effects of this increasing momentum

The economic environment for European enterprises is going to change radically. They will henceforth have to integrate new data into their strategic considerations and their economic calculations.

Three particularly striking phenomena must be taken into account:

- enhanced trading activity;
- a remodelling of company resources and costs;
- unstable market structure.

The process of integration spontaneously induces the effects of competition creation and trade stimulation.[4] The first years of European construction (the 1960s) were conspicuous for the considerable progress made in freeing trade, in respect of both customs duties and quantitative restrictions, and this freeing of trade has facilitated the expansion of intra-Community commerce and a resultant growth in the European economies.

The new wave of liberalization and integration which characterized the end of the 1980s and the beginning of the 1990s should produce comparable effects. The process in operation is summarized in figure 1.2, which shows the direct, quasi-mechanical effects resulting from the creation of the single European market. It follows a traditional analytical procedure, explaining a company's results or the performance of an economic system in terms of the existing operating structures and the effects on the various parties involved. The reality is illustrated in a more complex manner at a later stage, but for the moment this evident logic suffices to explain how movement is

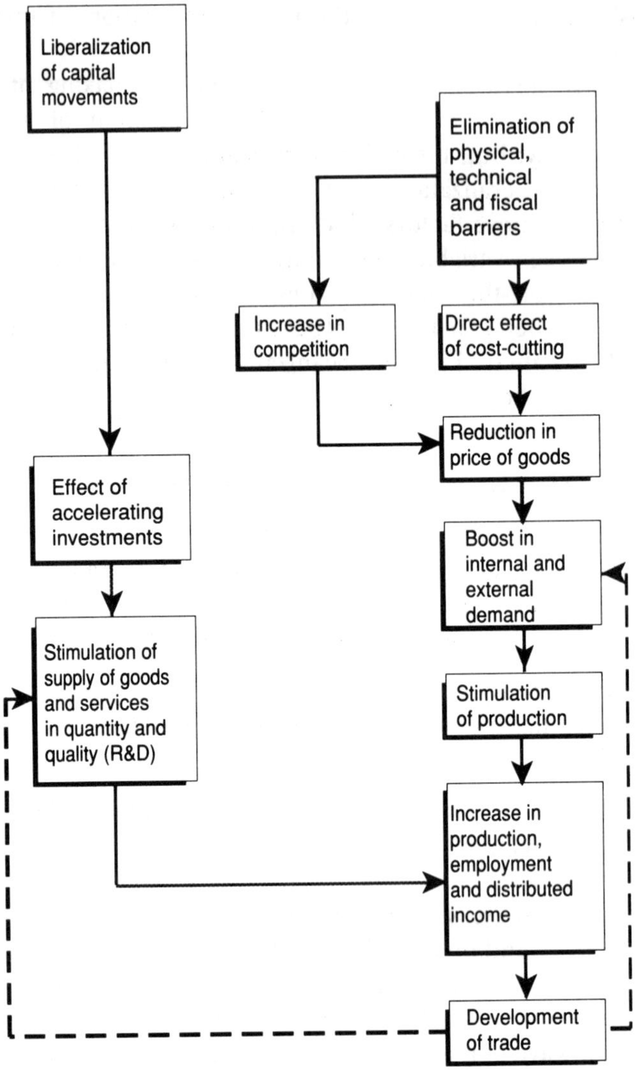

Figure 1.2 The direct effect of the single market on the development of trade
Source: Sabine Urban and Serge Vendemini, CESAG, Strasbourg.

stimulated by the absence of restraints or obstacles. It is in precisely this direction that the single European market is moving.

A second factor which will contribute to the trade development process is the increasing proximity of the markets. Of course, what has changed is not Europe's physical geography, but that of its cultures and mentalities. The scope of knowledge has been extended thanks to the movement of persons, the liberalization of services, the internationalization of the media, the development of means of communication and the dissemination of the resulting great debates or European events. Europeans are getting to know each other, to understand each other better, discovering a new fellowship, ceasing to regard each other as total strangers. Customs and practices are converging, as are consumption habits. At a stroke the European markets seem less distant, less mysterious, less risky. The initiatives of penetration which have been made into these increasingly understood and recognized markets through a structure of increasingly pertinent information are consequently encouraged.

Intra-European trading has been simplified and, at the same time, has seen a change in attitudes. This situation offers an opportunity not to be missed.

This is not to say that the development of mercantile activity is ever achieved without effort. The expenditure of energy is called for because a changing world enables the strongest or the most agile to dominate at the expense of those who rest too tranquilly or too cosily on the positions they have attained, positions which have become illusory. Europe is thus called upon to demonstrate a new conquering spirit, respecting those multiple internal cultural identities which have become component parts of an interdependent whole. The time has probably come to discover a form of liberalism less destructive than the traditional neo-liberalism, which shows signs of running out of steam in the Anglo-Saxon countries. In future, competition will rely on complex *partnership networks*. Thanks to the computerized management which is revolutionizing economies and social relationships, these networks will be one of the decisive keys to success and international competitiveness.

Existing theoretical work demonstrates that, among the economic advantages which are to be expected from the single market, one could number better allocation of resources, reduction in transactional costs, reduction in costs arising out of economies of scale, greater technical efficiency and an increased economic vitality.[5]

The first benefit, a better allocation of resources, will come about through the pricing system. In the Community of the single market competition, the lowering of prices and the standardization of price levels will force firms to be efficient. Only the more productive will survive; and the consumer will profit from this.

The choice by firms of the best centre of operations is also important. In practice, obstacles to intra-Community trade at present force firms to set up at or near the heart of the markets in which they wish to sell their products. In future, the liberalization of trading will enable them to set up in those areas in which costs are lower. All parts of Europe will therefore be able to enjoy an increase in revenue, thanks to the increased scope for comparative advantages of all kinds (wage levels, environmental quality, quality of life, cultural and training levels, etc.).

The second benefit, the reduction in transactional costs, is directly linked to the simplification of procedures. At present, firms which are active across Europe waste a great deal of time (and consequently money) filling in customs forms, modifying their products to make them conform to the standards applied in the various countries, controlling diversified stocks to satisfy administrative requirements, and adjusting the presentation or interpretation of their accounts according to the countries concerned. Liberalization of trading in goods and services and European economic and monetary union will eliminate or reduce these burdens.

The third type of advantage is linked to the new dimension of the European economy: economies of scale may be achieved through the effect of size on manufacturing or marketing units. It will be possible to benefit from the rationalization of processes, the spreading of structural costs or fixed charges (product design, for example) over larger quantities, economies of range, and so on to generate substantial reductions in expenditure, and thus the average cost of products, at least in certain sectors.

Finally, the great European market should stimulate technical efficiency and economic vitality through competition. It is well known that (over-)protected markets lead the suppliers of goods and services to adopt a passive and somnolent attitude, to maintain traditional practices; whereas competition favours reappraisal and encourages improvements of all kinds which foster efficiency, creative imagination and therefore innovation.

Nor is the issue solely one of competition. As will be demonstrated in the pages which follow, it can also be claimed that partnership agreements, if rationally conceived and well managed, enable maximum benefit to be gained from each partner's specific proficiencies and for these to be enriched mutually, with benefits in terms of timescale and costs.[6] In so far as competence is accepted as the deciding factor in international competitiveness, and thus in growth, the importance of strategic alliances and co-operation agreements in the economic renaissance of Europe becomes apparent.

In short, once reallocated to productive use, these freed resources will facilitate the harmonious raising of the general level of consumption and investment in accordance with the macroeconomic equilibrium, especially as regards the stability of prices, the balance of payments and budgetary balances. This will generate gains in collective well-being.

Empirical estimates of the costs involved have been made at the instigation of the European Commission.[7] The following approximate amounts have been calculated:[8]

- direct costs of frontier formalities and associated administrative costs: 1.9 per cent of total intra-Community trade, or around 9 billion Ecus;
- costs borne by industry as a result of identifiable barriers (rules, technical standards, etc.): an average of 2 per cent of production costs, or about 40 billion Ecus;
- gains arising from a better exploitation of the economies of scale: reduction in costs of between 1 per cent and 6 per cent, or about 60 billion Ecus.

The whole picture is summarized in table 1.2.

The impact of the single market through the indirect effects of resource and cost restructuring makes it possible to adjust figure 1.1 as shown in figure 1.3.

It will be noted that the above analysis is strongly imbued with the distorting effects of the paradigm used, namely the competitive market model. Certain variations in the minor key of this splendid melody, played so triumphantly in an optimistic major key, must obviously be taken into account.

Let us first of all point out that, if the concept of a 'non-Europe' has a cost, so also a Europe in the throes of integration has a cost, even though (in terms of cost/benefit ratios) the net benefits come out on top at the end of the day. The integration aimed for involves an extremely complex process which calls for considerable adaptation efforts – costs – in other words, on the part of the various participants. The extension of the socio-economic domain, together with the information and decision-making networks to which this leads, will entail substantial administrative costs (input and processing of the

Table 1.2 Material gains resulting from the 'internal market'

	Ecu bn	% of GNP
Phase 1 Gains arising out of the lifting of barriers restricting trade	8–9	0.2/0.3
Phase 2 Gains arising out of the lifting of barriers affecting production as a whole	57/71	2.0/2.4
Gains arising out of the lifting of barriers (sub-total)	65/80	2.2/2.7
Phase 3 Gains achieved from economies of scale and increases in production	61	2.1
Phase 4 Gains obtained from the effect of increased competition on industrial restructuring (economies of scale), on business inefficiency and on monopoly situations	46	1.6
Gains from the integration of the market (sub-total)	62[a]/107	2.1[a]/3.7
Total gains		
For the seven member states[b] at 1985 prices	127/187	4.3/6.4
For the twelve member states at 1988 prices	174/258	4.3/6.4
Mean point	216	5.3

[a] This alternative estimate of the total of phases 3 and 4 cannot be divided between the two phases.
[b] Seven member states (Germany, France, Italy, the UK and the Benelux countries) represent 88 per cent of the internal gross product of the twelve. The figures in the table refer solely to these seven states, particularly covered by the research.
Source: Commission of the European Communities, study by the Commission's General Directorate for economic and financial affairs.

relevant data, reorganization of services, mastery of languages, travel, inter-cultural management training, etc.). Furthermore, it is well known that changes provoke the phenomena of resistance to change which obviously create some measure of dysfunction. Competition is accepted instinctively only by the winners, the stronger of the protagonists. The weaker ones or losers, those who get trampled underfoot or even eliminated from the game, naturally endeavour to organize areas of protection or to block the system. Similarly, the unification mechanism which should promote the 'new European economy' will not operate instantaneously. It will be some time before the favourable effects are felt. During the interval which will be needed to finalize adjustments, it is possible that the logical composition of the system could be altered.

But even supposing that the competitive model of market economy is finally accepted in all its severity of operation, one must not ignore

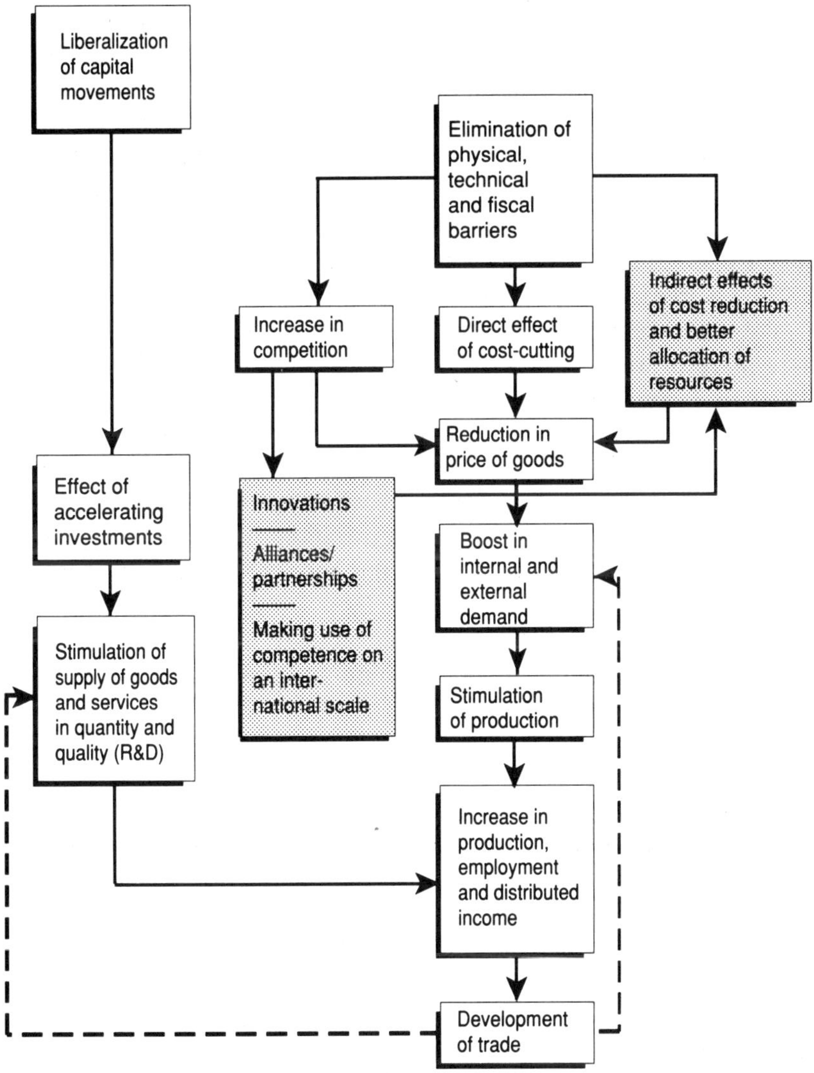

Figure 1.3 The dynamic impact of the single market
Source: Sabine Urban and Serge Vendemini, CESAG, Strasbourg.

certain dangers of sliding off course where the effects of this are concerned. Four points in particular must be stressed.

1 The development of intra-Community trade will, as we have noted, stimulate growth in the member states and thus in the distributed income. In other words, the European standard of living will be raised. This increase in demand will very probably provoke an increase in imports, that is to say, a diversion of the beneficial effects of the single market towards competing foreign economies.
2 The economies of scale and the reduction in the cost of intra-Community transactions will also work in favour of external competitors who establish sales networks within the Community area.
3 European manufacturing structures on the whole lack flexibility. The working year and the span of working life are shorter than in the main competing countries of the world, while the standard of welfare provision and associated social security contributions are much higher. The proportion of old people is important. The expenditure necessitated by the preservation of a crowded and polluted environment is also high. The mentality of many is based on an excessively secure, indeed backward-looking, performance. In short there needs to be a modernization of organizations and a mental rejuvenation in order for the improved competitiveness to prove beneficial.
4 Europe will not be able to recoup quickly the time lost in such decisive fields as R&D and the training of adequate numbers of highly qualified professionals. The time lag here could be considerable.

It will be gathered from this second aspect of the effects that European states must close ranks and steer more closely together if Europe as a whole is to win out. Vested interests offer only illusory protection and are dangerous in terms of potential development. Waste of resources will become suicidal. Agreement on this point is vital.

A competition-based economy with increased levels of competition will inevitably provoke a restructuring of the fabric of production. The prospect of a reduction in selling prices after 1992, combined with the eagerness of European industrial groups to procure an effective position by means of a global dimension, is encouraging an impressive movement towards concentration, towards acquisitions and mergers with companies thus transformed into 'allies'.

This tendency is particularly noticeable among larger companies, which have the capacity to organize or reorganize the markets and reduce the destructive effects of cut-throat competition. It is therefore curious that, although competition is declared in influential political and scientific circles to be necessary and beneficial, it is denigrated and distorted by the most influential of those actively involved. Fiat has a monopoly in the Italian automobile sector and yet its chairman, Giovanni Agnelli, claims to subscribe to a true liberal capitalism. Together with IRI, the largest industrial holding company in Italy, the four 'giants of Italian capitalism' (Giovanni Agnelli, Carlo de Benedetti, Silvio Berlusconi and Paul Gardini) control 80 per cent of the shares quoted on the Italian stock exchange. In Germany, the three great chemical companies (Hoechst, Bayer and BASF) efficiently organize the contents of their portfolio with the benevolent connivance of the Federal cartel office.[9] In every EC member state there is a tendency to organize those dominant business sectors from which the authorities, for economic, social and strategic reasons, cannot disassociate themselves. This tendency takes the form of industrial development co-ordination policy on both a private and a public level.[10]

The economic integration of Europe is certainly going to accentuate the current move towards restructuring.[11] Fresh macro- and meso-economic balances and imbalances will appear. The great market, single and multiple at the same time, will engender inter- and intra-branch rearrangements. The opening-up of the frontiers of Europe will lead to greater competition but with fewer competitors. New sectors of activity will proliferate, stimulated by foreign investment attracted to this revitalized economic region; others will wither and die.

The growing interpenetration of socio-economic systems which is apparent on a worldwide scale will be particularly acute in Europe. It will result in some real and abrupt changes which are potentially difficult to live with. The danger of undesirable pressures must therefore be forestalled, the inevitable socio-economic upheavals made bearable. To this end, the major industrial groups, quoted on the stock exchange and connected to a multinational capitalism, make extensive use of capital alliances. Smaller firms (the 'small' and 'medium-sized') have, understandably, tended more to resort to co-operative and contractual alliances, of a type discussed in the chapters which follow. This is not a minority or less interesting tendency: quite the reverse. In the business 'best-sellers' it is hailed s a promising groundswell,[12] the saga of firms in the competitive milieu being recounted in the following stages:

- 1920 to 1945: competitiveness through size;
- 1945 to 1970: growth through marketing;
- 1970 to 1980: competitiveness through strategic planning;
- 1980s: competitiveness through specialization, the exploitation of niches;
- 1990s: competitiveness through co-operation partnerships.

Could this new style of competition management (balancing competition with collaboration) be just another passing trend? Probably not; because, beyond the social necessity to organize the markets, current technological changes demand that a considered, long-term view be taken of economic developments. The essential regulation cannot be left to the whim of a market economy governed by 'pure and perfect competition', broken down by the influence of innumerable players. On the contrary, the more turbulent the environment, the more these players seek assurances and tranquillity. The public authorities have been widely involved since the 1930s and have not been lacking in influence. In every country powerful intervention has been rushed to the aid of the strong whose authority was in danger, or to the weak under threat.

At present these centralized policies are under attack and have shown their limitations. They need to be supplemented or complemented by decentralized action, more effective because it is able to handle the growing complexities of the real world. Contractual accords and partnerships made between grass-roots players fit into the logic of this new system.

The Policies of European States Reviewed: Protected Niches Disappear

The Europe of 1992 is eroding some secure positions, intruding upon traditions and established practices. The Commission has decided to challenge assistance from public authorities, especially state aid. Subsidiries, direct or indirect, explicit or surreptitious, can be as protectionist as customs duties or quotas. Competition must rule, must break down the barriers between markets, whether local or national, public or private. The liberal doctrine followed will also lead to the general admission of foreign capital, i.e. external investment. 'Fortress Europe' is indeed hospitable; some say not enough, others too much.

An end to national public procurement

This represents a considerable venture in economic terms. The report by the Commission on 'the cost of a non-Europe' estimates at 9 per cent of GDP the value of acquisitions by government departments of the member states alone, which increases to 15.5 per cent of GDP if the purchases made by public utilities are included.[13] These are average figures: in the case of Germany the total value would be 12 per cent of GDP, for Belgium 17.5 per cent, for France 14 per cent, for Italy 15.5 per cent – and for the United Kingdom 22 per cent.

Under 20 per cent of public sector procurement contracts have been awarded to other than national suppliers.[14] Opening up access to these contracts thus creates new potential outlets, substantial in the case of certain sectors such as transport, telecommunications, construction, public works, and all types of plant and equipment. At present these areas are highly compartmentalized. Two reasons are put forward to justify preference for national suppliers. First, government procurement is financed out of public funds and it therefore seems natural (and electorally defensible) for this money to be ploughed back, in principle, into national companies. Secondly, such contracts represent a major facet of the state's economic policy. They enable it to promote demand and investment, to come to the aid of disadvantaged regions, to try to combat unemployment, to encourage new technologies, and so forth.

In future, the Community institutions plan to strengthen the guarantees of equal opportunity to suppliers from other member states, to ensure that public procurement and the associated procedures are less ambiguous and more open and to extend these guarantees to many sectors of economic activity (including services). While these measures should enable considerable progress to be made towards opening up the arena to outside bids for government procurement contracts, both for goods and for services, the capacity for resistance of local, regional and national procurement bodies must not be underestimated. The Commission has none the less declined to challenge breaches of policy in the field of public procurement.

The expected effects of opening up the procurement channels are set out diagrammatically in figure 1.4. They are very attractive. It

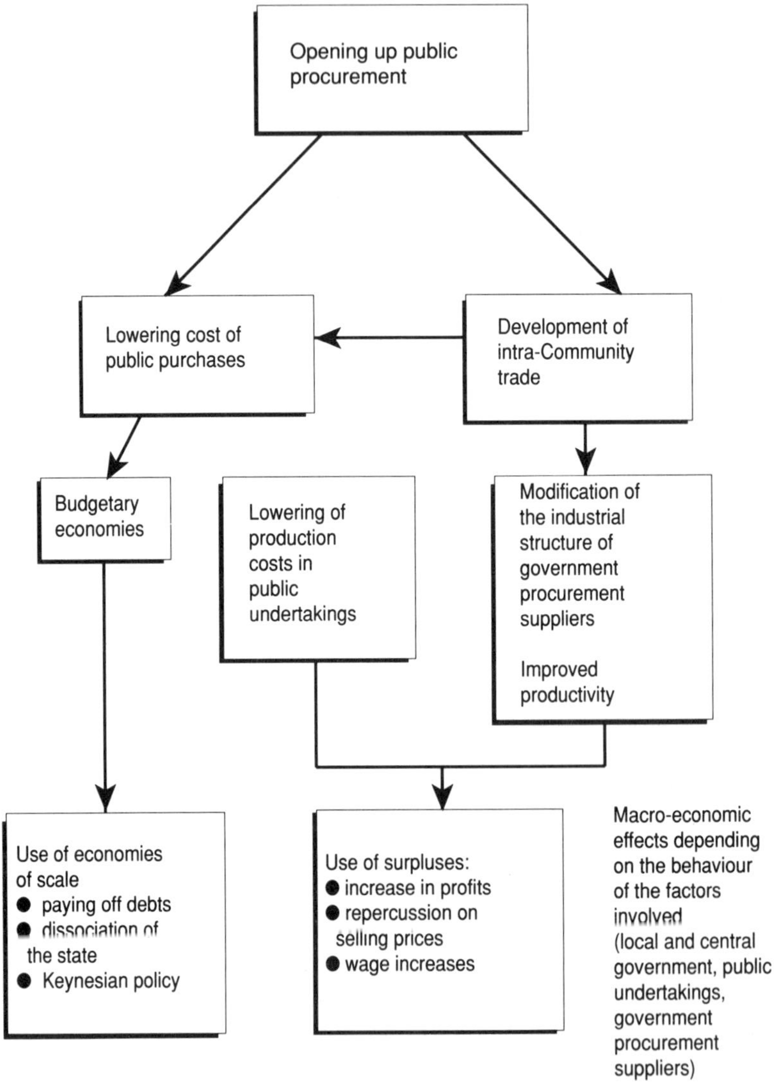

Figure 1.4 The macroeconomic effect of opening up access to public procurement
Source: CEPII, *Economie propsective internationale*, no. 33, January 1988, p. 9.

must be added that the imperative of critical size which exists in an increasing number of high-technology sectors (i.e. those with high R&D costs) strongly supports the Community policy.

Dilution of domestic markets

The concept of 'Europe 1992' benefits from good marketing. Public opinion polls carried out in member states show that hopes outweigh fears; the perceived advantages are seen as greater than the feared disadvantages.

This confidence is felt not only within the EC member countries themselves but also by others such as the members of EFTA (Sweden, Norway, Finland, Austria, Switzerland), the United States and Japan. The world is coming to see Europe as an increasingly attractive and privileged area.[15] Thus two movements are having a joint effect: the relocation of production within the EC, prompted by the measures described above and rapidly growing foreign investment from the United States, Japan, Sweden, South Korea and Taiwan.[16]

Since 1985 there has been a strong redirection of American capital towards the European Community. The United Kingdom and Germany continue to be the preferential recipients but, as unification progresses, the spread of investment is tending to become less uneven: France, Italy and The Netherlands are all improving their positions. The EC countries have become the main centres of production for American industrial subsidiaries abroad. The presence of American companies is particularly noticeable in the promising sectors of chemicals, agricultural foodstuffs, automobiles and information technology.

Japanese firms, too, have greatly increased their investments in the EC since the middle of the 1980s. 'Europe after 1992' fascinates Japanese executives who are not insensitive to certain rejection phenomena which are appearing here and there.[17] They are increasing their pressure 'from within' by boosting the number of their installations of all kinds (see table 1.3). Their strategy is as much political as economic; it is long-term and aggressive.

Furthermore, the increased competition from certain newly industrialized countries such as South Korea and Taiwan should not be underestimated. Since 1986, these countries have had to overcome the raising of protectionist barriers in their export markets.

Table 1.3 Japanese direct investment in Europe: preferred locations for different corporate functions (survey of 127 corporations by Nihon Keizai Shimbun)

	West Germany	Britain	France	Spain	Italy	Netherlands	Belgium	Total
Head office	61	56	19	0	5	13	15	169
Production	51	58	30	49	26	9	14	237
Sales	88	62	58	17	28	23	20	296
R&D	86	44	23	5	7	5	12	182
Finance	27	80	6	0	1	47	12	173
Total	3[illegible]3	300	136	71	67	97	73	
(Japanese production facilities: real number[a]	67	92	85	41	24	27	22	411

[a] Survey by Japan External Trade Organization, March 1989.
Source: *Japan Economic Journal*, N° 1337, 1358, 1989; Hypo-bank, Economic Research Department.

An increase in Korean and Taiwanese installations in Europe is likely. Sweden, Finland, Norway and Switzerland have also declared a firm wish to take up positions in the single market.

On the whole, non-European companies intend to profit from the largesse offered by this market comprising 320 million consumers with a privileged standard of living. 'Industrially, the Common Market does not therefore consist of twelve but, in fact, of seventeen.'[18] This means that European firms are finding themselves in a formidable 'domestic' environment. Sectors of activity are under attack from all sides, competitive positions are more and more under threat. The instability of market shares is accentuated by the profound change within member countries in relations between the state and companies. 'The realm of trading is increasingly escaping from political control.'[19] 'Less state intervention' doubtless implies less bureaucratic waste; but it also implies less support. This evident fact is not entirely innocent, to the extent that state aid does not merely play a defensive role, protecting certain parties, but also plays an offensive role, stimulating economic vitality and correcting the inequalities brought about by a model of competition in which economic factors have disproportionate resources and consequently disproportionate power.

The fact remains that, if the state is experiencing a reduction in its ability to arbitrate and to regulate in a unified Europe, firms will have to organize or reorganize themselves; they will have to collaborate in order to gain strength; in other words, to resist and to attack. But the transition from one set of regulations to the other is likely to be difficult.

The challenges of technology

The world economy has in many periods been dominated by Europe: first mercantile Europe; later industrial Europe; and then an inventive and innovative Europe. A positive impetus was provided by the perfection and exploitation of the steam engine which shaped the first industrial revolution, founded on coal, carried by the railways and centred on the textile industry. The second industrial revolution was shaped by electro-mechanics, founded on oil, carried by the motor car and supported by the chemical industry.[20] The third revolution is taking place before our eyes. The 'material' content of industrial activity is tending to diminish in favour of its 'intellectual' content –

information technology. The shaping factor now is electronics. New 'spin-off' technologies are adding to capabilities in fields already explored and are opening up those sectors which employ new materials (such as fibre optics, carbon fibres) and new tools (the laser).

Information technology is causing fundamental changes. It is exploiting the scientific knowledge acquired over several decades in the fields of signals, codes, languages and memories. From this spring revolutionary processes and products. Although this technology is based on physical resources alone, it has produced data processing, micro-electronics, robotics, office automation, telematics, etc. The use of these techniques is making the primary agricultural sector more productive, with automatic harvesting, milking and sheep-shearing, satellites which enable a better use of land to be made. The secondary sector has been transformed: oil refineries and cement works have been automated; numerically controlled machines and robots are deployed in the goods, equipment and consumer product industries; manufacturing boasts automated and flexible press and machine shops, computer-aided manufacture, automated assembly. Office automation is invading the tertiary sector, revolutionizing the management of companies, banks, insurance companies and post offices; and the non-productive social sector activities (tourism, health, etc.) also increasingly use these techniques. They are crucial in making industrial countries competitive.

When these techniques, based on data and code processing, are related to elements from the living world (micro-organisms, animal and vegetable cells, subcellular fractions, and soon tissues and organisms) they are referred to as 'biotechnology'. Developments in this area are causing radical transformations in agricultural energy and agricultural foodstuffs, high-quality chemicals, energy and biomedical matters. In the near future, the synergy between computer data-processing and biology (biotics) will result in high-performance products of which biochemical microprocessors are but one example. The interface between advanced software, systems experts and artificial intelligence will revolutionize everyone's relationships with others and with the world.

The use of microelectronics, robotics and biotechnology will no doubt alter the landscape of industrial society.

It is essential that thought be given to the fundamental characteristics of these technologies, the offspring of information science, which differentiate them from traditional industrial technologies. They are accelerating human capabilities and the efficiency of human activities at an enormous rate. And they consume only a relatively small amount of materials and energy in doing so. Their cost is, at most, that of the support for the information which they carry. These factors give rise to considerble repercussions.[21]

In the first place, these technologies upset traditional economic mechanisms. Such technologies are no longer merely the basis of manufacturing processes. New spin-off products are invading the market: tape-recorders, robots, videocassettes and videodiscs, educational microcomputers, interferon, new vaccines, to name but a few. Secondly, the cost and selling prices of these products have fallen abruptly. Such variations have obvious implications for businesses which, in order to stay in the game, are being constrained to enter into all kinds of agreements with competing firms. The case of Intel is an example: because of its financial weakness in the price war, this firm, the market leader in the field of integrated circuits and advanced memories, had to enter into an agreement with IBM for it to provide the technology for the manufacture of electronic chips.

A profound change is also occurring in the area of productivity and in the direction it is taking. What part does this play in a process of antibiotics fermentation, efficiently programmed with its chain synthesis and immobilized enzymes? It makes production automatic and continuous. The concept of productivity is moving upstream, to the point where innovation, programming and apparatus are combined. One of the bases of pricing, marginal costs, is disappearing.

In the future the decisive factor will be innovation, rooted in a vast R&D network, in collaboration between industry and public authorities and between centres of higher education and research.[22] Partnerships will be boosted, even in the world's liberal regimes (the United States, Germany, Japan). The talk is of 'cross-fertilization'.

But Europe is at a turning-point in its history; it has allowed itself to be challenged, indeed, overtaken. The balance of power is changing; the emergence of Japan as a power in the world economy constitutes a major factor in the evolution of international trade and spheres of influence.[23] In certain commercial sectors – motorcycles, cars, commercial vehicles, consumer electronics, cameras, clocks and watches, telecommunications equipment, active electronic components – Japan has gained an overwhelming supremacy. In other sectors (electrical equipment, househould electrical goods, computers, etc.) the penetration is more than simply significant. Over thirty years Japan has methodically renewed its production infrastructure and enhanced its industrial effectiveness by taking advantage of the opening up of world markets so strongly recommended by GATT. It is presented as an efficient model of specialization. Its strong points are appropriately spread between consumer goods, consumer durables and intermediate goods (its weak points being primary products).

According to analyses conducted by the Paris-based Centre d'Etudes Prospectives et d'Informations Internationales (CEPII), Japan's strong points have formed powerful 'poles of competitiveness' which have brought in their wake a whole series of activities located either upstream or downstream. From the point of view of long-term profitability, firms have woven durable and effective collaborative relations with each other, capable of supporting the cost of mastering high technology. It is these high-tech products, in such great demand, which symbolize the third industrial revolution; it is these which are going to turn future economic life and social behaviour upside down. Japan would seem to be well placed and determined to assume the role of director, the dealer of cards on a world scale. This is clearly demonstrated by trading trends, by international investment and by the patent rights which it holds. The 'intelligence revolution' is leading Japan into first place.[24] The protagonists are the Tsukuba science park and the very new Japan Key Technology Centre. They will soon be complemented by the Kansia science park (between Kyoto and Osaka) which has fantastic technological ambitions, has at its disposal impressive financial resources centred on research programmes which are regarded as the keys to the twenty-first century (optoelectronics, artificial intelligence, biocomputing, etc.) and consequently benefits from a formidably efficient organizational set-up. 'Techno-competitiveness' overshadows price comparisons.[25]

Europe must henceforth defend itself, using its powerful resources, in order to recoup the time lost in certain technologies of strategic importance; and it does not have long to do this. Japan has effectively explored the partnership route and it is both possible and necessary for Europe to follow its lead.

'Willingness to face up to world-wide competition, especially that from Japan and the United States, is the main factor in the unification of Europe.'[26] The decline of welfare state aid is the spur to firms to make their own response if they have no wish to become mere satellites, remotely-controlled by a few distant, modern leviathans.

Markets Controlled at Community Level

In their evocatively titled book *Crise, Krach, Boom* ('Crisis, Crash, Boom') Michel Albert and Jean Boissonat declare: 'Europe 1992 is launching the single market to combat the concept of national states. It will dismantle them.'[27] Those concerned must therefore seek to find a new balance. Jacques Delors predicts that by the year 2000 80 per cent of Europe's economic laws and regulations, perhaps even its social and fiscal ones, will be enacted by the Community. Present-day national rights will, in the very near future, become European 'regional' rights.

The Community principle will, little by little, subconsciously affect the thinking of individual nations. Increased powers of Community bodies will compel states to reassess their own powers in the light of the European financial and monetary system. Companies will have to conform to the new Community policy on standards, and to relinquish much of the state aid currently provided – a process of adjustment in which alliances and technical co-operation will be central. They will also have to review their lobbying policy at EC level.

Solutions to the Destabilization of National Markets

Economic and monetary union will destabilize national markets in goods and services and in capital (see figure 1.5). This process will severely disrupt existing economic and social conditions that have developed hitherto on the level of individual states, and new ways of dealing with this impact will be needed.

A similar urgency in the pursuit of new common practices arises from the peaceful revolution at the end of 1989 which freed Eastern European countries from a totalitarian yoke; if a new European policy is not formulated in this context there is the risk of a renaissance of nationalism and bilateral procedures, leading to a break-up of the vital community of interests.

New common policies will, of necessity, be developed and then defined jointly; individual nations will consequently find their room for manoeuvre much reduced.

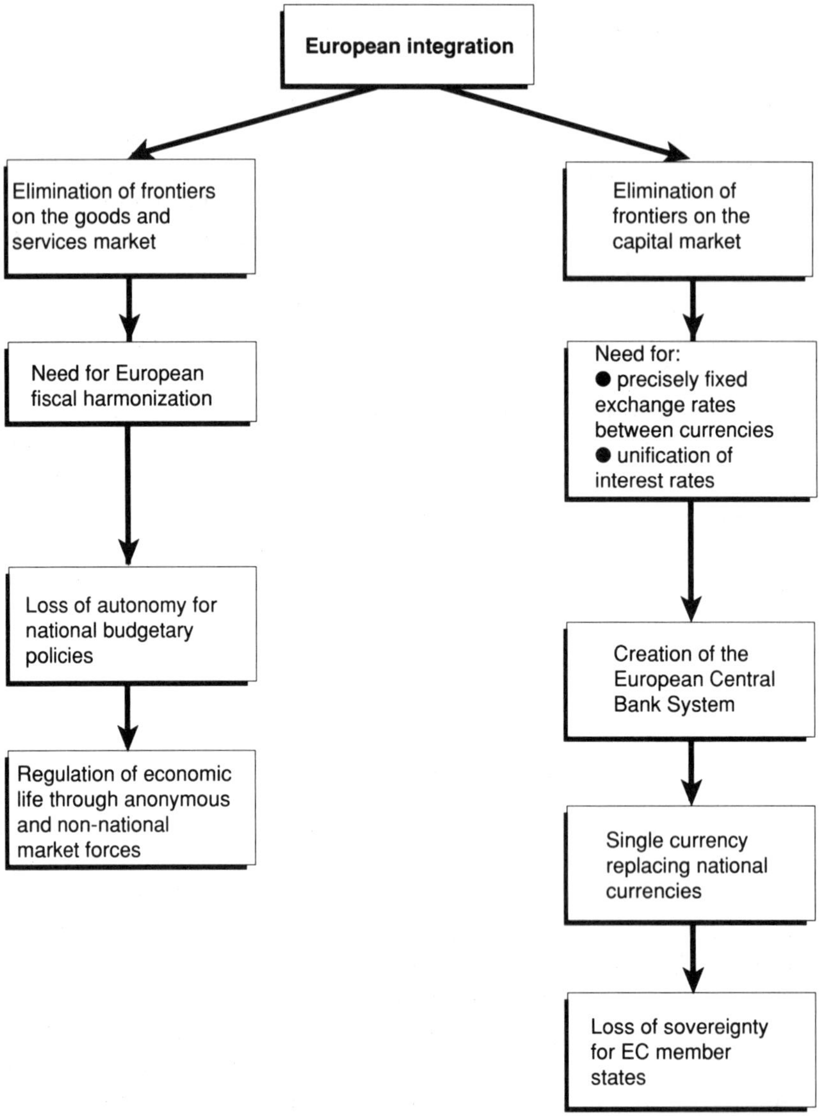

Figure 1.5 The impact of European economic and monetary union
Source: Sabine Urban and Serge Vendemini, CESAG, Strasbourg.

The erosion of national sovereignty through monetary union

The aim of monetary union is an ambitious one, historically unprecedented between developed nations. The problems in achieving it must be stressed. The intended process, based on voluntary co-operation, assumes the progressive transfer of decision-making powers from member states to the Community. In other words, the existing national identities will be affected and, over and above this institutional transformation, the very substance of social reality will be influenced. The right to mint money has always been a privilege which demonstrates sovereignty. The printing of money determines the degree of liquidity of the economy, that is to say its credit and payment facilities; consequently, it stimulates growth and employment or, on the other hand, produces disruptive speculation, linked to strong inflationary pressures. The general level of prices, interest rates and exchange rates depends on the productivity of the economic system concerned and on the monetary policies practised by each national central bank.

The formulation and application of a common monetary policy will necessarily involve new operating procedures, supplanting the independent strategies of individual member states, aimed at their own national objectives. 'From the moment any bank in the Community is able to receive deposits from any customer in the Community and grant him loans in any national currency, the high level of territorial correlation between the sphere of influence of a national central bank, the area in which its currency is used and that in which "its" banking system operates will have disappeared.'[28] The outcome will be the adoption of a single currency – perhaps the Ecu – issued by a European central bank, independent of any national political power. The existing central banks in the member states will lose, at a stroke, their autonomy and their ability to influence national economic data by manipulating interest rates, exchange rates or liquidity. Households and commercial companies alike will exchange their national banking and financial partners for European ones. National interdependency and community of interests will be transformed into Community interdependency. The question is, who will benefit from this altered context?

The creation of regional and sectoral imbalances through economic union

The shape of European economic union is not yet determined at the time of writing. The purpose of the EC inter-governmental conference in December 1990 was to map out the process of achieving economic and monetary union (EMU), with a view to political union.

Economic union, married to monetary union, will (according to the terms of the Delors Report) combine the characteristics of a completely free common market with a set of rules essential for its proper operation. This economic union will involve the adoption of a competition policy and other measures aimed at reinforcing market mechanisms. It will be necessary to ensure that the operation of the market is not obstructed by the action of private or public economic influences. In particular, there will be a need to impose strict limits on the recourse by certain sectors to public subsidies, as these create competitive imbalances and result in the inefficient allocation and use of scarce economic resources.

The theory of this is inescapable; but as a statement of practice it is naïve in taking no account of the virtually universal practice of giving state aid (in the form of subsidies, tax relief, free allocation of resources, etc.) to firms which are deemed to be of national interest. (The competitive advantages of companies are increasingly being built up through governmental aid; Japan in particular has demonstrated the effectiveness of this type of industrial policy.) The elimination of these arrangements, currently made in the context of national and independent budgetary policy, render certain industries vulnerable when exposed to worldwide competition; its operation is therefore not impartial. It is worth recalling a report from the organization 'Reconstruct America', published on 12 June 1990 under the aegis of Harvard and MIT economists, which stated that between now and the year 2000, deprived of official aid, US industry is likely to be widely overtaken in key sectors, such as high-definition images, fibre optics and superconductors.

The determination of common policies aimed at structural adjustment and regional development has been declared a necessity by the Commission. Yet it seems difficult to square the realization of these objectives (which devolve variously upon the European Regional Development Fund (ERDF), the European Social Fund (ESF) or the European Agricultural Guarantee and Guidance Fund

(EAGGF) with the resources being made available. According to forecasts, 'structural action' will account for only 25 per cent of the Community's budget in 1992, and this budget itself represents little more than 1 per cent of the Community GDP (around 2.5 per cent of the national budgets). The total is meagre.

A third requirement for economic union is the co-ordination of macroeconomic policy, consisting of restrictive rules on budgetary matters. To put it more simply, it is imperative that there is a better co-ordination of budgetary policies. This improved co-ordination should be based on three main medium-term trends:

- preferential financing of public deficits by non-monetary means;
- stabilization and reduction of public debt;
- research into an expenditure and receipts structure more favourable to supply conditions.

The definition of member states' budgetary policies will then be monitored by the Community, to a greater or lesser degree according to the country. In one group will be those countries which tend towards a budgetary surplus: the United Kingdom, Denmark and Luxembourg. A second group will comprise France and Germany, whose deficits are relatively moderate and stable. The third group of countries, which embraces Italy, Belgium and The Netherlands, will, according to the Commission, be obliged to stabilize their deficits before they will be able to envisage any reduction (the problem is urgent in the case of Italy). In the last group will be Spain, Ireland, Portugal and Greece, where the level of public debt and the conditions for financing it are particularly disturbing.

According to the Delors Report, the Community ought to be in a position to oversee the general economic situation, to assess the compatibility of developments in the various countries with the common objectives and to formulate economic policy guidance. Who will lay down the law? One is tempted to believe it will be the stronger nations, the weaker ones being obliged to bow to the common will.

Initially, the proposed arrangements will have the effect of restricting each country's budgetary (and hence political) autonomy. Moreover, they will lead to the separation of the two existing, complementary initiatives: that relating to co-operation among companies and that relating to co-operation among nations. A new initiative must be developed, based on original research into common interests and interdependence, in order to provide a coherent overall framework for *all* such developments.

This burgeoning network of monetary and economic activity is likely to extend rapidly beyond the institutional framework of the EC to spread over the wider European territory. On 14 June 1990 Jacques Delors declared in a speech in Sweden that 'the next step in European history must be the conclusion of the agreement creating the EEA (European Economic Area)'. In October 1990 the agreement for which the Commission President had hoped, between the EC and the EFTA, was concluded, creating the world's largest free trade area. The field of co-operation is widening; but, for the time being, it remains no less under the control of the Community organizations.

European Rules on Competition and Performance

Competition rules applicable to companies of member states are as old as the Community itself (see Treaty of Rome, Articles 85 and 86). Since those early days, certain alliances or agreements have been proscribed, others (beneficial agreements) authorized; but it is the Community which is the judge. Likewise, it is the Community which will grant the right to assess the validity of aid given by public authorities. Work on the harmonization of standards will henceforth be carried out on a European level; to be effective, lobbying will have to take place in Brussels or Strasbourg. In short, major initiatives will be taken more and more at the European level and less and less at national level.

Prohibition of anti-competitive agreements

Agreements between enterprises which are likely to restrict or distort competition within the common European market are already prohibited. The scope of this prohibition is extremely wide, covering the means of distribution of products; pricing policies; and agreements aimed at sharing the market or eliminating unofficial imports.

The European rules in this area are restrictive and the powers conferred on the Commission are considerable. It is empowered to:

- initiate investigations as well as prosecutions;
- require firms and companies to supply any information required in

full; refusal, incomplete information or delays are subject to penalty (fines escalating with the length of delay);

- make on-site inspections, during which the Commission's agents have the right of access to a firm's premises and all its documents;
- take interim measures for the preservation of competition in specific areas.

The Commission has not hesitated to impose stringent fines on delinquent enterprises.

Some exceptions to the general principle of prohibiting restrictive agreements are accepted, however, and these are of interest for our analysis. The Commission has the power to authorize certain 'beneficial practices'. What are these? There are three criteria that an agreement must fulfil to be accepted as a beneficial practice (once the enterprise concerned has notified the Commission of a draft agreement and supplied it with all the detailed information required):

- it will improve the production and distribution of products and/or promote technical progress;
- the enterprise reserves for users or consumers of its products or services an equitable share of the profits resulting from operation under the agreement;
- it will not eliminate competition – even potentially – with respect to a substantial proportion of the goods or services involved.

The Commission has in fact accepted that not all types of agreement need necessarily be notified to it, and has since published exemption regulations for each category. (These categories include some inter-enterprise co-operation and subcontracting practices; agreements of 'minor importance'; certain specialization and R&D agreements.)

Co-operation between European firms is thus expressly encouraged on the grounds of its economic value. For example, the Commission has adopted a favourable stance towards specialization agreements which, in general, help to rationalize the production and distribution of products. Firms may thus concentrate on the manufacture of certain goods or services in order to reduce their production costs and selling prices. It should also be noted that the Commission has adopted an exemption rule for each category which tends to favour co-operation between small and medium-sized enterprises and subcontracting. It has also adopted an exemption rule by category for certain collaborative R&D agreements, in particular:

- joint R&D on products and processes including mutual exploitation of the results;
- R&D on products and processes without mutual exploitation of the results;
- the collective exploitation of the results of previous R&D agreements entered into by the same enterprises.

Since 1984, the Commission has also accepted agreements for reducing structural over-capacities, provided that effective competition remains and users retain a real choice of suppliers. In the same spirit, the Commission also exercises a restraining jurisdiction (without any exemption mechanisms and thus any notification requirements) over 'abuses of dominant position'. Abuse is always censured and penalized, with no possibility of avoiding the application of the principle under any circumstances.

Evidently, the conduct of companies is judged and directed by the European authorities. Industrial firms cannot choose their position or restructure themselves as they wish. Holding or pursuing a large share of the market is regarded not as a performance indicator but as an indicator of 'dominant' position and thus as improper and reprehensible.

Indirect control of company practices: tackling state aid

Direct control of company practices is supplemented by indirect measures, aimed at imposing sanctions on states which grant aid (Article 92 of the EC Treaty). State aid is proscribed because it affects trade between states and distorts competition. There is thus an incompatibility of principle between these aid measures (whatever form they take: financial subsidies, guarantees, tax exemptions, reduced social security charges, loans at preferential rates or the holding of a controlling interest in a company's capital by public authorities) and the common market.

Some measure of compromise is nevertheless accepted in the form of special provisions. Certain of these (granted under a special authorization from the Commission) are very restrictive and concern only exceptional, particular cases, for example, aid aimed at making good the damage caused by natural catastrophes or other extraordinary events.

Other types of aid compatible with the functioning of the common market are also of interest and are widely used (they must be notified to the Commission in advance). These fall into four categories, as follows:

1 aid for disadvantaged regions suffering from high unemployment (the Mezzogiorno in Italy and the regions of what was formerly East Germany, for example);
2 aid aimed at promoting the realization of a major project of European interest (the Airbus, high-definition TV, etc.);
3 aid aimed at rectifying a serious disturbance in the economy of a member state;
4 aid aimed at encouraging the development of certain activities and certain economic sectors (steel, shipbuilding, textiles, synthetic fibres, automotive industry, environmental protection, R&D, etc.).

Article 93 of the Treaty of Rome grants a discretionary power to the Commission to require member states to cease or revise aid given. Illicit aid must be repaid by the benefiting enterprise. In the event of dispute, the parties concerned may refer the matter to the European Court of Justice in Luxembourg.

It is therefore clear that the progressive attainment of a single market will involve increasing weight and importance being given to the application of the rules concerning state aid. The current Commission guidelines for consideration of whether aid may be granted specify the following categories as potentially acceptable:

- Salvage and restructuring aid, authorized in exceptional cases and on condition that they are accompanied by a suitable restructuring plan.
- Regional adaptation aid. The Commission considers that the provision of new production plant and the extension of existing installations can contribute to regional development. The Commission therefore usually adopts a favourable attitude to such aid.
- Aid to investment and for the purposes of innovation, modernization or rationalization. The Commission exercises very tight control over aid for modernization and innovation.
- Aid for R&D. A favourable attitude is adopted by the Commission provided that a real distinction is made between R&D and modernization, that is, the introduction of new technology through investment in production.
- Aid for the protection of the environment and for energy conservation. Aid aimed at combating pollution in general (for

example, that which is agreed under the conditions set out in the provision for state aid for environmental protection) is regarded as acceptable within the framework of the existing regime. Each case is examined individually.

- Training aid linked to investment. The Commission adopts a generally favourable attitude towards initial and refresher training and professional retraining programmes, provided these do not merely reduce company costs.

Aid to improve performance is not viewed favourably; on the contrary, it is prohibited to introduce such aid and existing aid of this kind is to be progressively withdrawn.

Bearing in mind the direction Community policies are taking, member states will have to rethink their industrial policies. Countries with a centralized administrative structure, such as France, would seem to be less well placed in this regard than countries which are traditionally organized on more federalist or regional lines, such as Germany or Italy, where a decentralized and thus more flexible, structure enables the baton to be passed from central government to regional, district or city level. The European industrial area is being restructured on a regional basis.

Standardization: a European industrial tool

Trade is increasingly regulated by means of standards, as states and firms collaborate to impose their technical know-how at the required level.

Up to the 1980s, standardization was essentially a national tool, often used for protectionist purposes. A 'standard' is, in effect, a technical specification which has been agreed by the parties most concerned; it is intended to be used by the purchasers who have contributed towards the writing of it. When it is drawn up at national level, it is naturally protectionist. The Germans, in particular, are past masters of the art of making voluntary standards practically mandatory, for example by insisting on certification checks being made by laboratories which refer to such standards, or by ensuring that purchasers and manufacturers are united around these standards.[29]

Gradually, the international co-ordination bodies, the International Standards Organization (ISO) and International Electronics

Commission (IEC), have produced 'international standards', but these have only the status of recommendations. The European standards produced by the European Standards Committee (ESC) are, on the other hand, prescriptive and must be written into national standards. This important provision confers on the ESC and on CENELEC (the body concerned with electrical products) a powerful role in the removal of the technical shackles associated with national standards.

The Single Market Act has given European work on harmonization a powerful political boost by inaugurating a new Community harmonization procedure based on the rule of the vote of the qualified majority, rather than that of unanimity. By 1993, therefore, only a few national regulations should remain to create obstacles to trade. 'On 1 January 1993, it will no longer be possible, in principle, for any country to invoke national regulations and standards and their associated certificates against another member of the Community.'[30] Every member state must replace its national standards by European standards.

In an ideal world, European standards would be a true compromise between the various national standards and would be accepted by all. But to achieve this it will be necessary for companies (or their professional associations) to participate in the preparation of European standards. The importance of this point needs to be emphasized, for a standard is never impartial. Only rarely is it a purely technical document. A standard reflects the technological choices made by a country and its manufacturers. It is therefore a document which has an economic (and sometimes strategic) content and impact. Where, through lack of a jointly prepared European standard, a national standard carries the day, this will obviously give an advantage to the manufacturers in that country as they will not have to adapt, will be better able to master the technique used and will benefit from their standard's image of superiority (which understandably attaches to their products).

The technical rules of the game that will apply in the Single Market will be largely determined outside any one traditional national territory. Within the ESC/CENELEC work is being carried out by committees, the secretariats of which are attached to one of the national standards institutions. Currently, of the 156 technical committees, 20 per cent are attached to France (AFNOR), 40 per cent to Germany (DIN) and 17 per cent to Great Britain (BSI).[31]

These percentages indicate the significance of each country in this matter.

The current development of standards can, and should, be put to good use to reinforce the European industrial structure. No country in Europe has sufficient industrial or political weight to counter alone the great American and, especially, Japanese challenges. One way of picking up the gauntlet is to organize manufacturers and purchasers on a European level, possibly involving firms which have learned to appraise one another through co-operative agreements. It is significant that, in recent years, we have seen the formation of organizations for the preparation of European standards in the fields of aeronautics and information technology, fields which are seeing the gradual emergence of a real Community industry. Similarly, European manufacturers have decided to counter-attack with high-definition television in a consumer goods field which it seemed they would inevitably have to cede to the Japanese. Digital radio-telephony is another area of potential success, supported by Community standards which, by standardizing product quality, enable firms to achieve, among other things, economies of scale. Yet the range of products at which Community co-operation is aimed is very wide and is not restricted to electronics; it embraces vehicles, foodstuffs, pharmaceuticals, chemical products, construction and many others.

But convergence has to be rehearsed: cases are being pleaded, European bodies are being lobbied . . .

The need to lobby Community bodies

Given that the European Community will in future determine the basis of the legal framework for economic activity, professional organizations and firms, always the principal players on the ground, are going to have to set about lobbying – a concept still undervalued and not properly mastered in France, whereas countries such as Germany, Italy and the United Kingdom have already discovered effective ways and means of doing this.

To guarantee market transparency, the referees will need vigilant expert help.

The realization of the single market is going to intensify the battle which is waged continuously between the various industrial activities in each country (the differing types of energy, materials), between similar activities in two Community countries, and between countries in the Community and those outside. The competitors have not taken the Olympic oath. Many of them try to wear down their nearest rival (or even trip him up) and the referees – the national or European officials – honest though they may be, will see nothing of this and will find very good reasons why they should not impose sanctions or conduct an inquiry just to come to the conclusion that they are impotent.

Any mistakes made in the construction of Europe by an official who is ill-informed or misinformed, poorly supported or pushed too hard, every empty seat at a crucial meeting will result in the competitor from a member state finding the road barred to him, or that he has to negotiate an obstacle course, whilst his European rival or one from a third country will have a clear path before him.[32]

The job of a lobbyist, perfectly respectable in the Anglo-Saxon countries where economic agents are accustomed to free competition and to minimal intervention from the public authorities, is thought little of in France where the tradition is to rely on the wisdom of the senior civil servants (very often of high quality, it must be admitted), to whom the state has entrusted its services. In France, the lobbying function is customarily exercised by the representatives (specialized or otherwise) of firms or professional organizations. It is not usual to have recourse to independent, specialist lobbying agencies which may one day be trying hard to get the distribution of a product authorized and the next day, if they are so asked, to have the sale of it prohibited.[33]

Firms must include the practice of lobbying within the framework of their research into competitiveness. Their pursuit of cost reduction must bear on external factors as much as on internal factors. Among the first such factors to be taken into account are the costs associated with the legal and administrative environment: social and fiscal laws, protection of the consumer and the environment, workers' health care, etc. It is not easy to make cost comparisons across the various countries in the Community, or between costs here and in other, non-EC, countries. However, multinational corporations take this kind of analysis very much into account when choosing where to site their subsidiaries or their production units. It is imperative that, as long as European competition is increasing, firms put a ceiling on these costs or even eliminate them.

The strength of American industry is undeniable, as is the attention which the public authorities pay to it. Twenty thousand lobbyists operate daily in Washington, and they already have branches in Brussels.[34] For this reason, as for many others, it is essential that

Table 1.4 Impact of the single European market by sector

	Elimination of customs controls and tax harmonization	Technical standards	Public inter-vention and pro-curement	Public services and labour market	Movement of capital and company law	European R&D pro-grammes	Global appre-cia-tion
Industries:							
Agriculture and food	□ □	□ □	□		□		***
Energy	□	□	□		□		**
Iron and steel			□		□		*
Metallurgy	□						—
Paper and board		□					—
Glass		□					—
Chemicals		□ □				□	*
Plastic transformers	□				□		*
Mechanical and electrical plant	□	□	□ □		□	□	***
Specialist mechanical equipment		□			□		*
Precision and medical equipment		□	□		□	□	**
Computers		□				□ □	*
Telecommunications equipment	□	□ □	□ □		□	□ □	***
Professional electronics		□	□		□	□ □	**
Household equipment					□		—
Domestic electronics	□	□ □			□	□	**
Automobile manufacturing	□	□ □				□	**

Aerospace manufacturing		[]	[]			[] []	**
Shipbuilding			[]				–
Pharmaceuticals		[] []	[] []			[]	**
Textiles, clothing, footwear	[]				[]		*
Furniture	[]				[]		*
Publishing					[]		–
Construction, public works and services							
Construction/public works		[]	[]		[] []		**
Air transport			[] []	[] []	[] []		***
Other transport			[]	[]	[]		*
Telecommunications services		[]	[] []	[]	[]	[]	***
Retail trade			[]	[]	[]		*
Wholesale trade	[]			[]	[] []		**
Professions			[]	[] []	[]		**
Services to firms			[]	[]	[] []	[] []	***
Banks	[] []			[] []	[] []		***
Insurance	[] []			[] []	[] []		***

Key: no symbol: little or no specific impact
[]: considerable impact
[] []: major impact

A total has been obtained by adding the marks relating to each of the above criteria. This mark has been the subject of a global assessment, using the following grid:

–	total mark 0 or 1	little impact
*	total mark 2 or 3	noticeable impact
**	total mark 4 or 5	significant impact
***	total mark 6 or more	major impact

Source: *Bureau d'informations et de Prévisions Economiques/Problèmes économiques*, 5 May 1989.

Europeans get themselves organized in a concerted and unified manner, and do not act as scattered and uncoordinated individuals.

Notes

1 Enrique Baron, 'Europe 92, le rapt du futur', Collection Kairos, B. Coutaz, Arles, 1989.

2 For details, see for example: E. Gaillard, D. Carreau and W. L. Lee, 'Le Marché unique européen, Collection Etudes Internationales, Pedone, Paris, 1989; 'L'entreprise face à l'Europe; préparation au grand marché', *Les Référentiels*, Dunod, Paris, 1989 (permanently updated) under the direction of Jean-Marc de Leersnyder and Jean Thieffry; European Commission, *European Economy*, special issue, 'The Sectoral Impact of the European Single Market', Brussels, 1990; Centre d'Etudés Prospectives et d'Informations Internationales, Observatoire Français des Conjonctures Economiques, *Vers une fiscalité européene*, Economica, Paris, 1991.

3 See M. Penney, 'The Future for the EC: Corporate Tax Harmonisation', *Euro-business Review*, vol. 89, no. 4, pp. 38–41.

4 For a theoretical demonstration of this statement see, for example, Peter H. Lindert, *International Economics*, 8th edn, R. D. Irwin, Homewood, Ill., 1986; or Michael Emerson et al., *1992, la nouvelle économie européenne: une évaluation par la Commission de la CE des effects économiques de l'achèvement du marché intérieur*, Editions Universitaires de Boek, Brussels, 1989.

5 See L. A. Winters, 'Les effets du Grand Marché de 1992', *Economie Prospective Internationale*, no. 40, 1989, pp. 7–17 (previously published in the *Wales Business and Economics Review*, no. 2, Winter 1988.

6 Two conglomerates (GTE and NEC) have been analysed by C. K. Pralahad and Gary Hamel: see their 'The Core Competence of the Corporation', *Harvard Business Review*, May/June 1990, pp. 79–91.

7 Detailed studies are published in vols 1 (*Basic Studies*), 2 (*Studies on the Economics of Integration*) and sections of the European Commission report *Research on the Cost of Non-Europe*, Brussels/Luxembourg, 1988. A summary has been published by Pablo Cecchini, who directed the project.

8 It should be noted that the base year used for most estimates is 1985, during which the gross domestic product of the Twelve was Ecu 3,300 billion. The GDP was Ecu 2,900 billion for the seven principal countries which are usually used for evaluation (Germany, France, Italy, UK, Netherlands, Belgium, Luxembourg).

9 For Italy, see *A pour Affaires économiques*, no. 2, October 1989, pp. 51–66; for Germany, see S. Urban, S. Vendemini and F. F. Brost, *Elements sur les stratégies industrielles allemandes*, Morstadt, Kehl, 1982, pp. 87–150.

10 See Michael Porter, *The Competitive Advantage of Nations*, Macmillan, London, 1990.

11 To be convinced, the reader may refer to Emerson et al., '1992', pp. 35–136; Guy Crespy, ed. Observatoire des Stratégies Industrielles, *Marché unique, Marché multiple*, Economica, Paris, 1990, pp. 109–478; A. Francis and P. K. M. Tharakan, *The Competitiveness of European Industry*, Routledge, London, 1989; Alexis Jacquemin and André Sapir, *The European Internal Market: Trade and Competition*, Oxford University Press, Oxford, 1989.

12 See Craig R. Hickman and Michael A. Silva, *The Future 500: Creating Tomorrow's Organisations Today*, New American Library, New York, 1987, pp. 131–52.

13 European Commission, *The Cost of Non-Europe*, vol. 5: *Etude réalisée par quatre cabinets de consultants: W. S. Atkins Management Consultants, Eurequip SA, Roland Berger and Eurequip Italia.*

14 *Vade mecum* on government procurement in the Community, Commission Communication 87/C 358/01, Brussels, 1987, p. 1.

15 'A New Era of Global Competition', special edition of *Journal of Business Strategy*, March/April 1990.

16 See Crespy, *Marché unique, marché multiple*, pp. 43–108.

17 See *Journal of Japanese Trade and Industry*, especially vol. 8, no. 2.

18 Crespy, *Marché unique, marché multiple*, p. 23.

19 Ibid., p. 33.

20 See Gérard Lafay and Colette Herzog, *Commerce International: la fin des avantages acquis*, CEPII, Economica, Paris, 1989, p. 9.

21 Lecture given on 15 October 1982 by Jacques Robin, General Delegate of CESTA (Centre d'Etudes des Systèmes et Technologies Avancées), Paris.

22 See Danièle Blondel, *L'innovation pour le meilleur et pour le pire*, Economie mondiale, Hatier, Paris, 1990, pp. 208 ff.

23 Lafay and Herzog, *Commerce International*, pp. 95–115, 197–205.

24 See J-L. Moynot, 'Technologie: le Japon prépare le XXIe siècle', *Politiques industrielles*, Spring 1990, pp. 129–39.

25 See W. Kurth, 'La techno-compétivite', *L'Observateur de OCDE*, no. 164, June/July 1990, pp. 19–24.

26 John Naisbitt and Patricia Aburdene: *Mega Tendances 1990–2000: ce qui va changer*, First, Paris, 1990, p. 47.

27 Michel Albert and Jean Boissonnat: *Crise, Krach, Boom*, Seuil, Paris, 1988, p. 213.

28 Committee for the Study of Economic and Monetary Union, Report on Economic and Monetary Union in the European Community, Brussels, 1989 (Delors Report), p. 13.

29 V. Rigal, 'La normalisation, ou comment transformer une source d'entraves techniques en outil de la construction du marché intérieur', *Annales des Mines*, Special edition, Februry 1989, 'Les entreprises face à la construction européenne', p. 27.

30 F. Nicolas, Association Française de Normalisation, 'Gagner ou perdre au jeu des normes', *Annales des Mines*, February 1989, p. 81.

31 *Annales des Mines*, February 1989, p. 82.

32 G. Jourdan, 'Les organisms professionnels et 1993: Que vaut l'aiguillon de "Grand Marché" pour le char de l'Europe?', *Annales des Mines*, February 1989, p. 115.
33 Ibid., p. 116.
34 Ibid., p. 118.

2

The Impact of Market Changes on the Management of Companies

Rarely if ever have the pressures on European firms of the socio-economic environment and technological developments been as strong as they are in the current period of change. Activities are being restructured on a global level, with the supremely powerful multinationals sketching in sector by sector the shape of the triad formed by the United States, Japan and Europe.[1] Small and medium-sized firms are being forced to reorganize their activities in accordance with the strategies adopted by the larger ones. Major industrial moves are taking place, jointly with or in opposition to others, and every one of them is modifying the fields of competition and competence.

In some cases the environment remains very fragmented, with niches which favour small and medium-sized firms. In other cases it is evolving towards increasing specialization on a global level. In yet other cases it is market interconnection which dominates. And all this is happening very rapidly: the formation of the single market is not fundamentally altering the dealing of the cards but it is increasing the speed of the deal.[2]

The development of modified factors of competitiveness with the growing importance of non-material factors – intangible assets, network relations, cost/price factors, quality control – or the creation of highly fragmented markets offering particular openings have fostered the use of a now well-known classic strategy in ways specific to each company.[3] On the other hand, in the more complex sectors of activity, adaptation to current changes assumes a new relationship with the environment, an attitude reinforced both by the modes of expansion and by the organizational methods used by firms, which will in the course of this activity become ever less autonomous and more interdependent.

New Modes of Corporate Growth

The single European market demands of companies in the 1990s that they improve their skills and their industrial capabilities. These requirements are set out diagrammatically in figure 2.1.

Demand-led Euro-strategies

The vitality of Europe in the 1990s presents firms with a double challenge, both quantitative and qualitative.

Enlarged internal markets require increased manufacturing capacities

The nature of those markets which have still not been 'globalized' to a worldwide level is changing from a national to a continental one. The former national markets will progressively disappear into the Community whole. Firms in Europe must respond to this trend by increasing their manufacturing capacity if they are not to see their business overrun by competitors from afar. It must be remembered that, since 1982, industrial production in the Twelve has grown at a slower pace than that of the United States, of Japan and of the Asiatic 'dragons'.

An increase in manufacturing capacity inescapably calls for investment which, in turn, assumes means of finance and therefore savings. Meanwhile, the propensity to save is decreasing the world over:[4] a policy which wasted financial resources would accordingly not be welcomed. The internal financing capacity of companies (by means of ploughing earnings back into operations) is generally insufficient to face up to the growth-inspired demands; borrowing is therefore necessary, but is a very expensive option. Real interest rates have broadly speaking, become positive in recent years. The pursuit either of individual growth (internal growth of the company) or of external growth through the acquisition of existing units is consequently becoming very costly. It is expensive for the top companies which sometimes find it difficult to digest the results of their bulimic financial policies; it is almost unattainable for small and medium-sized firms.

The co-operative agreements route would seem to be both more reasonable and less egotistical, indeed, less destructive for the existing entities. The facts confirm this impression; with 1992 in

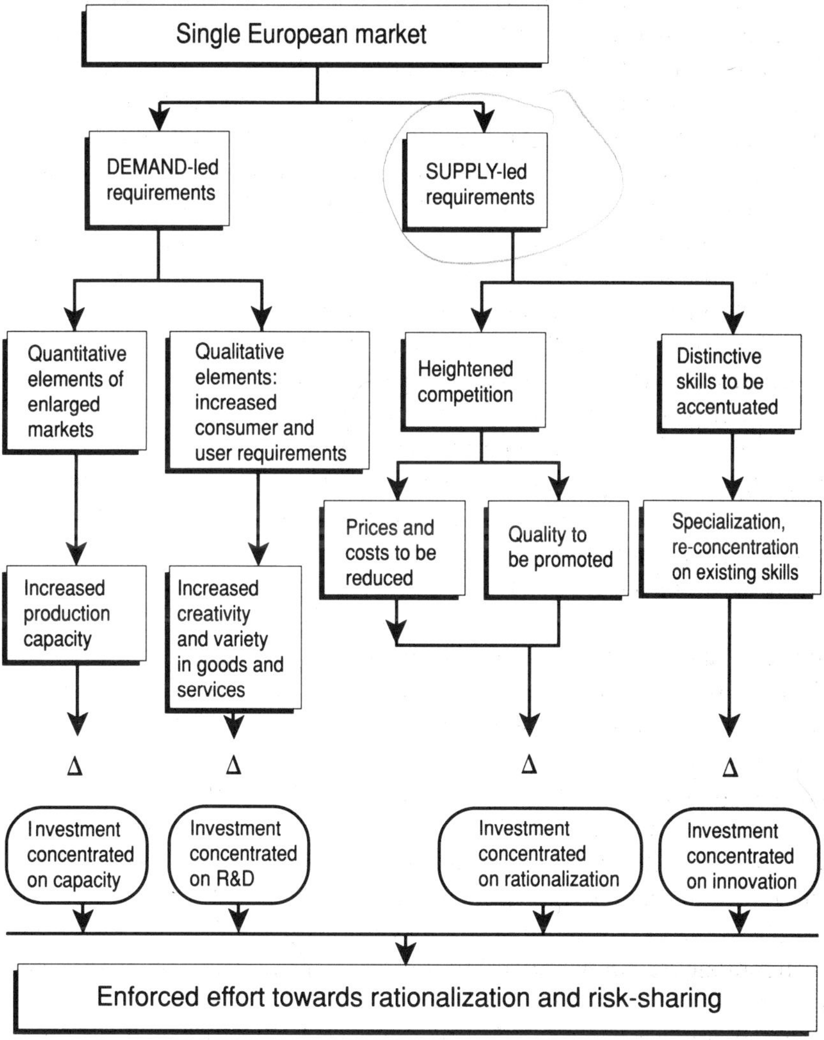

Figure 2.1 Euro-strategy: definition
Source: Sabine Urban and Serge Vendemini, CESAG, Strasbourg.

sight, co-operative manufacturing operations have been on the increase.[5] The emphasis on size which characterizes numerous industrial sectors has engendered a whole series of partnership measures, and this trend can only increase.

In the motor industry, for example, there is growing co-operation between manufacturers for the mutual production of parts, sub-assemblies or vehicles produced in small series: Renault/Volkswagen agreements for the joint manufacture of automatic gearboxes, Fiat/Peugeot SA for the joint manufacture of light commercial vehicles, Renault/Volvo for the joint manufacture of certain engines; and so on. Faced with the spirit of conquest shown by the major Japanese manufacturers – Toyota, Nissan and Honda – the European manufacturers must get moving. The creation of the single European market will accelerate the movement towards greater market homogeneity, imposing on European manufacturers the need to plan their product policy and their commercial policies on a European scale. In this kind of exercise the Japanese have already gained a formidable expertise, as reflected in the somewhat defensive strategies and protectionist measures (quotas) adopted by France, Spain and Italy.

In the field of telecommunications, the creation of the single market, with the systematic and reciprocal opening up of national networks and the adoption of a common system of standards, will both create opportunities for and impose constraints on considerably enlarged manufacturing capacities. Simultaneously, European demand is being developed through the modernization of the public switching networks and by the technical development of the services offered. Because of the national deregulation measures being taken (leading to the elimination of fragmented national markets) and the progressive standardization of materials, firms in this sector are having to make great efforts towards becoming international in order to cover the whole of the European market. Investments in capacity and partnership agreements are the logical corollaries of this. This trend is already being widely followed throughout the electrotechnical and telephonic sectors, led by three prime movers: Siemens, CGE (Compagnie Générale d'Electricité) and the ABB (Asea–Brown–Boveri)/Ericsson combination.[6]

In consumer electronics, the single market offers opportunities for the grand European ambitions for new activities such as direct broadcasting via satellite, high-definition television, domestic robotics (affording remote control of all domestic appliances), etc. – provided the necessary resources for getting a foothold in these fields can be mobilized. Considerable investment is called for. Even the top companies in this sector in Europe (Philips, Thomson, Nokia) seem to be compelled to work together, essentially for financial resource reasons. Thomson and Philips, for example, have decided to collaborate on research. None can really combat Japanese might alone.[7]

More discerning consumers require higher quality and better range

There is clear consumer demand for new products. An in-depth investigation carried out by Sandra Vandermerwe of the International Management Institute in Geneva confirms this trend in all the EC countries.[8] Consumers are becoming more demanding regarding the relationship between quality and price of products. They are demanding a wider choice of products, more extensive services and new products at an increasing rate. Industrial users are making similar demands, imposing strict requirements as to quality and price, more comprehensive and more convenient services, precise standards, 'just-in-time' deliveries, energy-saving, less polluting products, reduced harmful effects, etc.

Industrial producers are not waiting until 31 December 1992 before reacting to those demands. Creative developments are already in progress aimed at replenishing the range of products and activities which they have to offer. In Germany, for example, this movement was launched very noticeably in 1985.

The extent of consumers' qualitative demands may be illustrated by the foodstuffs sector, in many countries still very much subject to various non-tariff barriers and indirect taxes.[9] The disparity between rates of VAT and excise duty particularly affects wine, spirits and beer, tobacco, coffee and tea. There are innumerable non-tariff barriers (several hundred have been counted), which up until now have been applied in the form of restrictions on the use of specific ingredients, regulations concerning the content and description of products, laws relating to packaging, labelling, health provisions, etc. They particularly affect biscuits, ice cream, chocolate, pasta, soups and baby foods. The removal of these obstacles will bring in its wake increased competition and forced restructuring. So far as firms are concerned this will take the form of improvements in their scope for competitiveness and increased market cover; for the consumer there will be an increase in the range of products offered.

Supply-led Euro-strategies

External pressures, emanating not only from purchasers but also from competitors, are obliging companies to react in supply terms in order to guarantee their distinctive competitive advantages and skills.

The essential competitiveness of the manufacturing process

In the late 1970s and early 1980s in the United States and (to a lesser extent) Europe, in an environment conspicuous for the expansion of the financial markets and the resulting prevalence of galloping short-term thinking, the manufacturing function was somewhat neglected. More recently, following the priorities so strongly held by Japan and the new industrial countries, manufacturing is once more being regarded as an essential activity, both in America and in Europe.[10]

This change of attitude will not in itself solve all the problems of the manufacturing sector. New technology has to be integrated into the production processes, profoundly disturbing old ideas and practices. The dominant elements of productivity and efficiency must be supplemented by others, such as quality, service, realiability, adaptability, assimilation, etc. The need for imagination, method, flexibility and control is considerably increased. Production and its related logistics must be reviewed within the perspective of an international strategy rather than being determined by technical considerations, as was formerly the case. Production and decision-making systems are becoming more complex; the proper mastery of this complexity is becoming the key factor in competitiveness.

The competitiveness of manufacturing increasingly calls for long-term strategic planning and multiple, cross-disciplinary skills. Not only tangible assets, but also and especially the costly and risky intangible, informational assets, are assuming a decisive importance. It is therefore not surprising that firms, in their capacity as national production outlets, are increasingly conducting research into complementary activities and expertise. Industry is being re-centred on the company's core business, involving:

- the discarding of peripheral activities or sectors of activity which are insufficiently mastered;
- the development of basic expertise, supplemented by research into cross-fertilization between sectors (for example, the agreement

entered into by Peugeot SA (experienced in automation) and Dassault (experts in avionics); the alliance between Daimler-Benz and MBB);

- increased recourse to subcontracing or co-contracting, enabling complementary skills or manufacturing capacities to be used;
- an expansion in engineering, the role of which appears to become all the more indispensable to small and medium-sized firms as the variety of equipment or skills to be mobilized increases.

In short, the requirement for the means of production to be modernized in most sectors calls for massive investment. It is not merely the traditional sectors, possibly in decline, which call for the making of adjustments, but also the more modern ones in which Europe is already falling behind, such as semiconductors (integrated circuits, discrete components, optoelectronic components, integrated manufacturing systems (IMS)).

The 1985 crisis, which marked the end of a period of very rapid development (around 30 per cent per annum between 1975 and 1984), resulted, in Europe, in a regrouping of industry around three main corporate poles, the Dutch Philips, the Italo-French SGS-Thomson and the German Siemens; but still the critical size of each of these three manufacturing conglomerates is inadequate when compared with the Japanese or American manufacturers: in 1988 Philips was tenth on the world market, SGS-Thomson was thirteenth and Siemens twentieth.[11] These firms do, however, hold some aces; they have recently modernized their production capacity, with heavy investment since 1986 in Germany, The Netherlands, Italy and France and have a technological portfolio as good as any in the world. But to make their presence felt in the face of Japanese and American competition they need a European project. It was in this situation that the JESSI (Joint European Submicron Silicon) programme was launched in 1989. It has been shown that all the European participants need to embark upon collaboration and co-ordination ventures in order to master microelectronic technology (including manufacturing techniques) and also the materials and equipment to back up technological developments, together with those applications which enable the technology in advanced systems projects to be validated. Unfortunately, it is sometimes difficult to put industrial logic into practice. In September 1990, Philips decided, within the framework of a process of reorganization, to abandon the development and production of static RAM chips and thus to withdraw partially from the JESSI project. The two remaining partners, SGS-Thomson and Siemens, have decided to pursue their efforts in the memory field with the same objectives, but their resources have now been reduced. At the same time a joint venture project between Thomson-CSF and British Aerospace in the missile field has been opposed by the British government (which nevertheless accepted, without question, the transfer of ICL, the only major British computer manufacturer, to the Japanese Fujitsu group!). It seems that the convergence of European industries will be a difficult process.

The assertion of distinctive skills

Specialization is one response to increased competition. This is an offensive strategy based on the acquisition of product excellence which quickly enables a firm to outstrip competitors on the international markets. This is what happened in the tyre sector: Michelin took the lead with radial tyre technology, first in Europe, then in the United States and in Japan.

The acquisition of distinctive skills obviously has a high cost. It assumes first of all a major involvement in R&D in order to rise above the standard run of existing products. It is common knowledge that research is both costly and risky, the result not necessarily matching the outlay. The basic discoveries then have to be transformed into significant industrial applications, that is to say, the detection and creation of outlets by means of a pertinent and efficient marketing policy. This course of action presupposes top-quality human resources and a substantial commitment to initial, refresher and further training.

Technological research and human talent, then, are the two key factors which enable a company to avoid resting on its laurels, relying on the position or vested interests which it has acquired. Continual innovation has become essential. This requires a corporate context of accumulated skills, regularly updated, capable of releasing creative energy and thus the adaptation of products to changing circumstances. The perpetual stimulation of core competencies is the main source of competitiveness.

In certain sectors, however, for example the pharmaceutical and chemical industries, R&D has become excessively expensive and the necessary investment more and more onerous. Both the great multinational firms in these sectors and the smaller enterprises have reacted by refining and concentrating on their specialist field and by entering into partnership deals on an international level. It seems highly probable that the single market will see an escalation of co-operative agreements between European firms in such areas. 'On the one hand one could envisage a hardening of the trend towards concentration and putting research facilities to joint use in order to develop innovative products and, on the other hand, laboratories (with more limited resources) specialising in generic products.'[12] Co-operation will therefore take the form of a very active policy of pursuing patent rights and, in particular, the granting and acceptance of agreements to manufacture under licence.

In most sectors, the stakes involved in the process of adaptation, the volume of financial requirements and the extent of the risks run favour shared solutions and therefore partnerships. This tendency would also seem to result from the accelerating rate of change and thus the reduction in the available learning time, coupled with the time needed to amortize products (product life cycle). Companies need to come to terms with those who are in the know, at the opportune moment.

Revitalizing Managerial and Organizational Skills

The requirements of the single market in terms of corporate skills are expressed diagrammatically in figure 2.2.

The managerial and organizational constraints imposed by European economic union are obviously not exclusive to this situation. Every process of internationalization calls for a more or less detailed form of intercultural management. In the same way, the speed of technological change and the growth of complexity favour the use everywhere of flexible organizational structures capable of speedy adaptation.

The European problem is nevertheless particular for several reasons. The first is connected to the extraordinary cultural diversity of Europe. Nowhere else in the world is such a richness concentrated. From the north to the south, from the west to the east of this small portion of the planet, the variety is enormous. The integration of this diversity must consequently become a commonplace reflex, must infiltrate the daily routine, must affect everyone. Secondly, it should

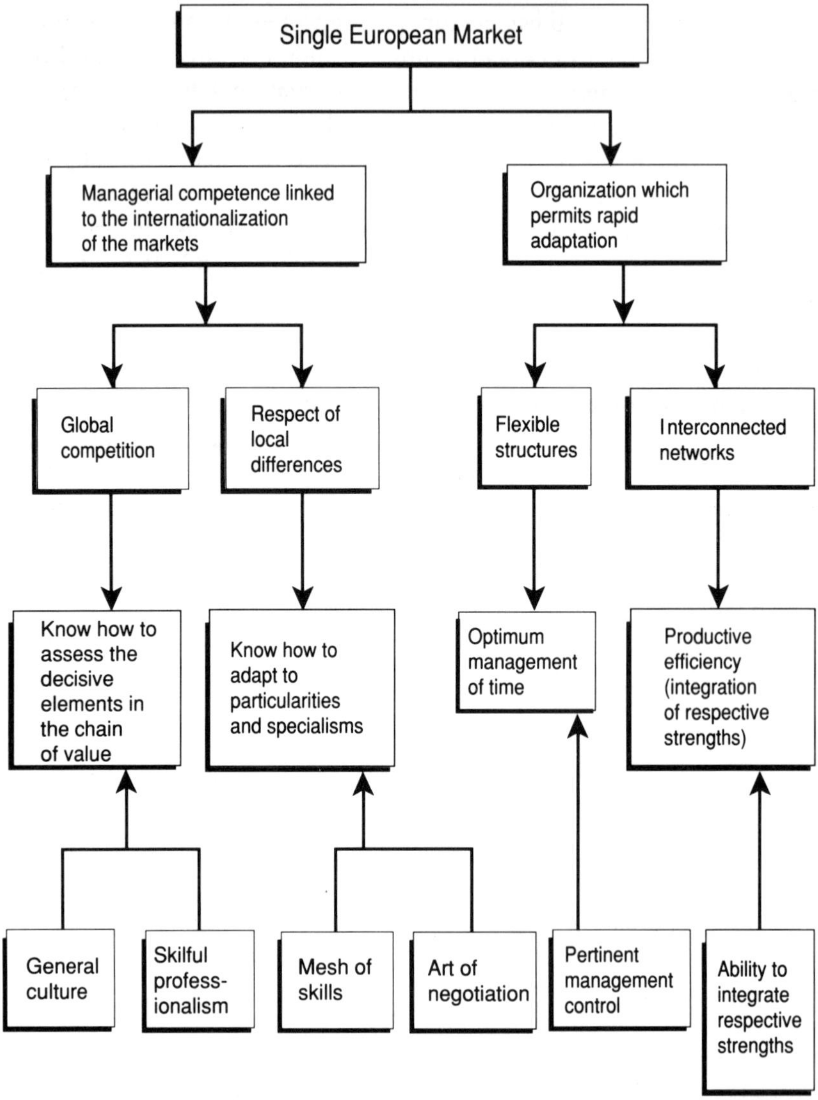

Figure 2.2 The single market and managerial skills
Source: Sabine Urban and Serge Vendemini, CESAG, Strasbourg.

be noted that this process is imposed institutionally. The stresses and strains are considerable and must be overcome in a relatively short space of time. There will be no escape from this. Thirdly, it must be stressed that this single European market is being built not on a 'green field site' but, on the contrary, on the foundations of a rich history made up of many battles for supremacy and power, of partitions and of the extension of empires and nations. The systems of values, of terms of reference, vary widely across the European countries. In many cases, that which is foreign remains alien. Fourthly, the highly-developed and industrialized countries of Europe, accustomed for many years to being rivals rather than partners, have always been drawn to specialized projects, often similar but not complementary.

The road to be followed is therefore not without pitfalls.

Requirements Arising from the Internationalization/Europeanization of Markets

European firms now have to function under conditions of global competition within their own geographical area and in other parts of the world. At the same time they have to have due regard for local specialities, exploiting distinctive features so as to make them a plus point in the battle against American or Japanese dominance. The linking of discrete skills is one solution to the problem; but in order to overcome the difficulties inherent in its implementation, there is a pressing need for high-quality, professional 'Euromanagers', able to negotiate the data arising from a system of cross-fertilization.

The inter-linking of skills in the pursuit of enhanced efficiency

Global competition is intensifying the demands made on Europeans for efficiency. The increased competition about to be unleashed upon the generally open European market also typifies the other world markets in which the Europeans are investing. The worldwide economic war is brutal; in order to win battles, strategy has always stressed the art of seeking allies capable of reinforcing offensive positions or of consolidating lines of defence.

Economic war is not episodic; it exists as a permanent phenomenon. Companies therefore have to seek allies, not piecemeal as the opportunities arise or to resist a passing threat, but systematically.

European firms pursue collaboration and co-operation partnerships out of a concern to attain an efficient critical size and the need (especially acute in a cultural environment with clear differences) to have regard for local identities or the wish for autonomy.

This kind of inter-connection has the advantage of bringing to fruition the activities of several partners, none of whom is subordinately linked to any other, either financially or legally. Through a range of relations which lead to the redefinition of the roles of the various players in the value-creating chain, extending from suppliers of services to the customers, this inter-linking enables the success factors of firms to be multiplied, notably by facilitating the transfer of skills or the sharing or diversification of activities.

In the contemporary literature, various authors draw attention to the increasing role played by the management of relations in the creation of wealth and the forging of a competitive edge. 'Increased productivity is nowadays no longer tied solely to the question of plant and equipment – automation and robotics for example. It has taken on an intangible dimension, linked in particular to the management of relations. . . . Relations are tending to become the dominant variables in productive systems.[13] 'The success or failure of the firm in a global context will be determined by its managerial capabilities, not by comparative advantages based on factors of production such as labor and natural resources. . . . The basic factor for attaining competitive supremacy will be management competence and leadership quality.'[14]

Europe is not merely an economic community; it is also a cultural community which therefore has every chance of entering into fertile co-operative relations, based on middle-of-the-road management styles as compared to the two extremes: the Japanese style which hinges on the systematic search for consensus at any price, and the American style rooted in activity, aggression and competition.[15] Coalition is easier where the bosses have been trained in the same culture or a similar one. Europe is certainly not a cultural entity.[16] It is marked by substantial contrasts traceable to two broad models: the Latin on the one hand and the Anglo-Saxon on the other. But these two extremes exist nowhere in pure and exclusive form; and the two tendencies are intermixing more and more.

A European has, as a general rule, a better knowledge of the characteristic cultures and demeanour of other European countries than of extra-European cultural factors. Working relations are facilitated by the closeness of cultures, of ways of thinking and of values which are respected. Partnerships on a European level can consequently become efficient rapidly.

By its very diversity Europe can also offer a wide range of complementary competencies, according to the traditions of each region or nation. The potential value of these varied abilities and qualifications is something which can be exploited because the management of efficient firms demands at the same time fighting qualities, administrative and organizational qualities, and negotiating qualities (see figure 2.3). Each of these varying kinds of abilities is more generously distributed in some regions than in others, these specialities being partially accounted for by historical factors.

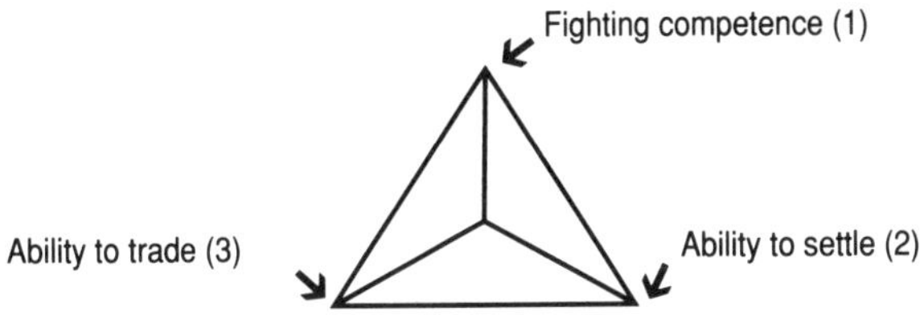

Figure 2.3 Cultural dimensions of competitiveness
Source: Sabine Urban and Serge Vendemini, CESAG, Strasbourg.

1 The fighting spirit, necessarily combined with a measure of aggression, will help the firm to develop, to move, to extend its field of activity, to increase its share of the market.
2 The ability to administer resources and to build up the firm, taking into account its environment, assumes an aptitude for mobilization, for listening, for conciliation, for power-sharing and enables the firm to stabilize the bases for development.
3 The ability to trade places the accent on the concept of mutual advantage, of mutual profits for the partners. Each gives and receives something without there being any winners or losers.

Distortions of this tetrahedron illustrate deficiencies in strategic management which are penalized by the conditions in which the economy and the company operate.[17] Co-operative alliances have the advantage of emphasizing these new requirements for stability. The trend is promising.

The art of negotiation assumes new prominence

The need to adapt to local particularities and to respect local differences calls for complete mastery of the art of negotiation, which is increasingly becoming a necessary element in a manager's armoury. This is a happy development in that negotation aims to reach agreement between parties by discussion rather than by aggression or destructive combat. Partnerships both demand and encourage this emergence of peaceful and positive relations between people and their organizations.

It is well known that cultural factors are significant in conducting negotiations.[18] The constituents of culture, such as values, way of thinking, system of communication, language and behavioural conventions are the key to understanding a foreign partner. There are therefore grounds for thinking that the increase in the number of intra-European contracts relating to research, manufacture or marketing will not only stimulate strategic alliances within Europe but will also lead to the weaving of a fabric of dynamic relations, capable of propelling the European economy towards a high standard of international performance.

The single market may be thought of as a crucible of negotiating skills, of use in a wider, global sphere.

New Organizational Structures: The Rise of Networking

The single market is calling for new kinds of organization in an economy increasingly based on flexible structures. Although economic theory usually starts with the product and the technical means of production, going on to analyse the relations developed by those involved in the economy (within firms and on the markets), reality is more and more reflecting the opposite priority: relations are themselves tending to become the central variables.[19] Participants in the economic game jointly play an increasing role in the design and development of products. One important illustration of this tendency is the growing overlap between R&D functions and marketing.

A networked economy, closely associating different manufacturer–consumer partnerships, stimulates the demand for quality by forming close links between all those who take part in the wealth-creation process, between sectors and also between countries. Nowadays value is created all along a complex chain of closely meshed links (*maillage*).

These networks are not merely value-generators; they also, by means of the flexible structures which can be set up through them, ensure an accelerated adaptation to change.

The single market provides a magnificent opportunity for European firms to exploit modern management methods which enable them to do something different, to do more and to do better. For the individual firm, achieving a good position in the international networks is becoming the top priority. Transnational alliances will henceforth define huge areas for co-operation between partners. Therefore new ways of co-ordinating activities and new types of management control must also be established.[20]

Networking: emulating Japan's success

Networking is designed as a permanent management strategy which favours collaboration and co-operation between partners, as opposed to the appropriation of financial and legal control. In an integrated network of autonomous but linked members each member has a margin of initiative but agrees to respect the operating principles and the behavioural standards accepted by common agreement.

The Japanese were the first to discover the virtues of organized networking – a policy to which they were led by force of circumstances but which has since been the basis of their success.[21] Following the Second World War the victorious Americans compelled the vanquished Japanese to dismantle completely all their major industrial groups (the *zaibatsu*) and reduce them to a host of small and medium-sized enterprises, with an absolute prohibition on the re-forming of integrated industrial entities. These new, smaller companies therefore found themselves compelled to work in concert but deprived of the possibility of linking their capital legally or financially; they had to operate through co-operation. To do this the Japanese invented 'managers' clubs' of twenty members who met once a month to 'tune their violins'. Each member of this 'top-level club' organized a second-level club of another twenty members, and each of these in his turn organized a third-level club of another twenty members. In this way several inter-firm co-operative networks are woven together, with original integration links, each network involving $20 \times 20 \times 20 = 8{,}000$ firms. In this way, networks are constructed which consist of entities specializing in different fields – financial, commercial, etc.

Eventually, the greater part of the Japanese economy was organized into networks. The ties which link these firms are still not determined by their financial interests in each other. They are based, in the first instance, on adherence to a common project, on the formulation of joint policies and strategies and on the mounting of tactical operations at group or sub-group level. These links also reflect the value of combining forces in information technology on the world markets.

These Japanese networks began the revitalization of declining industries, the diversification of products, innovation and assistance to new firms and thereby fashioned a great future for their economy. The integration principle which invigorates these networks underlines the strength of organized and negotiated competition in which industrial, financial and political thinking unites instead of competing and eliminating. The intention is to promote global competitiveness through a harmonious network structure.

Inter-firm networks in the form of co-operative alliances have been developing in Europe for a number of years. These are, of course, of especial interest to small and medium-sized firms for which membership of a network represents an inexpensive means of becoming international. These inter-firm alliances are well suited to meeting quickly and efficiently complex demands which are difficult to satisfy through the sharing of expertise, the adaptation of products to local demand, the search for greater compatibility between products and, in general, the penetration of multiple markets.

Decentralization and management control

According to the thinking outlined above and confirmed by recent industrial developments, inter-firm co-operation is going to spread. One consequence of this will be changes within companies in the administration of certain functions (by buying in or transfer of skills) and certain activities (for example, by pooling resources in order to reach the necessary critical size). It will therefore be necessary to supplement existing management tools, which are often tied to an analysis of the *company* and designed as an integrated group of activities, the overall performance of which is reflected in the general accounts, by tools appropriate for various *activities*, individual costs and margins of which should be known, in order that the firm can plot its overall direction and properly reconcile its different activities.

The conventional accounting systems currently in use within companies, whether they use the concept of variable costs, direct costs or overall costs, more often than not result in poor estimates of the unit cost of products. This inhibits decisions as to price, choice of supplier and the composition of sales. The new information and control systems must threfore concentrate on sub-assemblies, which correspond to predetermined phases in the production process, rather than the final product.

Bearing in mind the modern trends noted above, three suggestions may be offered.

First, strategic considerations will compel firms to set up an accounting system for each activity (activity-based costing).[22] The determination of the cost of activities, involving an assessment of the cost of transactions (transaction costing) and of the details of each operation (operation costing) will enable operational managers to take effective action concerning the operations for which they are responsible. In this way the competitiveness of each activity (taken to mean a series of tasks of the same type, performed with the preparation of a product or service in mind) can be improved by better mastery of costs and the precise formulation of competitive advantages. This necessary stage in the reformulation of a relevant costing system suited to the industrial conditions of the 1990s can also form the starting-point for determining the reallocation of resources within the firm and the conditions of collaboration to be negotiated between firms.

Second, knowing the cost of activities makes it possible to refine the competence profile of a firm. The concept of an 'activity' and the knowledge of the associated cost structure will make it possible to draw up comparative cost profiles between firms. Those firms in a position to negotiate co-operation contracts should be able to improve their own performance in comparison with their competitors' average performance, diagnose the strong points and the weak points in their management of certain functions, and check whether the discrepancy noted in relation to the mean standard is attributable more to the effects of volume or to the effects of experience. Thus it becomes possible to think in new ways about the allocation of resources and to provide responses to the questions posed: should the activity be de-integrated, that is, subcontracted to an outside firm? Should a target be a greater volume of activities (in order to obtain a better spread of the fixed costs)? Should the firm negotiate cost-sharing with a partner?

Third, an analysis of the cost of an activity enables managerial control to be exercised at the level of the co-operative agreements. Management control cannot be restricted to an enterprise's internal activities (usually divided up by product or by focus of responsibility), even where the enterprise is integrated into an increasingly complex network of partners who influence its overall profitability. There is good reason, therefore, for looking at some concrete instances where a management control system for the activities concerned is set up, sharing costs and gains among the partners. A greater objectivity and a better definition of the strategic decisions made by the enterprise as a whole should result.

The ABC (activity-based costing) approach developed by R. Cooper and R. S. Kaplan in the new design of cost management systems[23] is a very useful guide to light the way for profitable management action oriented towards partnership. The ABC approach is applicable across the spectrum of functions and activities, and reveals the links between the demands made by the different activities on the organization's resources and the revenues generated by each company's functions.

Activity-based cost management systems provide companies with management information and managerial control possibilities. ABC reveals unexpected peaks of profitability and craters of loss in a company's operations; managers should use it as a guide to re-price transactions, to alter product and customer mix, to discuss co-operative alliances in order to reduce excessive demands on their organizational resources.

In such ways, co-operative alliances may be forged in a very efficient and profitable way, as demonstrated in part 2.

Notes

1 See G. Crespy, ed. OSI, *Marché unique, marché multiple*, Economica, Paris, 1990, p. 41; CEPII, *Economie mondiale: de Berlin à Bagdad*, Economica, Paris, 1991.

2 This subject developed by G. Crespy in *Marché unique, marché multiple*, pp. 24ff.

3 M. Porter, *Competitive Advantage*, Free Press, New York, 1985.

4 See *Finances and Development*, IMF and World Bank, Washington, DC, June 1990.

5 Institut für Wirtschaftsforschung, Schnelldienst, Munich, November 1989, p. 15; June 1991, pp. 3–11.

6 Crespy, *Marché unique, marché multiple*, pp. 197–219.

7 Ibid., pp. 415–27.

8 S. Vandermerwe, 'Strategies for a Pan-European Market', *Long Range Planning*, vol. 22, no. 3, 1989, pp. 45–53.

9 Crespy, *Marché unique, marché multiple*, pp. 251–81.

10 See Wickham Skinner, *Manufacturing: The Formidable Competitive Weapon*, John Wiley, New York, 1985.

11 Crespy, *Marché unique, marché multiple*, p. 404.

12 Ibid., p. 246.

13 A. Bressand, C. Distler and K. Nicolaidis, 'Vers une économie de réseaux', *Politique industrielle*, Winter 1989, p. 156.

14 A. C. Hax, 'Building the Firm of the Future', *Sloan Management Review*, Winter 1989, p. 77.

15 See William Ouchy, *The M-form Society*, Addison-Wesley, Reading, Mass., 1984; F. G. Gauthey and D. Xardel, *Le management interculturel*, PUF, Paris, 1990.

16 See Geert Hofstede, 'Organising for Cultural Diversity', *European Management Journal*, vol. 7, no. 4, December 1989, pp. 390–7.

17 See STRATEGOR, *Stratégie, structure, décision, identité*, Interéditions, Paris, 1988, pp. 473 etc.

18 See A. Jolibert and M. Velasonez, 'La négotiation commerciale: Cadre théorique et Synthèse, *Recherche et Applications en Marketing*, vol. 4, no. 4, 1989, pp. 51–70; B. M. Hawrysh and J-L. Zaichkowsky, 'Cultural Approaches to Negotiations', *International Marketing Review*, April 1989, pp. 28–42.

19 Bressand et al., 'Vers une économie de réseaux', pp. 115–68; R. E. Miles, 'Competition: A New Industrial Relations System for the 21st Century', *California Management Review*, Winter 1989, pp. 9–28; Hax, 'Building the Firm of the Future', pp. 75–82.

20 Serge Feneuille, 'A Network Organization to Meet the Challenges of Complexity', *European Management Journal*, vol. 8, no. 3, September 1990, pp. 296–301; Wim G. Biemans, 'The Management Implications of Networking', *European Management Journal*, vol. 8, no. 4, December 1990, pp. 529–40.

21 See V. Laboucheix et al., *Traité de la qualité totale*, Dunod, Paris, 1990: chapter 20, by G. Archier, pp. 205–13.

22 See Robin Cooper and Robert S. Kaplan, 'Profit Priorities from Activity-Based Costing', *Harvard Business Review*, May–June 1991, pp. 130–5.

23 R. Cooper and R. S. Kaplan, *The Design of Cost Management Systems*, Prentice-Hall, Englewood Cliffs, NJ, 1991.

PART II

The Bases for Inter-Company Co-operation on an International Level

Introduction to Part II

In part I we analysed the thinking behind the single European market and illustrated the measures which enterprises should take in adapting to it.

Taking an overall view, two major elements stand out:

1 The single market will in effect widen the scope of the enterprise:
  - on the demand side, enterprises will have to think in terms of a bigger market with a more varied customer base;
  - on the supply side, the change in the number of participants will result in an increased potential for competition in the short term (obligations as to price, quality, etc.) and in the medium term (build-up of distinctive advantages).

2 The single market will force firms to bolster their expertise, especially:
  - their internationalization expertise;
  - their organizational expertise;
  - a strategic expertise.[1]

The last type of expertise applies to both internal strategy (all those decisions which bear on the management of activities in the sense of balancing production and costs) and external strategy (decisions which bear on the relationship of the activity to its environment).

It is in this context that co-operation is frequently cited as an original and effective procedure. However, such co-operation still has no status. Sometimes looked at from the standpoint of conditions for success,[2] sometimes from the standpoint of intentions[3] and competitive positions, sometimes from the standpoint of the factors which determine the power of the collaborators,[4] co-operative agreements are not seen to be founded on an explicit necessity with regard to their shape or their strategic objectives. In other words, it is often the very number of co-operative agreements, and its recent share increase, which is used to justify the interest which the strategies of co-operation have aroused.

The aim of this second part is to establish the whys and wherefores of co-operative agreements in the context of the new European competitive situation.

Chapter 3 analyses the economic and technical factors which lead to internal and external solutions in terms of co-operation. To this end a particular theme is developed in which the enterprise as a legal entity will no longer be regarded as the ultimate point of reference. An approach is set out by means of which it will be possible to enhance the prospects of the enterprise's operation as regards both its internal congruity and its relationship with the environment, sometimes at the level of the activity, sometimes at the level of a function, sometimes on the global level of the company.

Chapter 4 explores the institutional and cultural factors which lead towards co-operation and influence the form and content of a co-operative practice. Are we progressing towards a new model of competition in which confrontation will gradually be replaced by the search for complementarity? In other words, can we speak of the emergence of co-operative management and the development of new strategic models?[5]

Notes

1 M. Bommensath, *Votre entreprise face à 1992*, Editions de l'Organisation, Paris, 1988, p. 125: 'in a war calling for prompt responses, like those which deregulation and prospect of a single market without frontiers are already prompting, strategies play a paramount role in the taking up of good positions or the acquisition of lacking skills.'

2 H. Perlmutter and D. Heenan, 'Cooperate to Compete Globally', *Harvard Business Review*, March/April 1986, pp. 136–52.

3 A. Jacquemin and P. Buigues, '1992: Quelles stratégies pour des entreprises européennes?', *Revue française de gestion*, June/July/August 1988, pp. 5–15.

4 G. Hamel, Y. Le Doz and C. Prahalad, 'S'associer avec la concurrence, comment en sortir gagnant?', *Harvard l'Expansion*, Autumn 1989, pp. 24–32.

5 G. Archier and H. Serieyx, *Pilotes du troisième type*, Seuil, Paris, 1986, pp. 193–206: 'Vers de nouveaux modèles stratégiques'.

3

A Theoretical Model of Co-operative Alliances

A firm is a legal entity, endowed with a certain decision-making autonomy, with capital and with a mission. It is responsible to its environment and to its shareholders. This summary of corporate identity in fact masks a more complex reality; many strategic or management choices are made, not at the overall company level but at that of a characteristic activity or operational function. Every part of the company has its own motivation and one must see things from the viewpoint of each level in order to understand the need for different forms of co-operation. The first section of this chapter therefore proposes a three-level pattern of study for the firm, by means of which the grounds for co-operative alliances and their form may be understood.

Three significant forms of co-operation stand out:

- *adaptation co-operation*, based on the need to ensure a competitive position for each of the firm's activities;
- *functional co-operation*, justified by the quest for an essential congruity between the various functions within an activity and at company level;
- *co-ordinated co-operation*, suggested by the congruity of the combination of activities within a company.

The second section of this chapter will be devoted to an analysis of these three forms of co-operation and their justification in the quest for competitiveness.

The connection between the single European market and the development of inter-enterprise co-operation is usually demonstrated by reference to a series of facts: the increased number of agreements and the attention given by the media to such agreements,[1] or to the evolution of a new and rational market economy policy. The more advanced work on this latter asepct highlights three principal market economy policies: confrontation, avoidance and co-operation.[2] Confrontation is implicit in the 'domination by cost' theory and is also at the centre of the recommendations which arise out of portfolio analysis models, since these offer essentially three options: to develop, maintain or abandon a product. Avoidance is aimed at getting round the competition and avoiding the added cost of confrontation. Two main means are used; the allocation of distinctive features to the products and the concentration on certain market segments. Finally, co-operation is aimed at increasing the resources, augmenting general skills and strengthening inter-enterprise relations, thus mitigating the constraints of size and uncertainty.

Within this framework three types of co-operation may be identified (see table 3.1). The 'allocation' type of co-operation takes account of adaptations in terms of regrouping or fragmentation and revolves around minimizing the costs of transactions. The 'symbiotic' type of co-operation is based on the concept of resource combination and is aimed at accelerating access to those skills which are sometimes onerous to acquire and take a long time to implement. The 'alliance' type of co-operation is aimed at setting up contractual relations with competing firms.

A number of investigations and interviews we have carried out indicate that it is possible to go beyond this approach to co-operation.

Table 3.1 Types of co-operation and the corresponding economies and strategic moves

Partners' fields of activity	Type of co-operation	Type of economy achieved	Corresponding strategic moves
Same competitive field but different sector of activity	Allocated	Economies of transactional costs	Regrouping
Different competitive fields	Symbiotic	Economies of range	Diversification
Same sector	Alliance	Economies of size	Specialization

Source: G. Koenig, *Management Stratégique: visions, manoeuvres, tactiques*, Nathan, Paris, 1990, p. 189.

This chapter will be devoted to investigating the objective factors which create the need for co-operation and to widening the concept of co-operation by proposing a new typology.

In order to establish the need for co-operation, the scenario developed will concentrate on the firm as a whole and will locate the question of co-operation at the heart of the process of resource allocation. To this end a representative matrix of the enterprise will be set out in the first section, distinguishing three levels of attention: that of the activity (the comparable level on which competition occurs), that of the function (the level where skills are brought into play and where costs are incurred) and that of the company (the organization where overall congruity arises from the combination of activities).

The need for co-operation in order to reduce costs, to speed up adaptation or perhaps as a new factor to further the company's specialization or diversification choices, will be exemplified by the dynamic management of the enterprise in the face of universal competition, subject to the restrictions imposed by the new competitive environment. The second section accordingly sets out a new typology of forms of co-operation, develops the relationships between types of agreement, as determined by the allocation of resources, and specific forms of agreement, and finally illustrates the five classic legal supports for the implementation of agreements.

The Three Performance Levels of the Firm: Activity, Function and Company

A Representative Matrix of the Activities of the Enterprise

The key concepts: activity, function, company

The enterprise, in the form of a company, may be visualized by means of a matrix (see figure 3.1). The first dimension represents the activities for which the company is competing; the second dimension corresponds to the functions, that is, the principal phases of creation of added value.

The *activity* is an entity identified according to five criteria; product, technology, interface of functions (global cost profile), group

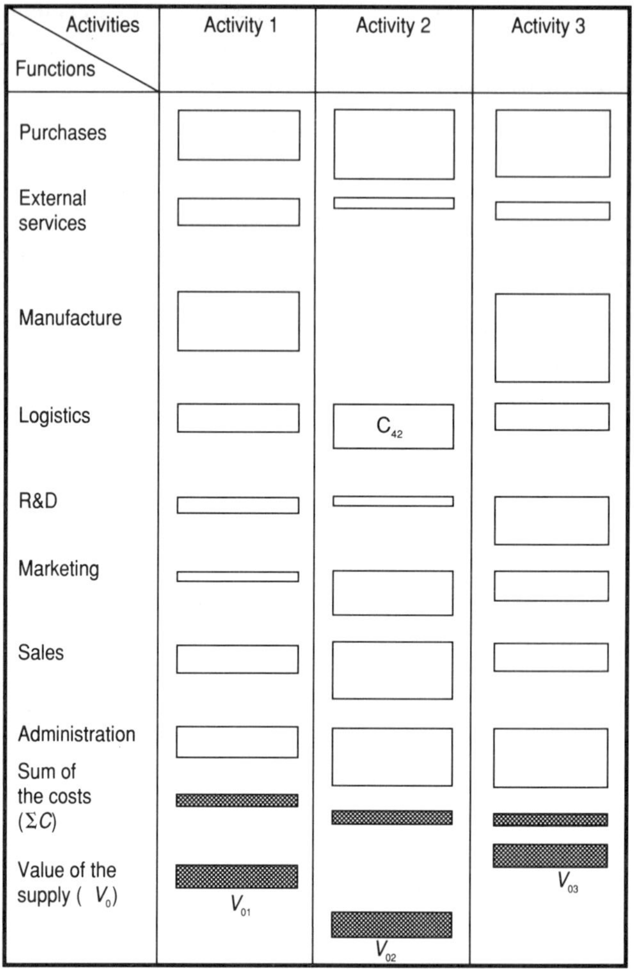

Figure 3.1 Matrix representation of the firm
Source: Sabine Urban and Serge Vendemini, CESAG, Strasbourg.

of users (concept of consistent sales policy) and geographical area targeted. The term *function* refers to every operation which the enterprise has to carry out to provide an activity. The full list of functions to be carried out is illustrated by the cost profile of the activity. The *company*, as a legal entity, covers all the activities and organizes functions for each activity.

Competitiveness lies at the level of the activity; the key factors for success are to be found in the interpretation of the cost analysis. The overall competitiveness of the company lies in the way its activities are co-ordinated and in the congruity of the management of functions, each being subject to the constraints proper and specific to each activity.

Figure 3.1 represents the actual configuration of the resource allocation matrix. Each box corresponds to the cost of the function for each activity. Reading down the columns gives an analysis of the cost of exploitation for the activity concerned. Reading across the line gives the apportionment of a particular function over the various activities.

The key dimensions for the interpretation of the figure are as follows:

- The value of the supply (V_o) per activity is obtained by dividing the turnover for the activity by the number of invoiceable units of a similar nature.
- The cost of a function within one activity (C_{ij}) corresponds to the cost of the function *i* for the activity *j*; it is represented by the boxed area (e.g. the logistical cost of activity 2 = C_{42}).
- The total cost (ΣC) is equal to the total of the boxes which relate to the management of an activity (e.g. ΣC_{ij} for activity *j* over the eight functions listed).
- The cost analysis corresponds to the relative cost burden of a function in relation to the total costs associated with an activity (e.g. burden of the logistical cost for activity 2 = $C_{42}/\Sigma C_2$).
- The net margin ($V_o - \Sigma C$) for an activity *j* ($V_o - \Sigma C_{ij}$) corresponds to the true financial profitability; expressed as a percentage it is represented by ($V_{oj} - \Sigma C_{ij}/V_{oj}$).

The juxtaposition of these different evaluations makes it possible to identify several essential variables:

- the profitability proper to each activity (analysis of $V_o - \Sigma C$);
- the significance of the function *i* in the control of the costs of each activity;
- the valorization level of the activity (analysis of the ranking of V_o).

The final element in the interpretation of this matrix is the concept of competence,[3] which supplies the decision-makign tools. Access to this competence assumes an efficient mastery of the functions involved and a pertinent analysis of the existing quantitative and qualitative barriers to entry into the sector.

There are three *quantitative barriers* to entry: the influence of volume and experience; the influence of input costs; and the influence of introductory costs. The influence of volume and experience traverses the distinction between the fixed costs associated with the function (according to the given activity) and the variable costs. The relative proportion of fixed costs to variable costs determines the slope of the function (cost of the function *i* for the activity *j*/quantity produced). The higher the fixed costs, the more sensitive the inclination is to volume and the steeper the curve: the higher the variable costs, the more gradual the slope and the less sensitive to the volumes produced in activity j.

Activity / Function	Activity 1		Activity j	Activity k
Function *i*	competence (*i*,1)			

Figure 3.2 Function management: key elements
Source: Sabine Urban and Serge Vendemini, CESAG, Strasbourg.

In other words, the more demand made on fixed costs by the function concerned in the activity in question, the more urgent the quest for a suitable volume in order to attain a minimum performance level for the function within the activity concerned. This reference level, known as the appropriate divisor of the fixed costs, is the technical critical size. It is pertinent for each activity and for each function, but not globally. In order to obtain levels of profitability proper to its various activities, the company is thus obliged to cope with several technical critical size constraints.

Two additional elements are needed in order to come to terms properly with the reasoning of the model: the fixed costs threshold (the level of activity beyond which the fixed costs move into a different band); and the apportionment of fixed costs, that is, the spreading of the fixed costs for a single function over several activities.

The second quantitative barrier is the influence of input costs. This relates to factors outside the firm, such as institutional and geographical conditions.

Finally, the influence of introductory costs refers to the impact of geographical location on the cost of a function. This is particularly relevant in the case of logistical functions (distance from the customer bases, etc.).

The *qualitative barriers* relate to the know-how required to take on and improve the working of a given function or activity. By way of example, a qualitative barrier to the sales function in respect of a given activity might be the total accumulated sales contacts which create a responsive climate and thus provide a certain short-term stability and security of turnover.

As a general rule, the more a function, in its implementation, can avoid externally set objective procedures (e.g. production standards set by the supplier of a machine), the higher the qualitative barriers for that function within a given activity. Thus qualitative barriers dominate in the case of functions where there is a degree of freedom as regards the conditions and methods of implementation.

Analysis in terms of competition

Strategic conditions for the firm, both external (the choice, maintenance and separation of activities) and internal (the administration of the functions to ensure they are up to standard for an activity) are obtained by means of a dynamic application of this matrix-based model.

The objective components of internal decisions (management of functions) and external decisions (management of activities) stem from a comparison of the elements on the matrix for the firm under study with those of its principal competitors. A comparative and costed analysis of the matrix elements for the competitors parallels the analysis of the competition. The costed dimensions which come out of this analysis are as follows:

$A = \sum_{i=1}^{n} \frac{(V_{oj} - \Sigma C_j)\, i}{n}$ = average structural net margin ratio for the activity j (n = number of major intervening factors on the activity j);

B = standard deviation from this average A;

$$C = \sum_{i=1}^{n} \frac{(V_{oj})\ i}{n} = \text{average value of the supply on the activity } j;$$

D = standard deviation from this average C;

$$E = \sum_{i=1}^{n} \frac{(\Sigma C_j)\ i}{n} = \text{average level of costs on the activity } j;$$

F = standard deviation from this average E.

Using a combination of the data described above it is possible to draw up a typology of activities in competitive terms.

- *Fragmented activities* are characterized by numerous competitors (n is significant) with a poor level of concentration (all the parties involved in the activity are of similar size). Confirmation of fragmented activities can be obtained by checking the dimension D: standard deviation from the value of the high level of supply. The tremendous variety on the market demands a 'made to measure' product. A real commitment of the producer makes it possible to adapt the product to suit the customer and negotiate prices with a considerable degree of freedom. Moreover, two further elements go to make up the conditions of a fragmented activity; low barriers to entry (readily available techniques, easily accessible central functions at competitive cost) and the absence of economies of scale, with cost increases only tenuously linked to the size of production.
- *Emergent activities* are identified by means of a large number of potential competitors (high n) together with a great variety of technical options (high F).
- *Mature activities*[4] are characterized by a smaller number of competitors (lower n). Knowledge of the product unifies purchasing conduct and imposes a sort of market price. Competition is therefore based on cost management (D: low standard deviation from the value of the supply; F: high standard deviation from the average costs).
- *Activities in decline* generally have an asymmetrical aspect (few competitors, with certain companies dominating) and a low rate of growth. This leads to a low average structural net margin ratio (low A).

- *Worldwide activities* are those in which the principal participants are scattered around the world. Once the geographical dimension has been defined, all the other classifications (fragmented, emergent, mature, in decline) may be applied.

Table 3.2 illustrates the characteristics by means of which the principal types of activity may be identified within the analysis of the competitive framework, namely, by comparison of the elements of the matrix.

Table 3.2 Analysis of the competition and identification of the status of activities

Characteristics \ Activities	Fragmented	Emergent	Mature	Decline
n	high	high	average	low
D	high	high	low	low
F	low	high	low	low

n = number of parties involved.
D = standard deviation from the average for the value of the supply. Indication of ability to escape from the price criterion.
F = standard deviation from the average costs which indicate the degree of freedom in implementation.
Source: Sabine Urban and Serge Vendemini, CESAG, Strasbourg.

The suggested method of analysing the competition, by drawing up matrices representing the principal parties involved in the activity in question, also helps to identify the key factors for success in each activity. This identification is made by means of an analysis of each activity which discriminates between individual parties where, on the one hand, the value of the supply/level of costs combination shows a net margin higher than average and, on the other, individual parties with a low net margin ratio.

The main keys to success are to be found on three levels (see figure 3.3):

- the competitive environment, exemplified by the number of participants *n* and by the type of dominant relationships between them, e.g. whether there is an acknowledged market leader;
- the value of the supply, illustrated by the absolute worth of the standard invoiceable unit;
- control of skills management, illustrated by the cost levels, the

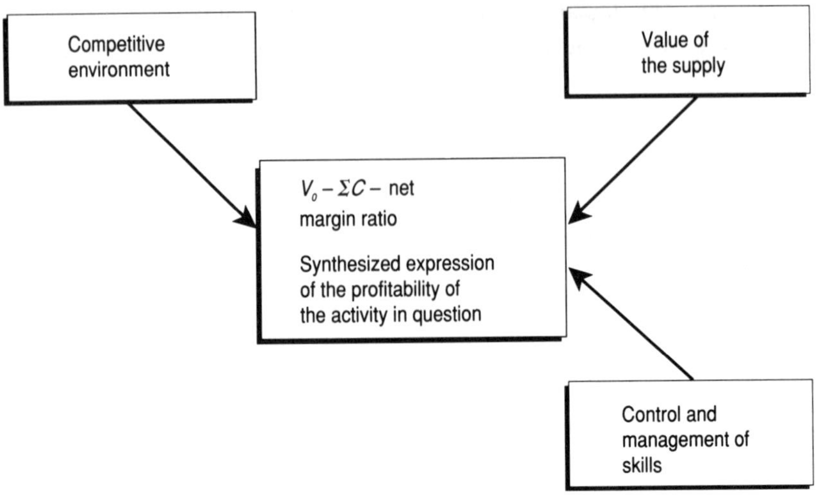

Figure 3.3 The key factors for success by activity
Source: Sabine Urban and Serge Vendemini, CESAG, Strasbourg.

relative burden of the various costs and the absolute total costs $\Sigma (C_j)i$.

In other words, the key factors for success for the activity j are identified as pertaining to those enterprises which have a net margin ratio lower than average:

$$\text{KFS} = f(n_j, V_{oj}, C_{j1}, C_{j2} \ldots C_{jk}, \Sigma C_j),$$

where:

KFS = key factors to success,
n = number of major participants in an activity,
V_{oj} = value of the supply,
$C_{j1} \ldots C_{jk}$ = importance and cost of each skill,
ΣC_j = costs of the activity j.[5]

Sometimes competitive advantage depends on a restructuring of the conditions of competition (intervention at n), it being understood that, in a sector where there are no winners (average V_{oj} and low σV_{oj}), clarification of market shares becomes a priority. Sometimes competitive advantage depends on product differentiation (factors of segmentation and margin negotiating power) in order to avoid being subjected to the cost of 'zapping' (comparable product and competitive price). And sometimes competitive advantage depends on mastery and combination of skills (cost weighting and management).

The Dynamic Management of the Firm

The representation of the firm by means of a matrix highlights three levels of pressure which affect a developing enterprise. On the activity level the question of competitive ability is posed and concerns the concept of key factors for success and the control and management of these. In another connection, the management of functions is central to the activity in enabling the competitive conditions to be met, but it must be capable of being financed at company level. Management at company level poses the question of distribution of resources among fields of activity. The purpose of this section is to provide criteria of dynamic management for each level of interest – activity, company and function.

The management of an activity: the search for competitive capability

The process of this search is summarized in figure 3.4, which relates the key structural factors for success to the relative strong and weak points of the enterprise in question within the overall arrangement.

The structural key factors for success are determined by a differential analysis of the data relating to the activity (value of the supply, competitive environment, cost levels and analysis for the necessary functions), effected by comparing those enterprises which provide the activity with a high net margin and those enterprises which provide it with a low net margin. If the variables which distinguish these are the cost variables, the determining factor in the company's competitive capacity will ultimately be how well it manages its skills. It is therefore a question of appreciating, for the functions concerned, what proportion of the performance deviation is due to control of the quantitative barriers and what proportion is due to control of the qualitative barriers.

The second important concept is that relating to the comparison between the key factors for the success of an *activity*, and the key factors for the success of an *enterprise.* This comparison makes it possible to take operational decisions.

However, this argument is not entirely straightforward. The activity's degree of maturity often ranks the weight of the various key

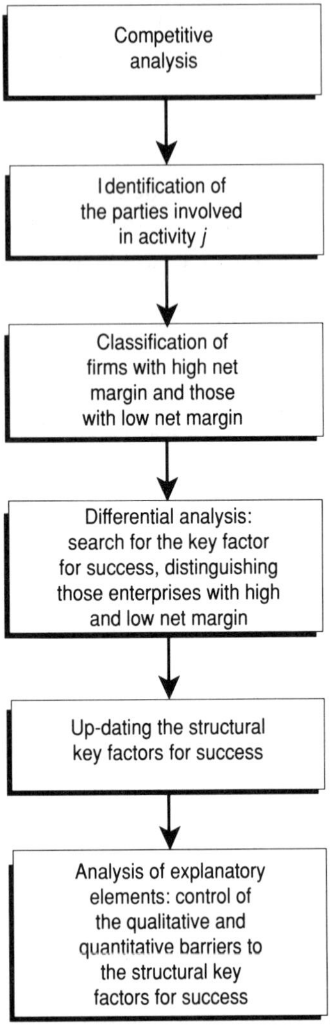

Figure 3.4 Methodology of the analysis of competitiveness by activity
Source: Sabine Urban and Serge Vendemini, CESAG, Strasbourg.

factors to success to the extent that quasi-standard management procedures for the activity may be formalized.[6] The argument here takes up the classification of activities described above.

In the case of fragmented activities (*n* important, products perceived differently, absence of economies of scale), four options may be exercised:

- seek greater standardization of the product in order to obtain certain economies of scale;

- develop product differentiation by widening the scope of the supply (regrouping and complementary services);
- go for specialization by concentrating on certain types of product (specialist image) or types of customer;
- increase size through mergers or acquisitions in order to alter the structure of the supply (number of participants and type of competition).

In the case of these fragmented activities, the main direction to be followed is determined by the ability to affect the structure of the supply (reduce the number of producers) or by the quest for standardization. As a consequence, according to the ability to alter the environment or otherwise, or the ability to affect the key factors to success (control and management of skills), four standard routes emerge (see figure 3.5).

In the emergent activities, characterized by high *n*, great variety of technical options, few commercial costs, the absence of a suitable infrastructure, poor customer experience, primacy rests on the production techniques side. The competitive capacity of such activities is usually improved through investment in technology (see figure 3.6).

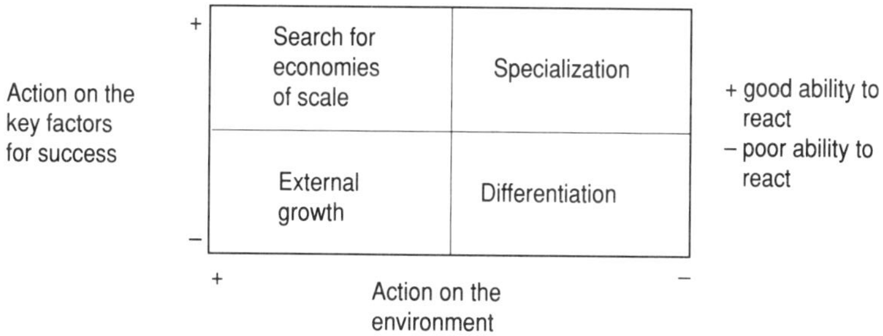

Figure 3.5 Dynamic management of fragmented activities
Source: Sabine Urban and Serge Vendemini, CESAG, Strasbourg.

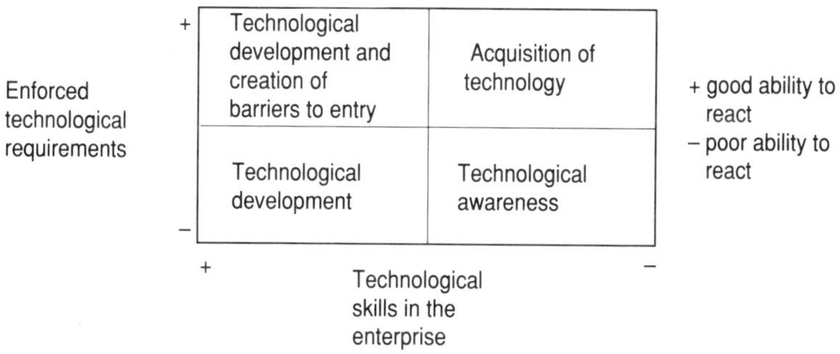

Figure 3.6 Dynamic management of emergent activities
Source: Sabine Urban and Serge Vendemini, CESAG, Strasbourg.

Mature activities are typified by the limited number of parties involved, products with similar characteristics and competitive advantages especially apparent at the level of costs and services. Competition conducted on the level of production conditions (cost of manufacturing, etc.) has often resulted in rigidity in production capacity, with problems in adjusting in the short term to the level required by demand. Medium-term solutions will depend on the firm's capacity for innovation and the prospects for modification of the key factors for success in this activity (see figure 3.7).

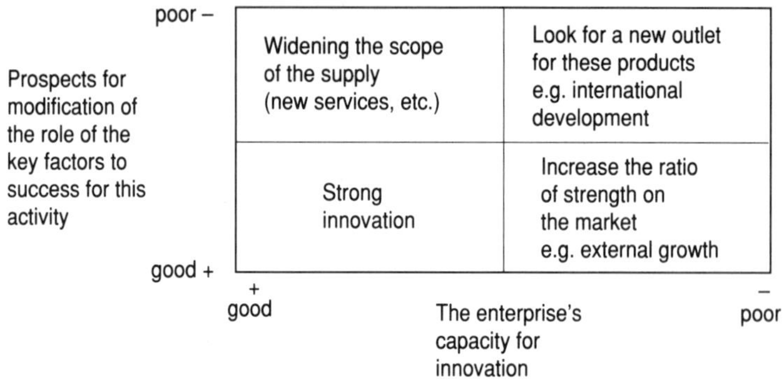

Figure 3.7 Dynamic management of mature activities
Source: Sabine Urban and Serge Vendemini, CESAG, Strasbourg.

Activities in decline are those in which the volume of sales is decreasing overall. The decline may or may not be fatal. In the case of a 'sick-bed' decline the movement into recession is slow, prices remaining stable with good margins. In the case of a 'fatal' decline, the loss of sales is considerable, prices are unstable and eroded by the competition, the products being very similar. As a consequence, there are four possible strategies, depending on whether the enterprise is in a 'sick-bed' or 'fatal' decline (see figure 3.8). Domination consists of controlling a greater part of the market, in such a way that changes in price or product can be made more easily. Specialization consists of fighting the decline by taking particular initiatives. Disinvestment consists of limiting the investment so that resources may be allocated to other activities. Pulling out is effected in the case of a fatal decline and a weak competitive position. It may take the form of reselling the activity to a new owner.

	The enterprise controls the key factors for success	The enterprise has weakness when compared with its principal competitors
'Sick-bed' decline	Domination	Disinvestment
'Fatal' decline	Specialization	Pulling-out

Figure 3.8 Activities in decline: the main solutions
Source: Sabine Urban and Serge Vendemini, CESAG, Strasbourg.

In the case of worldwide activities, the strategic orientation varies according to whether or not segments exist in particular locations and the national and international dispersion. The concept of critical commercial assets is often paramount.

Management at company level: the search for overall congruity

The enterprise possesses a capacity for competition in each activity. According to the status of each activity (in terms of structural aspects and the evolution of demand), analysis of the key factors required for success and the extent to which they are in place suggests some particular strategic options. Nevertheless, even if the strategic analysis is consistent, it is not necessarily the case that the addition of these strategic orientations will be consistent and viable at the level of the company, the legal unit of reference.

The central concept is that of the core business of the enterprise. This is expressed by a combination of all the skills employed at the level of each activity (see figure 3.9): all the expertise and skills which the enterprise can mobilize. The expertise ingredient of the mixture, where this is expressed at the level of the activity, corresponds to the position (ΣC_j, V_{oj}) of the market leaders and determines the ranking of the key factors for success (see figure 3.10).

The interconnected management of activities at company level must meet two major requirements:

- Financial congruity: does the interconnection of activities provide a balance in the flow of liquid assets?

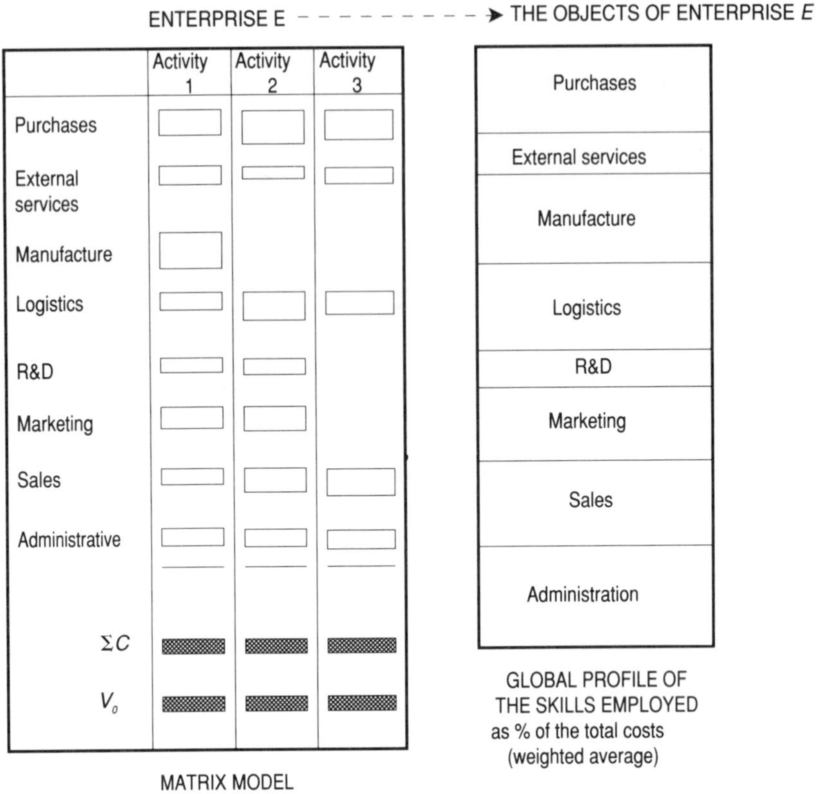

Figure 3.9 Core business: a know-how mix
Source: Sabine Urban and Serge Vendemini, CESAG, Strasbourg.

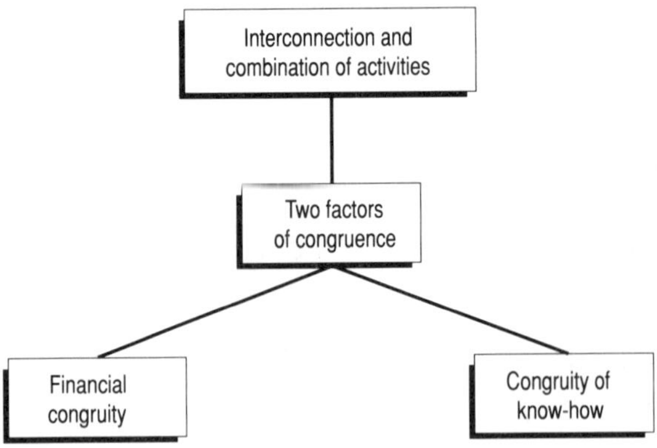

Figure 3.10 Dynamic management at company level
Source: Sabine Urban and Serge Vendemini, CESAG, Strasbourg.

- The congruity of know-how: is the combination of the types of know-how (essential in order to control the key factors for success at the level of each activity) manageable at the level of the company?

Financial congruity is fundamental at company level and is expressed in terms of the balance of the flow of liquid assets. In practice, it is the company which is responsible to its shareholders, the company which has to face up to external financial undertakings. Consequently, the management of the company's portfolio of activities has to be aimed at distributing the flow between activities but, above all, at ensuring a significant and positive cash flow in order to guarantee the continued existence of the enterprise.

Competitiveness at company level is therefore mainly expressed by its capacity to generate positive resources from the combination of the various activities. Here again we find a whole arsenal of portfolio models. The Boston Consulting Group (BCG) distinguishes four categories of activity:[7]

- *cash cows*, which are the principal sources of internal finance (earnings ploughed back) and which will also support developing activities;
- *stars*, which become the factors that generate liquid assets;
- *dead-weights*, which weigh down the overall balance, generally providing neither growth nor margins;
- *dilemmas*, activities where decisions as to commitment or withdrawal have to be made according to whether or not competitive trump cards are held.

According to the BCG analysis, the traditional factors which affect cash flow are the market growth rate and the relative market share. Following on from this, the work carried out by the Strategy Planning Institute, Cambridge (Mass.) puts forward two principles:

1. Cash flow is negative in rapidly growing markets unless the share of the market becomes significant, in which case cash flow becomes strongly positive.
2. On slow-moving markets cash flows generally become positive. The greater the share of the market, the more important they become.

In the matrix-type model presented here, an analysis of the activity's rate of growth may be undertaken by estimation, comparing

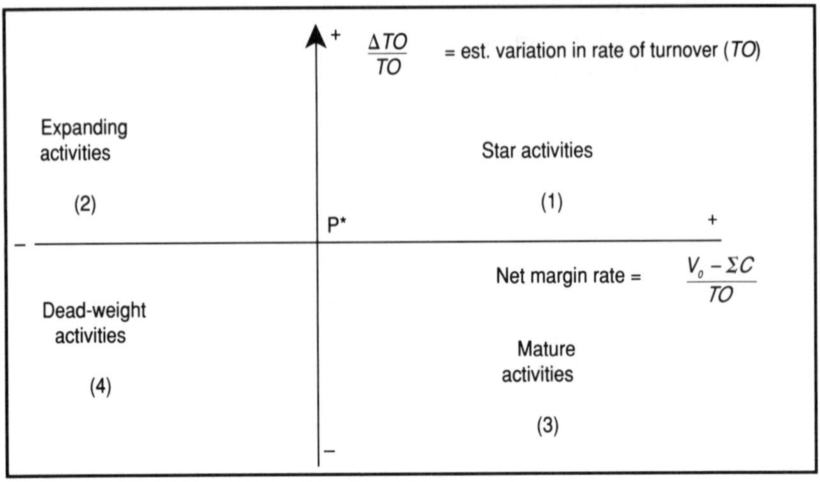

Figure 3.11 Analysis of activities demonstrating their contribution to cash flow
Key: + = high; – = poor; P* = mean point which corresponds to the activity whose rate of expansion is near average and whose profitability is near average.
Source: Sabine Urban and Serge Vendemini, CESAG, Strasbourg.

the rates of growth achieved with the main influences on the activity concerned.

Taking into account the dual dimension (estimated rate of growth of the activity and net margin level), the typology of the activities therefore takes shape as shown in figure 3.11. Area (1) represents the 'star' activities with high margins and the prospect of high growth. Area (2) corresponds to activities where turnover growth may be high but where the conditions of profitability are not stable (as regards the value of the supply and/or the conditions of exploitation). Area (3) is where the activities produce high margins but without much prospect of growth. Area (4) poses problems because it denotes a poor contribution to margins and poor market prospects.

The firm seeks to combine activities with a view to providing a balanced flow. In this context, portfolio methods are above all tools which the general management can use in its deliberations, illustrating balanced or unbalanced portfolio configurations. The consultants Harlé, Chevalier and d'Hoeraene suggest a portfolio structure using the ratios shown in table 3.3.[8]

The principle of assimilation of new activities should take its inspiration from the principle of 'burgeoning' put forward by Octave Gélinier.[9] The diversification procedure covers, in fact, three possibilities:

Table 3.3 Analytical table of the management of activities within a company: states of equilibrium

Activity	General rate of growth (%)	Necessary contribution to turnover (%)	Necessary contribution to margins (%)	Ideal customer distribution (%)	Resource employment
Developing activities $\Delta TO/TO >$ av.	$\geqslant 8$	20	30	50	2/6
Stable activities $\Delta TO/TO \sim$ avg.	0–8	50	50	30	3/6
Activities in decline $\Delta TO/TO <$ avg.	$\leqslant 0$	30	20	20	1/6

Source: E. Harlé, G. Chevalier and d'Hoeraene *Comment adapter l'entreprise à l'évolution des marchés?*, Dunod, Paris, 1988, p. 64.

- Vary the product: develop other versions (more points of reference) in order to cover the varied customer expectations. This corresponds to the normal dynamic management of an activity.
- Burgeon by using the company's existing skills: this involves taking on new activities, maximizing the company's know-how in the field. It represents a closely linked diversification.
- Diversify into other fields: this relates to the assimilation of new activities, not linked to the field already mastered. It represents a conglomerational diversification (see figure 3.12).

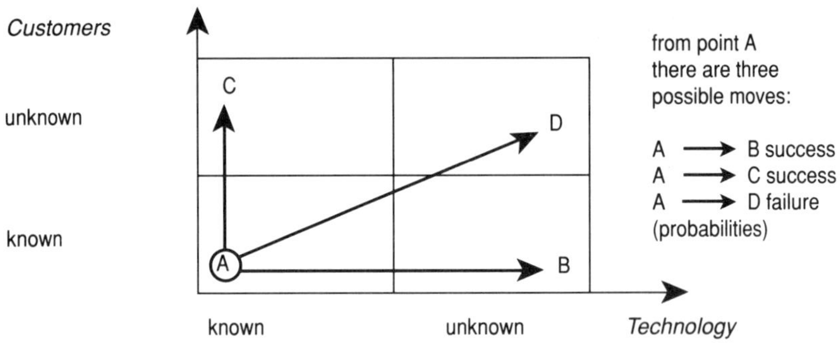

Figure 3.12 The burgeoning theory
Source: O. Gélinier, *Stratégie de l'entreprise et motivation des hommes*, Editions d'Organisation, Paris, p. 132.

Gélinier puts forward the following three principles:

1 If your current activities have growing markets, do not diversify if you want to fulfil the ambitions for growth. Vary the products and widen the markets without changing the type of business.
2 If the current activities have reached a turnover ceiling, diversify into similar kinds of products, expanding into those fields which remain associated with the core business.
3 'If you stick to known technology in order to cope with the commercial unknown, or if you stick to the known commercial paths in order to tackle unknown technology, there is a good chance of success. But if you plunge into the twin unknowns your risk of failure is high.'[10]

In other words, burgeoning is the development by the firm of a new activity to which the vigour of the firm's existing skills contributes.

Gélinier estimates an 80 per cent success rate for the proceeds of burgeoning, against 20 per cent for 'external' diversification.

The burgeoning must be organized and two pitfalls avoided: (a) cutting the buds by financial pruning; and (b) burgeoning in all directions and so coming to grief through over-dispersion.

Management of the functions: de-integration

The thesis presented here is based on an appreciation of the impact that planned moves at activity level will have on the cost of a function, or alternatively how the management of functions conditions the management of activities. Up until now the proposed model of resource allocation has taken the activity as the key to the allocation. However, the part played by the function in overall competitiveness is primordial.

At the level of the activity, the management of functions is essential in order to meet the competition requirements (control of costs and of the key factors to success) but it must be possible to finance this at company level. The ceasing of an activity might adversely affect the control of a function and thus be harmful to its overall financing. Because each function is spread over several activities, the interface between activities is central to the analysis of the functions.[11]

The management of functions is often looked at in terms of cost reduction, whereas the aim should rather be cost control in order to obtain a lasting competitive edge without destructuring the expertise of the firm (see table 3.4).[12]

Technically, the strategic management of functions is obtained through the representation of the enterprise on the matrix, an analysis of the key factors to success for each activity, an analysis of the business (the expertise which determines the structure) and, finally, through the creation of performance standards (by comparing and studying the competition).

The generalization of accounts by activity, targeting the cost analysis, will encourage hedging and will determine the conditions for the function's cost control in terms of de-integration. A de-integrated enterprise is one which concentrates its resources where it has the greatest competitive advantage and which handles non-distinctive functions by way of shared costs or by processing them externally. The de-integrated enterprise compares the internal cost of sales per function with the cost of external processing. In economic calculations

Table 3.4 The management of functions

	Classic management of functions: obsession with cost reduction	Strategic management of functions: control of the competitive edge
Objectives	In the short term, application of ratios and of cost-reduction rules. e.g. as % in relation to previous year	In the long term, specifying the key factors to success per activity based on accurate analysis of the competition
Method	Various cost-cutting exercises; elimination of certain discretionary activities	Detailed analysis of the firm's total cost flow, of partial costs per activity; having regard to the interface between activities
Talents needed for the successful implementation	Analytical ability; steadiness; strict management control	Ability to read the future of activities and to anticipate the key factors to success

Source: IMC, *La maîtrise des coûts*, IMC Business Communications, Geneva, 1989, p. 13.

the de-integrated enterprise makes a distinction between the 'within' (place where the main expertise is managed) and the 'without' (place where certain functions are handled).

In the conceptual framework of de-integration, the traditional firm has recourse to external bodies (enterprises or organizations) which are of a more suitable economic size to process the same type of function at less costs. Thus an electrical equipment wholesaler, whose business is oriented towards fault-finding nd advice, might decide to farm out his storage and delivery function, arranging for it to be handled over a wider range of activities (and thus at less cost) by a specialist transport undertaking. In some cases special bodies will be formed (meta-enterprises like the Prato model in Italy, involving the textile industry) to provide the handling of secondary functions (e.g. finance, information technology) at lower cost. The slimmed-down, de-integrated firm can consequently concentrate on its principal functions and gain flexibility and clarity in its cost of sales. It is undeniable that the de-integration model is superior to the accumulation function model.

Forms of Co-operation Linked to Levels of Operation

The single European market will introduce three major changes at the level of the company:[13]

- a modification of the framework of competition;
- a modification of the conditions for exploitation;
- a *de facto* modification of the firm's competitive position.

These major upheavals, which will have repercussions throughout the firm, may be pictured as shown in figures 3.13 and 3.14.

Figure 3.13 focuses on changes to the framework of competition. The removal of customs controls, the acceptance of new standards and the opening-up of the markets will all alter the size of the markets, give an impetus to de-integration and favour standardization.

Figure 3.14 illustrates the topography surrounding the changes to the conditions of exploitation; free access to inputs and services and the lowering of the cost of currency exchange will render an overall reduction in costs possible. The first effect will undoubtedly be the raising of the minimum size of company in order to remain competitive in terms of cost. The second consequence will be the pursuit of control over logistics and distribution so as to radiate over the wider markets. Finally will come differentiation on the grounds of quality: the ability to produce in modular form in order to adapt to a variety of demands, or perhaps closeness to the end-user (e.g. local after-sales service in the case of industrial products).

It is therefore unrealistic to imagine that the firm will be able to progress from a local or national level to attain European distribution by promoting all its activities. Experience has shown that geographical expansion involves a re-centring of activities. The most realistic hypothesis suggests that, in the case of small and medium-sized businesses whose resources are limited, adaptation may be achieved through a refocusing on their fields of excellence, or the particular business of the firm.[14]

However, the changes to the firm's competitive position arising out of these new circumstances will vary considerably depending on the firm's current position in terms of its business and degree of involvement with the exterior. Bommensath has drawn up a useful typology relating the currently dominant position of firms to gaps in the skills available to them in the context of the new competition

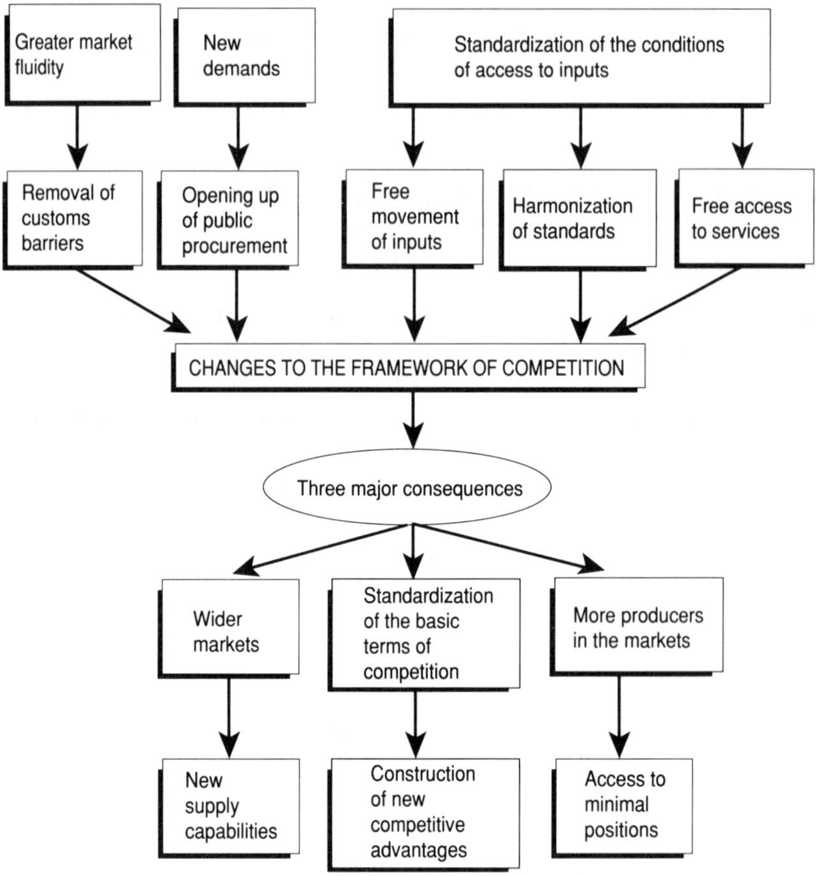

Figure 3.13 Illustration of the changes to the framework of competition at company level arising from the single market
Source: Sabine Urban and Serge Vendemini, after G. Petit, 'Stratégie 90: Developpement europóean de l'entreprise'. *Moniteur du Commerce International*, no. 93, July 1990.

situation (see table 3.5).[15] In the first type, deregulation will make apparent serious skill gaps. In the second type, adaptation is achieved through accelerating product innovation. In the third type, long-fragmented markets have blocked innovation. Parity of financial burdens and the end of protectionism will provoke more structured, more industrialized competition. So far as the fourth type is concerned, the change has already taken place, the next goal being

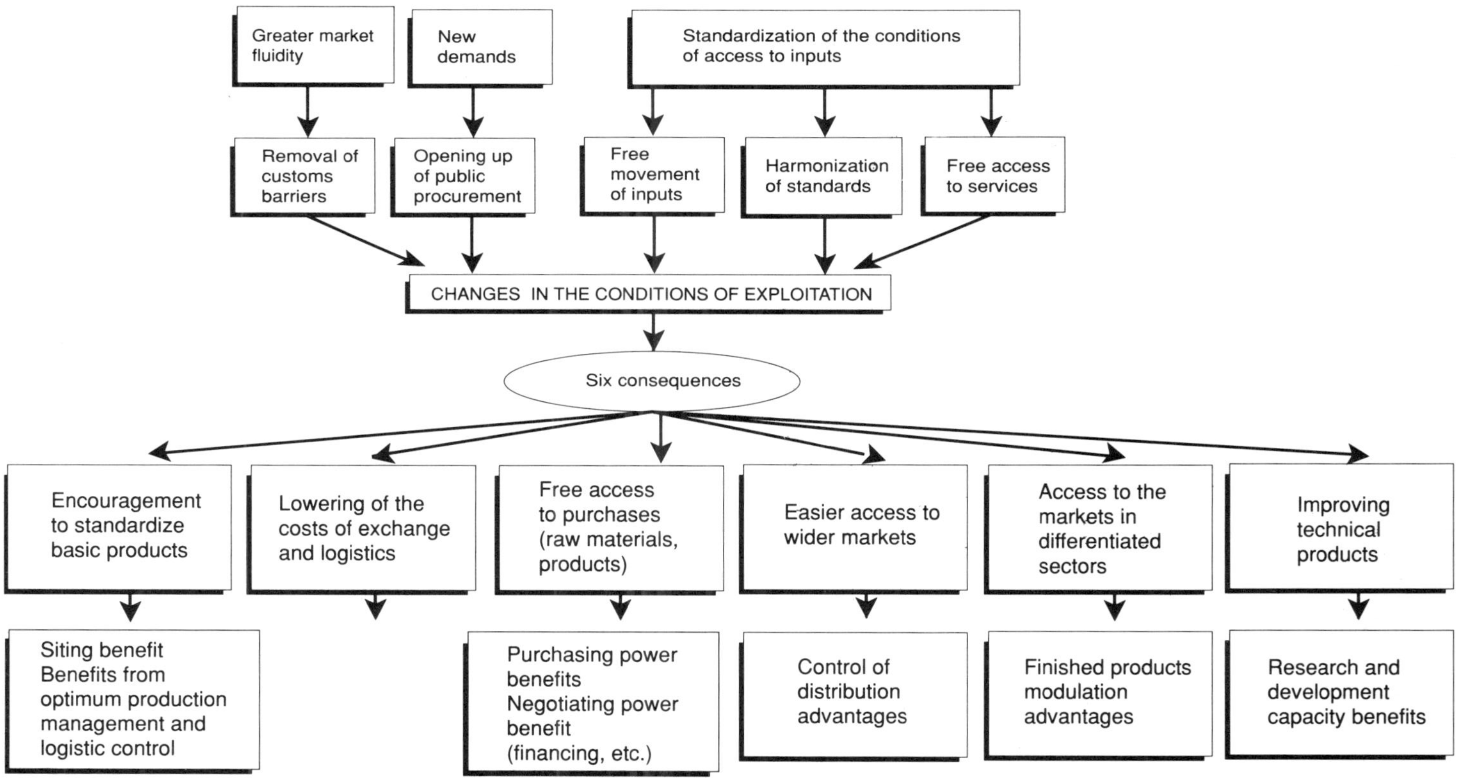

Figure 3.14 Illustration of the changes in the conditions of exploitation arising from the single market
Source: Sabine Urban and Serge Vendemini, after Petit, 'Stratégie 90'.

Table 3.5 The single market and its effect on business: changes to the firm's competitive position

	Degree of internationalization	Fiscal/regulatory environment	Business and skill gaps
1st type	Protected and national firms: road transport, etc.	Fundamental deregulation after a long history of interventionism and protectionism	Substantial gaps in skills; profound changes including cultural (modernization, innovation, internationalization)
2nd type	Firms hampered by regulations: food industries, etc.	Moderation or elimination of restrictions; deregulation	Compensation for skills inhibited by regulation, e.g. innovative skills in food industry enterprises
3rd type	Underdeveloped or poorly internationalized firms: textiles, etc.	Parity of fiscal and other charges	Gaps in international skills; modernization etc.
4th type	Developed and internationalized firms: insurance etc.	Distortions to be reduced	Use of competitive edge over European competitors
5th type	Firms engaged in European-style business: radiotelephones, etc.	Key problem of European standards and research in the face of Japanese competition	Need to build more complex skills, often associated with several businesses

Source: after B. Bommensath, *Manager l'intelligence de votre entreprise*, Editions d'organisation, Paris, 1987.

access to a European dimension. In the fifth type, firms already have a European dimension, the issue here being the creation of a lasting competitive advantage over the extra-European competition.

However, firms have entrenched perceptions of this imminent environment and of appropriate responses to it (see figures 3.15–3.17). External solutions (partnership, merger) attract as much support as internal solutions (restructuring, reorganization) (see figure 3.16). Furthermore, the aims of specialization and of achieving critical size are fairly general. In this context, collaboration is often mentioned as a means of accelerating adaptation. In the following sections we shall show that a diagnosis at company level suggests three kinds of co-operation and types of agreement.

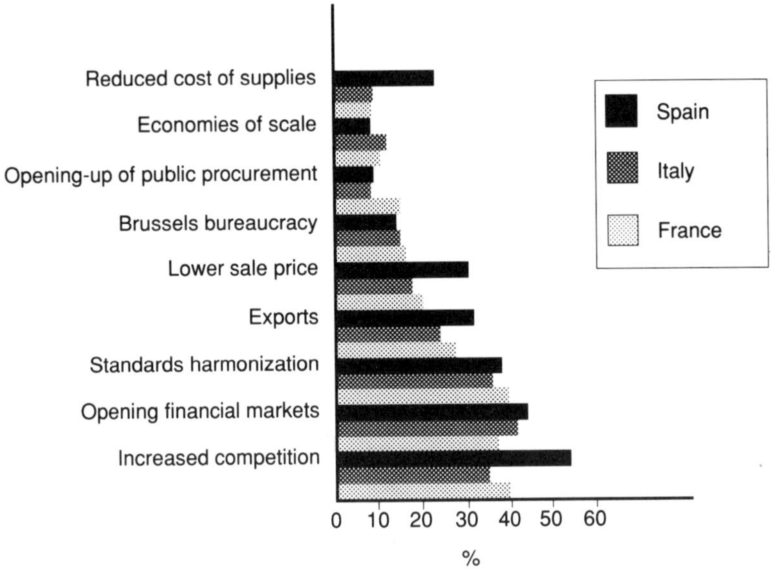

Figure 3.15 Perception of the single market: results of a study (question: what elements of the single market are deemed important?)
Source: Ernst and Young Audit et Conseil.

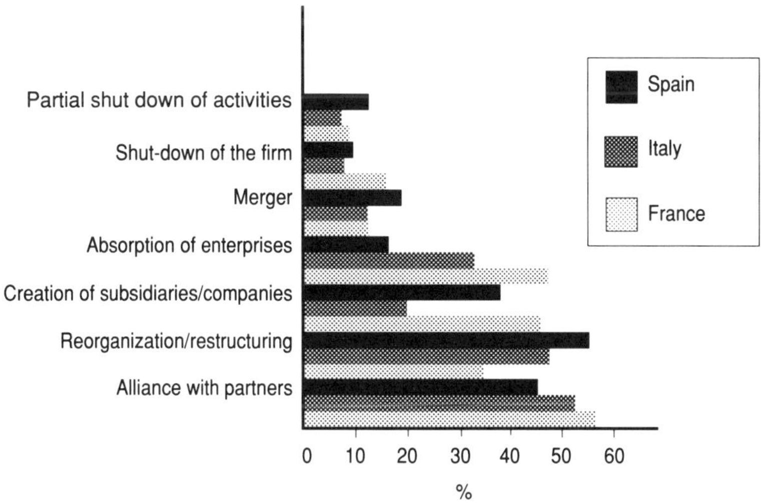

Figure 3.16 Anticipated major strategies: results of a study
Source: Ernst and Young Audit et Conseil.

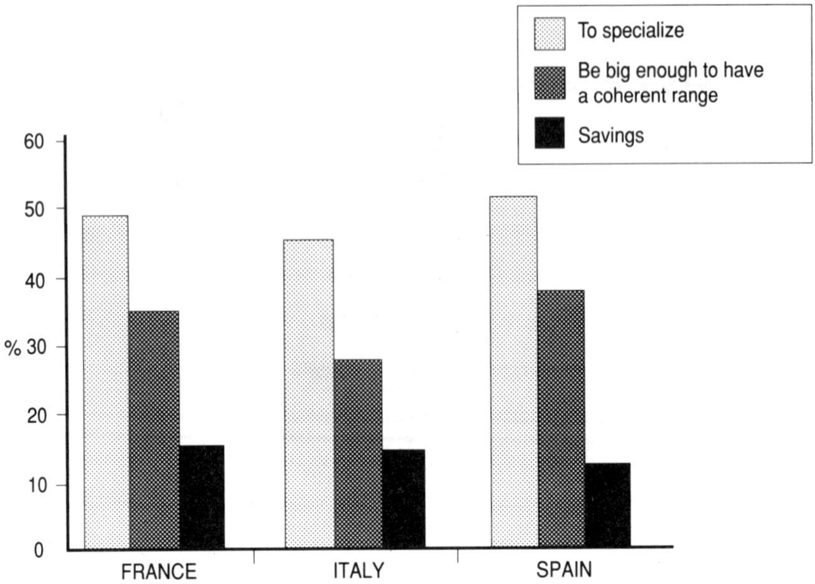

Figure 3.17 Prospects for 1993: results of a study
Source: Ernst and Young Audit et Conseil.

Levels of Resource Allocation and Types of Co-operation

The company matrix enables us to identify the main questions which are posed at the level of a developing firm. In each field of activity, the competitive capacity of an enterprise is demonstrated by the combination of the key factors for success. By 'key factor for success' we mean the differentiated value of the supply (expressed in the price level) or an efficient combination of production factors (a relatively good cost level). The competitive capacity of an enterprise is assessed by comparing the skills required (determined from an analysis of the main competitors) with the skills possessed.

In this assessment a distinction must be made between the minimum factors which are needed to survive in this activity (which most competitors are able to control) and the differential factors which give a competitive edge. As a general rule the minimum factors are the commonplace factors, while the key factors for success correlate with the differentiating skills. A general classification of commonplace skills, differentiating skills and developing skills has arisen from recent studies.[16]

At the level of the company, there is a sharing of resources or a sharing of expertise between several fields of activity. Those skills which are shared or spread over several fields of activity must be subjected to transverse evaluations (cost of the function for each activity and at company level). An analysis of the matrix highlights several types of disparity between skills possessed and skills needed.[17]

- The first type (development disparity) relates to the lack of those skills which are required in order to manage the growth of the activities, without there being any change in the ranking of the key factors to success (e.g. increasing the supply capacity within an activity).
- The second (strengthening disparity) refers to the need for skills to consolidate control of the key factors to success in respect of existing activities (e.g. setting up a distribution network, finding an opening in an export market).
- The third (repositioning disparity) corresponds to the lack of those skills required to bring about a change in the status of the key factors for success for the existing activities (e.g. to move from a pricing policy to a policy of differentiation through the services associated with the products).
- The fourth (deployment disparity) concerns the lack of those skills needed to succeed in new activities. Numerous studies have shown how difficult it is to find short-term solutions for this type of disparity (see the section on 'burgeoning' above).[18]

The new competitive environment will intensify certain disparities. The diagnosis of each firm's 'European context' will be made in terms of a rapid attainment of a balance between resources and skills to be enhanced and/or acquired.

The constraints imposed on small and medium-sized firms by the lack of resources in the short term thus force them to identify quickly their activities of excellence (those in which there is good control of the key factors for success and a competitive edge) and the so-called 'strategic' national or international markets (those in which they hold the necessary key factors for success). In this context the ability to create, to acquire and to co-operate will be central to these adaptations.

- Creation (of a subsidiary, for example) will provide a good degree of control over operations but it often takes a long time to obtain a satisfactory return on the investment.

- Acquisition makes it possible to reach a significant level of development quickly but the cost is often high. Moreover, it often places a heavy demand on 'management energy'[19] in order to attune working methods, cultures or several different management systems.
- Co-operation through a system of alliances, whether in a limited or more complex agreement, enables the objectives (critical size, cost reduction, etc.) to be achieved more quickly. There may be a heavy demand on managerial energy (for there is a constant risk of conflict: see part III) but the initial investment frequently remains low and flexibility is improved.

The co-operative solution will become the favoured one for small and medium-sized firms because it gives them access to new markets, new functions (a distribution network, after-sales service, etc.) and a better position more quickly, without taking on the risks and costs associated with an acquisition or the creation of a new organization.

Our research leads us to the conclusion that co-operation is the new way of adapting to the uncertainties of the market economy. Three constant features stand out:

1. Co-operation is an effective means of pushing back the firm's temporal horizon and of stabilizing the markets.
2. Co-operation reduces the risks and the time involved in the management of functions and/or the introduction of products.
3. Co-operation is a means of accelerating the acquisition of technical or commercial expertise.

Using the representative matrix of the enterprise (at company level, activity level or function level) the typology of co-operation which emerges is as follows:

- *adaptation co-operation* covers the management of and changes to activities;
- *functional co-operation* rationalizes the management of functions;
- *co-ordination co-operation* harmonizes the management of the portfolio of activities and is aimed at the viability of the company.

A diagrammatic representation of this typology is given in figure 3.18.

The studies of co-operative alliances conducted by CESAG (the Centre d'Etude des Sciences Appliquées à la Gestion at the Robert Schuman University, Strasbourg) cover two particularly interesting

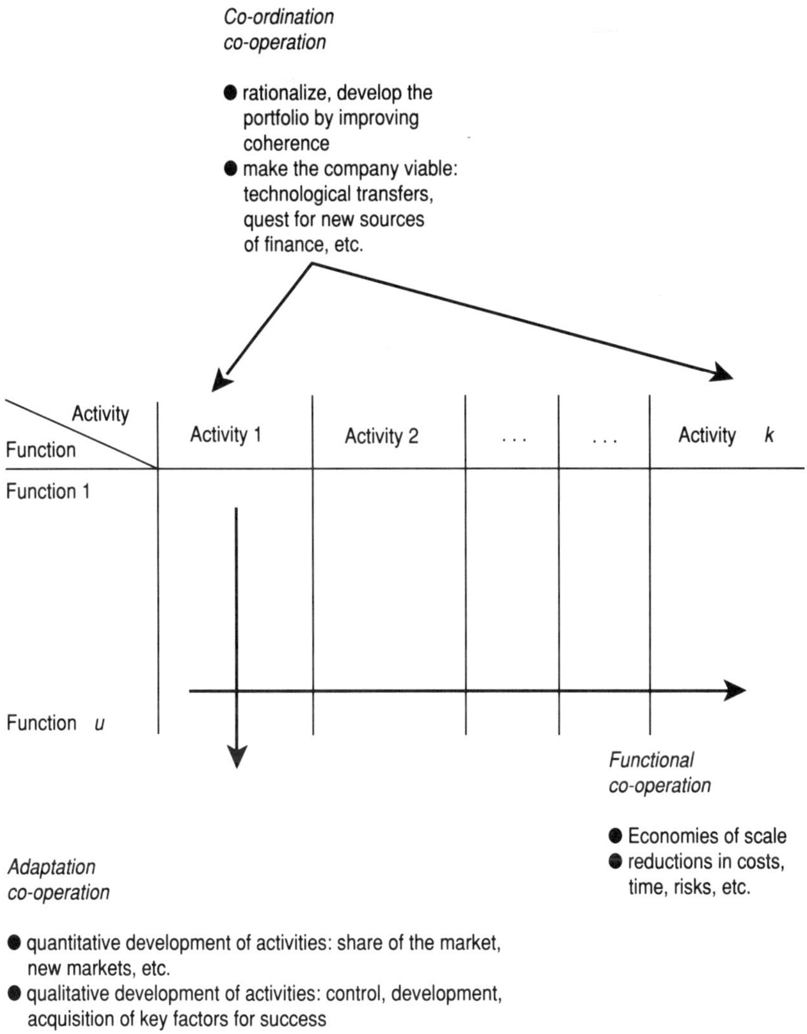

Figure 3.18 Representation of the three types of co-operation
Source: Sabine Urban and Serge Vendemini, CESAG, Strasbourg.

areas of observation: Western Germany, which has provided the pattern for European industry since the end of the Second World War, and Italy, which, for a number of years, has demonstrated entrepreneurial vitality and astonishing industrial creativity. The German sample was set up using the RKW sample of 2,000 firms (the members of the Rationalisierungs Kuratorium der deutschen Wirtschaft) and resulted in the processing of the replies to 200 questionnaires and thirty-six interviews. The Italian sample, set up with the aid of Confindustria in Rome and the Centre Studi sui Processi di Internazionalizzazione (CESPRI)/University L. Bocconi in Milan, was aimed at 4,000 industrial companies and led to the processing of 816 questionnaires and thirty interviews. The detailed results of these studies have been published by us elsewhere.[20] Other recent studies have demonstrated that there is already a preponderance of adaptation co-operation agreements aimed at accelerating acquisition of a new competitive capability (see figure 3.19).[21]

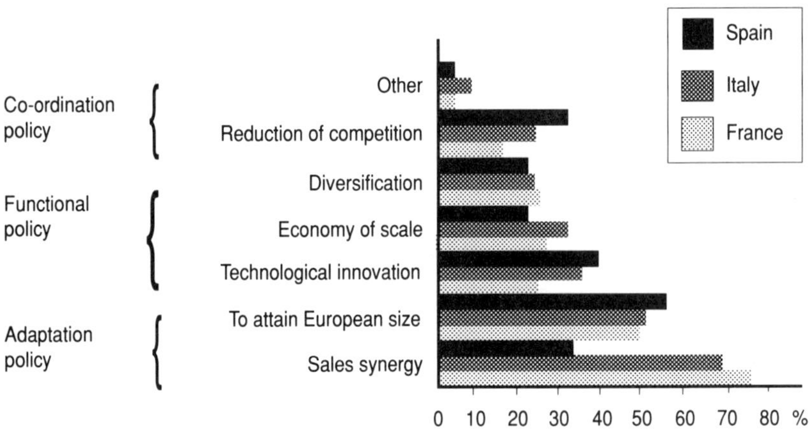

Figure 3.19 The hierarchy of types of co-operation: the current perception of the content of alliances
Source: Ernst and Young Audit et Conseil.

Adaptation co-operation

In the context of the new competitive environment described in the first part of this work, adaptation co-operation is aimed at resolving two main objectives for competitiveness at the level of the activity:

- to facilitate access to better quantitative positions: better supply capacity, development of market share;
- to promote access to better qualitative positions: control, development and acquisition of key factors of success.

Consequently, adaptation co-operation is aimed especially at accelerating the development and bolstering of downstream skills (sales and distribution) and of upstream skills (technology).

The development of downstream skills calls for the setting up of a supply facility and a multi-branch sales chain in the markets, especially those abroad. Specific studies into the means of access to these markets demonstrate the predominance of adaptation co-operation as compared with other types, such as traditional forms of export or the formation or acquisition of subsidiaries.[22] Small and medium-sized firms will have to develop their marketing expertise to improve their chances of gaining a foothold in those foreign markets identified as strategically important by an analysis of the competition. The usual intermediaries, export agents of the traditional type, are losing their central role in favour of direct siting and local alliances. Direct siting has increased by 20 per cent over three years which illustrates a break in behavioural patterns and arises out of a new strategic culture.

The development of upstream skills calls for great attention to be paid to technology. In practice, control of the various and innovative technologies will secure a real and lasting advantage within industrial undertakings. Without getting involved in a general discourse on technology, the weight of the various factors may be placed in order of importance and a distinction made between the main categories of firms (see table 3.6).

In the case of industrial firms dominated by product and process innovation, the acquisition and development of technological resources are expensive and far exceed the research and development budget. Technological skills have their own life cycle. They materialize, separate and become commonplace before declining. The cycles have a tendency to become shorter. A more rapid amortization of technological investment is consequently essential if the firm is to be in a position to finance future developments. To this end, a higher commercial profile (higher turnover) or spreading the cost of technological investment over several activities (synergy) will help towards a higher overall technological level.[23]

Three paths to better technological capability emerge: improving the means of access to technology (beyond just internal research and development, subcontracting research work, acquisition of technology, etc.); the promotion of innovation; and collaboration.

Table 3.6 Performance discrimination factors by type of enterprise

	Type of enterprise			
Variables	Services	Industry (investment/intermediate)	Industry (consumer)	Distribution
The basic business	Tangibility of the service	Product and process innovation	Product quality; renewal of the range; management; distribution	Adaptation to the market
The assets	Corporate name; securities	Know-how; flexibility	Trade marks plant	Logistics; siting
Source of profit	Economy and time management	Component standardization; growth	Price control; productivity	Stock rotation; Margin mixture
Human qualities	Creativity; loyalty; availability	Technical skill; polyvalence	Specialization; respect for procedures	Team spirit; responsibility

Source: after O. Gélinier, *Strategie de l'enterprise et motivation des hommes*, Editions d'Organisation, Paris, 1990, p. 279.

Functional co-operation

This type of co-operation is aimed at reducing the cost of one or more functions within an activity and/or within the company as a whole. The problem of the management of functions has been covered earlier in this chapter. Here we look at the methods practised, listing the ways in which the cost of a function is controlled and better managed.

It is always difficult to think at the level of the function, since the management of functions has to be exercised at the level of each activity in order to meet the exigencies of competition (necessary control of costs and control of the key factors for success), and is fundamental at company level: these functions contribute to the crystallization of know-how which ultimately defines the business carried on.

Within a company, the cost of a function is often shared between several activities. The concept of shared cost is thus a determining factor in function management at the company and activity levels. Three possibilities may be envisaged:

- efficient cost-sharing, which refers to sharing among the activities the cost of those functions which correspond to the key factors for success;
- impartial cost-sharing, which refers to the equitable sharing among activities of the cost of non-distinctive functions,
- anti-economic cost sharing, which refers to the enforced search for lateral distribution of the function (forced spread over several activities) to the point of de-specializing the activities, so as to centralize the functions and expenses within the company.

The option of co-operating in order to strengthen an activity's competitiveness (to handle the function at a cost lower than the internal cost) therefore currently appears to be one of the keys to strategic management (strengthening the activity's competitive position) and to internal management. However, the option taken (handling the function alone or with others, internally or externally) must take into account the role the function plays in the other activities or there is a danger of disjointing the company and generating other over-costs.

The interconnection of functions is therefore of critical importance in the determination of company policy, since it structures the whole firm. Figure 3.20 enables a diagnosis to be made of the method of

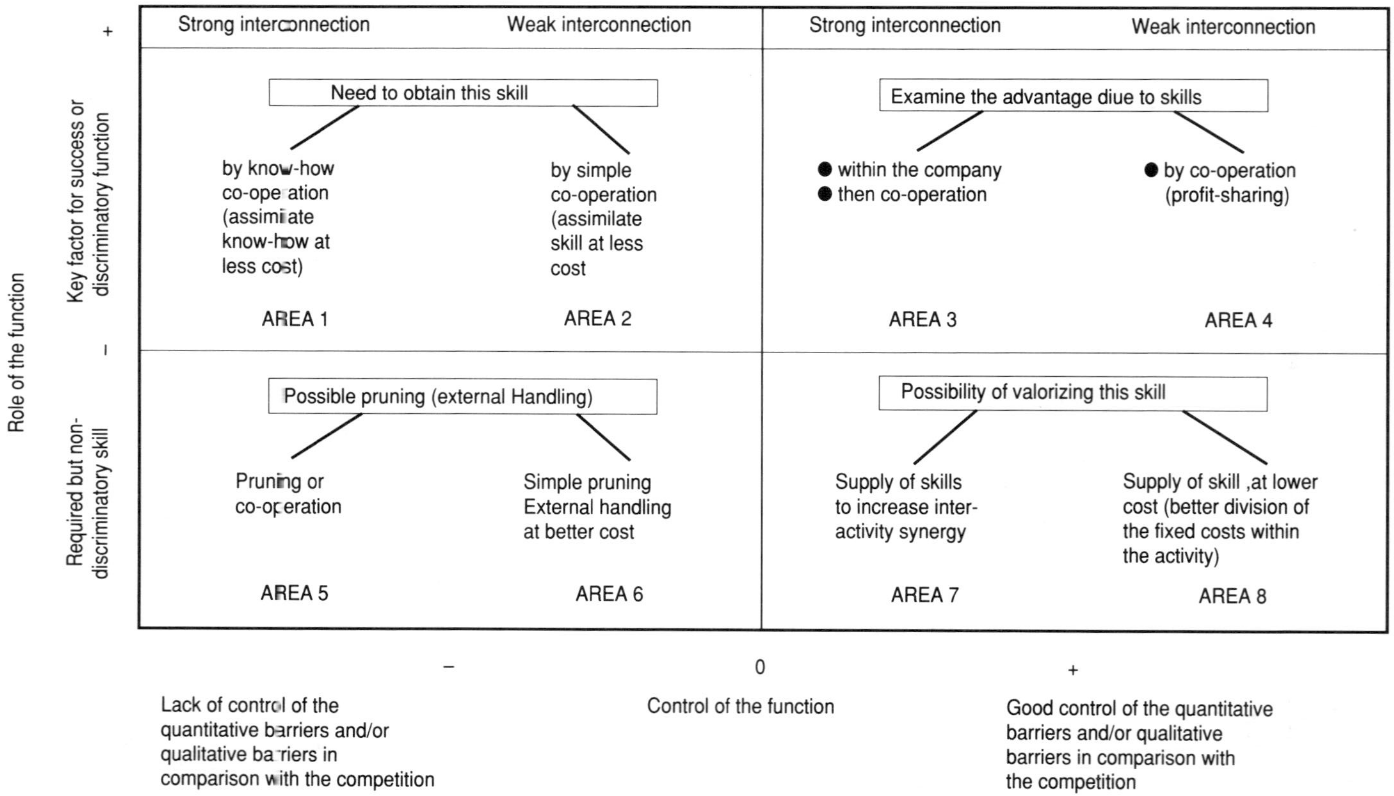

Figure 3.20 Diagnosis of the function and solutions in terms of co-operation
Source: Sabine Urban and Serge Vendemini, CESAG, Strasbourg.

dealing with a function according to whether or not it is a key factor for success, how the function has performed (in relation to the best competitors) and whether the function is independent or related to other activities. This analytical table suggests procedures to be used to obtain a skill, to develop it or to exploit it. Co-operation is therefore:

- a negotiated procedure accelerating access to a function by learning (area 1) or at lower cost (area 2);
- an efficient procedure which goes beyond a function (area 3) while introducing partners (area 4), in exchange for other advantages;
- a procedure which generates economies of scale (areas 7, 8).

The concrete content of the forms of function co-operation is illustrated by table 3.7.

Table 3.7 Major functions and principal content of functional co-operation

Major functions	Content of functional co-operation
Purchases	Joint purchase of supplies Common external logistics (routing of supplies)
Production	
Technology	Patent licence Engineering contract
Process	Common internal logistics Common installations Joint manufacture Communal assembly, quality control and despatch
Sales	Shared customers Combined sales force Joint distribution circuit Joint penetration of a geographical market

Source: Sabine Urban and Serge Vendemini, CESAG, Strasbourg.

Co-ordination co-operation

The company must combine its activities in order to ensure financial coherence, with a balance of generated and invested cash flow, and congruity of know-how. The springboard is obviously the company's business.

Two philosophies guide the combination of activities; the philosophy of specialization and that of diversification. In both cases co-operative procedures nowadays play a central role as accelerators of adaptation.

Two methods typify the management of activities directed by the aims of specialization: strict specialization (development of the current business) and flexible specialization (expanding into other types of business).

In the strict specialization model, the firm can either co-ordinate its existing activities more efficiently in order to establish the current business more soundly, or it can create capabilities. Specialization by better co-ordination may be achieved by acquisition or by co-operation. Whatever formula is used, two objectives are pursued:

- to bring together complementary advantages, for example distribution networks covering different geographical areas;
- to co-ordinate similar advantages, as in the case of the European arms industry, where French and German industrialists are joining forces in order to create the helicopter activity.

In this context co-operation appears to be increasingly effective. It enables the collaborators to benefit from the advantages which growth brings, without having to bear excessive investment, especially where research and development is an important factor. Co-operation makes it possible to amortize the costs inherent in a new project over wider markets from the start.

Specialization through the development of capabilities is the classic model. When the markets are relatively stable the enterprise is encouraged to invest internally. It therefore bears itself the risk of over-capacity, of sluggish return on investment and the cost of imitation (mimicry strategy). Here again, co-operation appears to be the effective formula. This is usually possible and preferred when the participants are few in number and the firms are in an analogous competitive position, with the same advantages. There is no question that co-operation can enhance the coherence of projects, avoiding duplication and competition between investment projects.

With a flexible specialization policy, the firm aims to consolidate its business by enhancing its scope. A firm usually enhances its scope by introducing a strong innovative element within the specialized activity, either on the technical side or on the sales side. In this context, co-operation can be the means of spreading the cost of gaining knowledge but often also accelerates the development and commercial validation of this innovation (as, for example, with the introduction of the VHS standard, promoting the widespread use of the domestic video cassette recorder). Co-operation between modest-sized firms may upset the relative balance of market shares, sharpening perceptions of innovation.

According to the alternative philosophy of diversification and co-operation, the company sees its development in terms of increasing the number of fields of activity. Studies of the relation between company diversification and performance have produced numerous results; the most significant are those of Rumelt (see table 3.8), who came to the conclusion that diversified firms with linked activities obtained better performances in the medium term.[24] More recently, Porter has asserted that diversification policies fall far short of obtaining the anticipated results.[25] At all events, although the effects of diversification are variable, the effects of linked diversification are not in dispute.

Table 3.8 Degrees of diversification

Degree of relativity[a]	Degree of specialization[b]		
	High (> 95%)	Medium (70% < 95%)	Low (≤ 70%)
Low (≤ 70%)	Insignificant		Firm with unconnected activities
High (> 70%)	Firm with single activity	Firm with dominant activity	Firm with connected activities

[a] Measured by the size of the largest group of connected activities figuring in the firm's overall turnover.
[b] Measured by the size of the largest activity figuring in the firm's overall turnover.
Source: G. Koenig, after A. Rumelt, *Stategy, Structure and Economic Performance*, Harvard University Press, Cambridge, Mass., 1974, p. 287.

The principle of linked diversification consists of using the expertise a firm already possesses for other activities. Where diversification is concerned, the main consideration is to know whether it would be in the firm's interest to exploit the resources and skills at its disposal in new activities on its own, or if it should encourage a partner to come in with it.

There is no question that access to diversification through co-operation offers two advantages:

- a reduction in the entry fee to an activity,
- access to economies of scope.[26]

These economies of scope in fact bring us back to the concept of synergy. Economies of scope relate to the reductions in costs which stem, not from an increase in the volume of an activity, but from the introduction of an activity which acts as a cost divisor for the other activities (from the interconnection with certain functions).

Types of Co-operation and Forms of Agreement

The previous section was aimed at defining the bases for co-operative agreements. Co-operation is born out of the constraints felt at the level of the activity (a need to develop qualitative and quantitative standards) or at the level of the functions (appearance, cost, control of the function), or else at the level of the company (the need to co-ordinate activities). This section will define the tangible foundations on which the various types of co-operation agreements are set up.

A typology of co-operation agreements

Eleven essential forms of agreement have been identified, according to their anchor point. These are set out in figure 3.21. These agreements may be aimed at adaptation, at the management of a function, or at optimizing the co-ordination of activities.

Form no. 1: research contract. A research contract is one by means of which one enterprise orders from another a piece of research in return for payment. It is normal to call the party which initiates the placing of the order the 'research placer' and the one who carries it out the 'research undertaker'. The scope of such a contract is virtually unlimited. It may be used for four purposes: information (placing all the available knowledge about a problem at the client's disposal); study (increasing knowledge in a specific field); control (checking performance to ensure the conformity of a product); and suggestion (various recommendations).

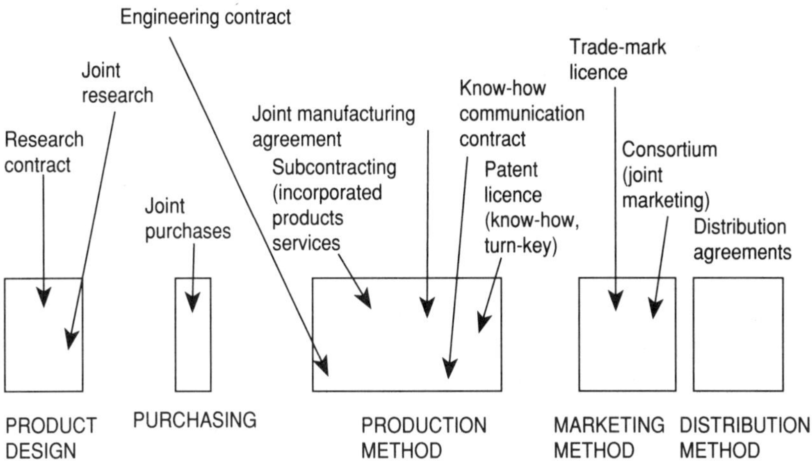

Figure 3.21 The eleven fundamental forms of co-operation
Source: Sabine Urban and Serge Vendemini, CESAG, Strasbourg.

In France, such a research contract may be described as a contract for services (it is not a mandate; it is not a contract of employment, for the researcher is not a subordinate; it is not a contract of sale). If the research leads to the manufacturing of a product, this contract becomes a contract of sale for the products manufactured.

Form no. 2: joint research agreement. Joint research agreements are generally referred to as 'research and development agreements'. They are usually entered into between two or more firms who thereby anticipate carrying out research into one or more given subjects together. The essential feature is the collaboration of the parties in a given task. These agreements may be distinguished from other research agreements which do not assume the participation of all the contractants (e.g. group agreements in which one company within the group carries out the research for all the companies in the group).

Joint research agreements can result in the formation of groups which may or may not have a legal identity, such as a company, partnership, *groupement d'intérêt économique* or holding company. These agreements are entered into for at least three reasons: the cost of research and development (difficult to finance at the level of a single company); the need for a minimum number of researchers to procure expansion; and the need for a minimum number of researchers for each speciality to ensure a result.

The field of application is the improvement of existing products, the search for new products and the refining of production techniques.

Form no. 3: joint purchasing agreement. This type of agreement is aimed at combining the purchasing power of several enterprises with a view to obtaining better terms (discounts). The legal basis is often a *groupement d'intérêt économique* (GIE: a legal entity (originally French) which falls between a company and a partnership and provides a flexible framework for individuals or companies wishing to pool some of their resources in order to develop their joint activities and profits. The statutory basis for the GIE now exists in all EC member states except Greece.) The agreement between the natural or legal persons who decide to form a GIE plays a predominant role; the GIE is a contract. In practice this contract represents a union of capabilities.

Where an enterprise does not itself have the necessary size to exercise adequate purchasing power, it may be persuaded to form a group with others. The aim of the partners to such a union is not to complement their specialist fields but to reach a desired volume.

Form no. 4: subcontracting agreement. In subcontracting, one firm entrusts to another the task of executing, in accordance with given specifications, part of a production and/or service process for which it retains the final economic responsibility. This type of agreement differs from a consortium or co-contracting agreement in which the firms are joint parties to the contract and are jointly and severally liable. Subcontracting operations are very varied: typical examples in manufacturing are the execution of cutting-out operations, production of parts, making an assembly or sub-assembly, etc.

There are two valid grounds for subcontracting: the quest for capacity (the party placing the order has limited capacity); and the quest for a specialist (the party placing the order calls upon a third party who is able to carry out certain tasks under better technical and financial conditions).

Form no. 5: engineering contract. An engineering contract is that under which an enterprise undertakes to provide certain services relating to the installation or start-up of various types of industrial plant and equipment. This type of contract covers three sub-types: the basic engineering contract, often limited to the provision of a survey and consultancy; the turn-key contract, under which the equipment is provided upon completion; and the product-in-hand contract.

There are several justifications for having recourse to this type of contract, among them that the engineering work promotes improved productivity in the firm which commissions it; that it improves the return on investment (capital goods are obtained at a better price); and that it enables benefit to be gained from new technological knowledge. These engineering contracts are often awarded following an invitation to tender.

Form no. 6: joint manufacturing agreement. Under a joint manufacturing agreement, two or more enterprises undertake to participate in the manufacture of one or more given products. This participation generally consists of using a common unit of production, or the rationalization of tasks (in which case specialization agreements come into play).

Such agreements have two aims: to strengthen the competitive capability (rationalization of the process, commencement of series production); or to join forces in order to undertake a costly manufacturing process which no firm could undertake on its own.

These agreements are delicate matters. The definition of the items to be manufactured and the specifications must be described extremely carefully and with the maximum of detail.

Form no. 7: patent licence. A patent licence is a contract under which the holder of a patent grants to a person or any other party permission to use it against the payment of a fee.

The large number of patents illustrates the success of this type of contract with firms. A licence is a means of valorizing an invention. The licence can favour a redeployment, or even a diversification of activities. For the licensing agreement to be valid, it is essential that a fee is charged to the licensee in return for the right to use the patent.

Form no. 8: trade mark licence. A trade mark licence is an agreement under which the owner of a trade mark permits another to use it, wholly or partially, in return for a fee. A trade mark is an effective tool in gaining or keeping customers. A trade mark licence is often associated with a patent or expertise licence. Sometimes the trade mark licence is the principal element around which more extensive co-operation is organized (e.g. franchising).

Form no. 9: agreement for the communication of expertise. An expertise (or know-how) communication agreement is an agreement under the terms of which the holder of the rights to a process passes on that expert knowledge with a view to assisting in the manufacture of a product or the provision of a service.

This arrangement is similar to a patent licence and is often drawn up as a licensing contract. However, although an agreement for the communication of expertise often accompanies a patent transfer or concession, no less frequent are agreements which relate solely to know-how without being linked to any parallel transfer of property. The agreement must specify the conditions under which documents (papers, plans, etc. necessary for the implementation of the process), equipment or personnel (often the grantor of the contract undertakes to train the beneficiary's staff) are transferred to the beneficiary.

Form no. 10: consortium agreement. A consortium agreement relates to accords entered into with a view to jointly gaining access to a market and capitalizing on this. Often one of the firms takes on the role of leader or pilot company.

These agreements play a determining role in increasing supply capacity. Three types of reason lie behind the development of this procedure: technical reasons (to corner new markets, especially export markets); financial reasons (the costs of a distant market sometimes exceed the capabilities of an isolated firm); and marketing reasons (supply capacity, to unify the image, to construct lines of communication).

Form no. 11: distribution contract. A distribution contract is one by means of which one firm undertakes to make available one or more points of sale to another firm which has products and services to offer the customers and undertakes to operate these.

Distribution contracts are very varied. If the distributor acts on behalf of the supplier and in his name, he is an agent (agency contract). If the distributor acts in his own name but on behalf of the supplier, he is a commission agent (commission contract). If the distributor acts on his own behalf, in his own name, by re-selling products which he has purchased outright, he is a concessionaire (concession contract). Other conditions may attach to the basic distribution contract: sole rights or otherwise, a greater or lesser degree of co-operation (technical assistance, formation of a franchise-type contract).

Different processes may be devised in order to establish and firm up the agreements for all these forms of contract. The main points are as follows:

1 The *heads of agreement*. Co-operation is, above all else, a manifestation of willingness. A heads of agreement document may be drawn up at the first exchange of views in order to determine the terms and timescales.
2 The *letter of intent*. An agreement setting out the broad principles of the future compact and the basic points. A letter of intent does not have the force of a contract; it is an undertaking on the part of the parties to come to terms within a reasonable period of time.
3 The *outline agreement*. Where contractual relations are to become prolonged, as is the case in a co-operation agreement, a convention may determine the general rules which will govern the operation as a whole.
4 The *formalities*. The importance of the undertaking demands a degree of formality. Unlike mere commercial relations, the parties cannot make do with simple procedures. The contracts have to receive special treatment; they must be drawn up with the utmost care and precision. In practice, a summary is prepared, describing the background and the aims of the operation and defining the spirit of the co-operation. Very ofen other documents are appended and the contract refers to these as regards technical or financial aspects, or concerning guarantees.

Co-operation agreements: a summary

Once the bases for co-operation agreements have been defined (the three typical objectives being adaptation, functional management and co-ordination) and the legal shape decided on (one of eleven possible forms), it merely remains to opt for the most useful, desirable and efficient legal structure.

The contract is but one of the possible ways of forming an inter-company co-operation. Figure 3.22 illustrates the five typical structures within which co-operation may take place.

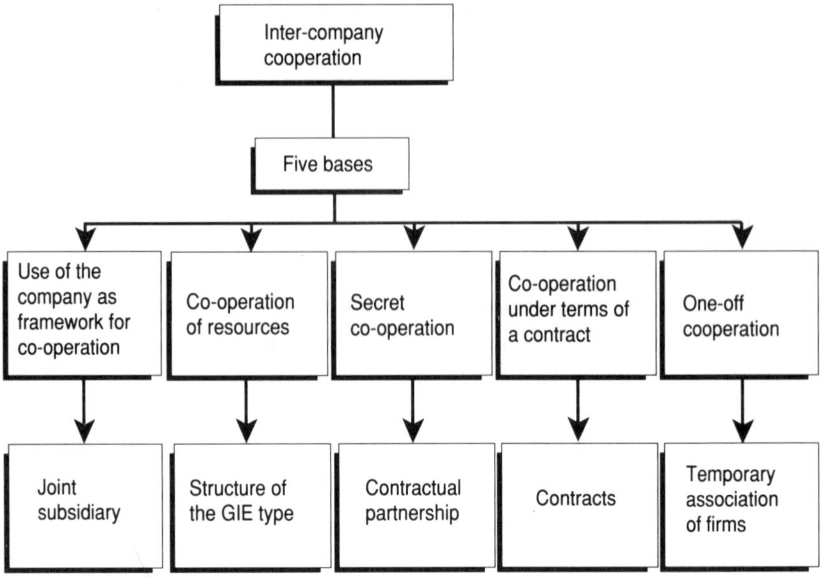

Figure 3.22 Summary of the legal bases for inter-company co-operation
Source: Sabine Urban and Serge Vendemini, CESAG, Strasbourg.

The *joint subsidiary* covers several concepts. In the widest sense it concerns a co-operation between firms within a legal structure known as a joint subsidiary, that is, a company controlled by two or more firms independent from each other. The concentration of resources within the framework of a joint subsidiary results in close relations between the partners. A very high degree of goodwill dominates this type of association.

This type of subsidiary may fall into six classes: joint sales subsidiary; joint production subsidiary; joint resource management subsidiary; joint subsidiary for the management of a complementary activity; joint subsidiary for a one-off operation; joint subsidiary as first step towards a merger.

A *groupment d'intérêt économique* (GIE) may be formed with a view to making use of all those resources calculated to facilitate or develop the economic activity of the members of the group and to improve or increase the profits from this activity. The GIE is often the basis for a joint exploitation of functions (purchasing, service management, etc.). It is one effective means of ensuring the continuous co-operation between firms and goes beyond a simple commercial relationship. Moreover, it helps to clarify the cost of providing certain functions (or a structure external to the enterprise) and facilitates the de-integration of traditional enterprises.

On the other hand, a GIE has the disadvantage of entailing the joint and several unlimited liability of the members.

A *contractual partnership* is a framework for co-operation which arises out of a choice made by the founders. It is a separate, unregistered company (participation may be made public or kept secret). This type of partnership is often used in the wine, timber and arts trades; also in the construction industry and in turn-key factory projects.

The contractual partnership may be used as a union of enterprises for a specific operation (major markets), in order to provide a function (sales on behalf of the members) or for the management of jointly owned property (wine storage vats, debarking centre for the timber trade, etc.). In France an association under the 1901 law is a similar legal entity; however, membership of an association of this type is known to all whereas the principal aim of a contractual partnership is to remain secret.

Co-operation under the terms of a *contract* provides an agreement with a great deal of flexibility, limiting the effects inherent in the existence of a legal entity. In order to be effective, the parties have to define precisely their objects and the resources to be used, but no legal collective structure will permit the parties to consult regularly in order to modify the agreements. In the same way, no decision-making body is imposed to dictate the application of inter-enterprise agreements: in this respect contracts differ fundamentally from co-operative entities which have a legal personality.

However, the lack of legal entity status does not mean the members are any less liable. Failure to execute the agreements may, apart from the sanctions provided for under the contract, be the subject of legal proceedings or, more frequently, recourse to arbitration.

The purpose of a *temporary association* agreement is to bring together different firms in order to carry out a given task which none could complete alone. The associated firms retain their total autonomy of management but temporarily join forces in order to carry out a particular operation. The association is entered into with the prospect of dissolving as soon as the precise objective has been realized. Such an association is not a company; it must also be distinguished from a GIE. There is no wish among participants to merge. A temporary association agreement may be represented by its objective (the given operation), by the method of achieving this (each member undertakes to provide discrete services) and by its duration (a fixed period).

Conclusion

The need for firms to adapt in the world of the single market, and the privileged position which co-operative procedures hold in this adaptation, lead us to highlight two main points:

- the growing role of legal factors, both in the internal management dimension and in the firm's strategic dimension: many problems will be solved by the forming of relations with other enterprises;
- the growing role which the management of relations will play in value creation and in the formation of competitive advantages.

Firms will become more and more involved in the administration of a variety of co-operative networks. These will be of three kinds: trans-company co-operation networks (co-operation all down the line with suppliers and/or customers), inter-company co-operation networks and meta-company co-operation networks (co-operation with external bodies which affect the functioning or the adaptation of the traditional firm). The exploitation of all these types of network in order to gain access to markets, to technical expertise, to better methods of handling the cost of functions, to more valuable information, and so on, will become a crucial problem for the firm.

Notes

1 G. Hamel, Y. Le Doz and C. Prahalad, 'S'associer avec la concurrence: comment en sortir gagnant? *Hanard L'Expansion*, Autumn 1989, p. 24: 'Vous ne pouvez pas échapper aux alliances stratégiques. Apprenez donc à en tirer parti . . .'

2 G. Koenig, *Management Stratégique: visions, manoeuvres, tactiques*, Nathan, Paris, ch. 6, p. 153: 'Les conduits d'acteurs et les politiques relationnelles: l'évitement, la coopération.'

3 F. J. Grouillart, *Stratégie pour une entreprise compétitive*, Economica, Paris, 1989, p. 188.

4 M. Porter, *Competition in global industries*, Harvard Business School Press, Cambridge, Mass., 1986.

5 The representation is close to that of Grouillart, *Stratégie pour une entreprise compétitive*, p. 237.
6 F. Bidault, *Le champ stratégique de l'entreprise*, Economica, Paris, 1988, p. 176.
7 C. Sicard, *Pratique de la stratégie d'entreprise*, Hommes et techniques, Paris, 1986, p. 141.
8 E. Harlé, G. Chevalier and J. d'Hoeraene, *Comment adapter l'entreprise à l'évolution des marchés?*, Dunod, Paris, 1988, p. 59.
9 O. Gelinier, *Stratégie de l'entreprise et motivation des hommes*, Editions d'Organisation, Paris, 1990, p. 130.
10 Ibid., p. 132.
11 M. Porter, *Competitive Advantage: Creating and Sustaining Superior Performance*, Free Press, New York, 1985, ch. 9: 'Interrelationships among business units'.
12 IMC, *La maîtrise des coûts*, IMC Business Communications, Geneva, 1989, ch. 4: 'Pourquoi la plupart des programmes de réduction des coûts échouent-ils?'
13 G. Petit, 'Statégie 90: Développement européen de l'entreprise', *Moniteur du Commerce International*, no. 93, July 1990, p. 23.
14 Ibid., p. 59.
15 M. Bommensath, *Votre entreprise face à 1992: Le marché unique européen*, Editions d'Organisation, Paris, 1988, p. 132.
16 J. Morin, *L'excellence technologique*, Publi-union, Paris, 1985; R. Calori and T. Atamer, *L'action stratégique*, Editions d'organisation, Paris, 1989.
17 M. Bommensath, *Manager l'intelligence de votre entreprise*, Editions d'organisation, Paris, 1988; Morin, *L'excellence technologique*.
18 M. Porter, 'De l'avantage concurrentiel à la stratégie', *Harvard L'Expansion*, Winter 1989–90.
19 Petit, 'Stratégie 90'.
20 S. Urban and S. Vendemini, *Etudes et Recherches du Commissariat Général au Plan*, no. 2: 'Entreprises allemandes et coopération industrielle à l'échelle européenne' ('German firms and industrial co-operation on the European level'), Documentation Française, Paris, 1986; 'Les entreprises industrielles italiennes et la coopération internationale' ('Italian industrial firms and international co-operation'), CESAG Working Paper, Strasbourg, 1988.
21 HSD Conseil, 'Le PME face à 1992', Erust and Young Audit et Conseil, Tour Manhotter, 92095 Paris, Ceder 21.
22 Ministère de l'Industrie et Commissariat Général au Plan, 'PMI 90: Vers la compétition globale', a survey concerning 845 small and medium-sized enterprises in France, Paris, 1989.
23 T. Durand, 'Management pour la technologie: de la théorie à la pratique', *Revue française de gestion*, November/December 1988, p. 5.
24 R. I. Rumelt, *Strategy, Structure and Economic Performance*, Cambridge, Mass., Harvard University Press, 1974.
25 Porter, *Competitive Advantage*.
26 D. J. Teece, 'Economics of Scope and the Scope of the Enterprise, *Journal of Economic Behavior and Organization*, vol. 1, no. 3, September 1980, pp. 223–47.

4

Examination of Co-operative Practices

Co-operation is a concept that national public authorities and the European Community are not promoting extensively; but the realities experienced on the ground remain largely unknown and systematic studies are rare. On the instigation of the General Commission for the Plan in Paris and the EC Business Co-operation Centre in Brussels, the Centre d'Etude des Sciences Appliquées à la Gestion (CESAG) at the Robert Schuman University, Strasbourg, has undertaken to fill this gap.

The studies carried out by CESAG cover two particularly interesting fields of observation: West Germany, which has dominated the European industrial scene since the end of the Second World War, and Italy, which in recent years has shown an astonishing entrepreneurial dynamism and industrial creativity.[1]

The research looked only at those forms of co-operation which are formulated with an international dimension. The analyses referred to below relate especially to the results of the Italian research because this was more productive in the study of the various types of agreement and their implications and, more significantly was undertaken more recently.

The first part of this chapter deals with the principal types of major agreement on the international level and is intended to highlight the characteristics of the co-operating enterprises and, in particular, the rationales implicit in these agreements. Examples of the main types of agreement are given by macro-activity. The second part of the chapter analyses the objectives pursued by the partners and endeavours to bring out the strong points of effective agreements.

Forms of Industrial Co-operation at an International Level

When trying to comprehend the practice of co-operation, various questions spring to mind:

- Among the major forms of co-operation (adaptation, functional, co-ordination), which are most commonly encountered on an international level?
- As a lot has been said about the policies of capital integration by major enterprises and financial groups, resulting in combines, mergers of interests, takeovers, etc., are co-operation policies associated with firms of a particular size?
- Is co-operation more particularly dictated for certain industrial sectors?
- Is co-operation linked to certain production methods?
- Is co-operation stimulated by the regional environment of firms?
- Are co-operation agreements more readily entered into in certain countries, related to the export activities of the firm?
- What are the main types of agreement by macro-activity (intermediate goods, capital goods, consumer goods)?
- How do each firm's interests fit in with the interests of its partners? Is it possible to arrive at an analysis of effective agreements?

The first section of this chapter addresses these various questions in two parts. First, we review the three types of co-operation and their practice on an international level, highlighting factors arising from research. We give figures showing the range of co-operative agreements in place and clarifying the attributes of the collaborating enterprises. Secondly, we examine the three main types of agreement by macro-activity, depicting the main courses which these agreements follow.

Co-operation Practice on the International level: Research Data

The extent of co-operative agreements

In chapter 3 we considered three types of co-operation through a matrix representing the firm:

- adaptation co-operation, covering the adaptation of the management and competitiveness of an activity;
- functional co-operation, aimed at rationalizing the management of functions;
- co-ordination co-operation, harmonizing the management of the portfolio of activities and aimed at making the firm profitable.

By means of an analysis of the basic contents of co-operative agreements with an international dimension, the Italian study carried out in 1988 (year of reference 1987) highlights the ranking of these three forms of agreement and the variations between small and medium-sized firms and major multinational companies (see table 4.1).

Table 4.1 The ranking of co-operative agreements with an international dimension

Types of agreement	All firms[a] (%)	SMEs[b] (%)	Major enterprises (%)
Adaptation co-operation:			
to develop market share	51.1	47.7	56.9
to gain access to new markets	36.0	41.2	27.5
to acquire new technologies	18.4	16.5	21.6
to diversify production	21.7	18.8	26.5
Functional co-operation			
to obtain economies of scale	30.5	27.7	35.3
to reduce costs, time, risks	16.5	11.2	25.5
Co-ordination co-operation			
to rationalize the portfolio	16.2	13.5	20.6
to make the firm's technology profitable	17.6	14.7	22.6
to obtain new financing	2.9	1.8	4.9

[a] As % of replies; n = 272.
[b] Firms with less than 500 employees, not belonging to a financial group.
Source: CESAG, Strasbourg/CESPRI, Milan, 1987.

Adaptation co-operation predominates over other forms of co-operation at the international level. Furthermore, some specifics emerge. The results recorded demonstrate that in practice there are differences in conduct and development policies between large and small firms. In the case of SMEs, weaker in terms of resources than the large firms, the conquest of new markets poses greater problems. The costs involved are high and partnership with a foreign enterprise therefore appears to be a sound solution. Large firms, on the other hand, are more concerned with the problems involved in rationalizing production and their portfolio of activities. They usually employ mass production methods and have a wide range of possible products to develop. There is therefore a temptation to organize the competition.

Again, the SMEs utilize more specific types of know-how. They are highly specialized and fill more or less narrow 'niches' in the market. They therefore have to exploit fully this competitive advantage without dispersing their efforts over those fields which do not coincide with that traditional line of business which they have fully mastered. Flexibility takes precedence over mass production, the quality and originality of the product being favoured against sheer quantity.

This difference in practices depending on size encourages an emphasis on the objective features of the co-operating firms.

Features of the co-operating firms

The main features of co-operating firms may be identified by means of four criteria: size, business sector, organization of production and tendency to export.

Size and co-operative practice. Italy is a country in which small businesses flourish. The 1981 industrial census revealed that firms with fewer than twenty staff employed 34.5 per cent of the working population in industry. This proportion rises to close on 60 per cent if one includes the staff employed by firms with between twenty and 100 employees.

This industrial employment pattern is fairly specific to Italy, compared with other developed industrial countries. The average industrial establishment employs 9.3 employees in Italy (in 1981); 28.4 employees in West Germany (in 1977); 56.8 employees in the UK (in 1979); 14.9 employees in Japan (in 1978). The Italian sample studied (see table 4.2) does not entirely reflect this fact. Medium-sized and large firms are shown to hold a position which is undoubtedly disproportionately important, no doubt due to the customary reluctance on the part of small and medium-sized firms to fill in questionnaires. But one may also suppose that, as a general rule, small firms feel themselves to be under less pressure to enter into formal co-operative agreements than large firms.

Table 4.2 International co-operations and size of firm

Size (no. of employees	All Italian firms[a] (%)	Sample firms				Co-operating firms[b]			
		1981 No.	%	1986 No.	%	1981 No.	%	1986 No.	%
1–49	87.2	139	22.3	164	25.0	16	13.2	19	14.0
50–99	6.9	165	26.4	170	25.9	22	18.2	38	27.9
100–499	5.[illegible]	240	38.5	252	38.3	52	43.0	48	35.3
Over 500	0.8	80	12.8	71	20.8	31	25.6	31	22.8
Unspecified[c]		83	–	50	–	21	–	6	–
Total	100.0	707		707	100.0	142	100.0	142	100.0

[a] *Source*: ISTAT, 1981 census, as % of total.
[b] Out of the sample studied 707 firms replied, 142 firms co-operated, 272 agreements (the first agreements deemed significant) were analysed.
[c] Where the sample firms did not supply this figure.
Source (except [a]): CESAG, Strasbourg/CESPRI, Milan.

In the light of this table it would seem that the practice of co-operation based on signed agreements requires a degree of organization which small firms do not possess, or only possess exceptionally.

Sector and co-operative practice. Looking at table 4.3, one sees a greater propensity to co-operate in the chemical, electrical engineering and general engineering industries, with the inclination to collaborate much less in the consumer goods industry.

To delve deeper into this relationship, the agreements have been re-classified according to Pavitt's nomenclature.[2] This distinguishes:

- highly specialized industries (specialized machinery and equipment, railway rolling stock);
- traditional industries (leather, timber, textiles, ceramics, furniture, footwear, toys, sports goods, jewellery, musical instruments, food and drink industries);
- scale-intensive industries (chemicals, rubber, iron and steel, metallurgy, consumer durables, cars and other motor vehicles, boats, radio and television, paper);
- science-based industries, with high levels of research (pharmaceutical products, cosmetics, data processing, telecommunications, electronic components, aeronautics).

According to this classification, the agreements covered by the study were distributed as shown in table 4.4. In absolute terms on the sample taken, the evolution of agreements is greatest in the high-tech or science-based industries. Nevertheless, one-quarter of the agreements were found in the traditional industries. Furthermore, co-operation agreements with an international dimension are often the key factors for these industries. They form the greater proportion of those agreements which are regarded as important.

Production processes and co-operative practice. Study of table 4.5 reveals three facts:

- Enterprises are the more open to co-operation where they have organized their productive activities in a decentralized manner. This observation applies regardless of the size of the firm: small firms as well as larger ones see in this an opportunity to increase the flexibility of their productive resources.
- Mass production favours co-operative decisions.

Table 4.3 Co-operating firms and sector of activity

Manufacturing industries	1971[a]	1981[a]	1984[a]	1987 sample	
				Total (n=707)	Co-operating firms (n=142)
Mining, mineral, chemicals	17.04	15.04	14.00	12.16	14.09
Minerals	0.15	0.08	0.01	0.30	–
Metallurgy	2.30	1.76	1.69	1.20	2.82
Non-ferrous metals	1.25	1.16	1.10	0.90	–
Non-ferrous metallurgy	9.15	7.96	7.63	6.61	4.23
Chemicals	4.06	3.88	3.50	2.85	7.04
Regenerated fibres	0.13	0.20	0.07	0.30	–
Engineering	30.75	34.08	33.43	34.99	54.23
Metal products	12.25	12.70	12.55	10.81	12.68
Machinery	8.51	10.13	11.14	12.01	23.24
Office equipment	0.19	0.30	0.10	0.16	0.70
Industrial plant	5.87	6.75	5.76	5.86	9.15
Motor vehicles	1.58	1.71	1.60	2.85	2.82
Other transport equipment	1.10	1.28	1.14	2.55	2.82
Precision machinery	1.25	1.21	1.14	0.75	2.82
Traditional industries	52.21	50.88	52.57	52.85	31.68
Food industry	4.70	4.72	4.96	5.11	2.11
Drinks and tobacco	3.10	2.40	2.25	3.60	5.63
Textiles	12.05	9.85	10.05	9.30	2.11
Leather	1.56	1.74	1.90	2.40	0.70
Footwear, clothing	11.83	13.43	13.71	6.91	6.34
Timber, furniture	8.00	7.91	8.00	10.81	5.63
Paper, publishing	5.30	4.85	5.07	6.01	2.82
Rubber	3.70	4.19	4.77	5.11	4.23
Other industries	1.97	1.79	1.86	3.60	2.11
Total	100.00	100.00	100.00	100.00	100.00

[a] Industrial firms with more than 20 employees.
Sources: ISTAT, CESAG/CESPRI.

Table 4.4 Co-operative agreements and industries

	No. of agreements		Including the three main agreements	
Type of industry	No.	%	No.	%
Science-based	252[a]	40	25	9
Scale-intensive	104	17	72	27
Specialized	118	19	76	29
Traditional	153	24	91	35
Total	627	100	264[b]	100

[a] 120 signed by Olivetti, 47 by Italtel.
[b] Among the 272 agreements regarded by the firms as important, 8 could not be classified.
Source: CESAG, Strasbourg/CESPRI, Milan, 1987.

- Enterprises which adapt their products to the specific needs of their customers are clearly less inclined towards co-operation than those which manufacture standard products. This tendency has already been strongly emphasized in the course of research on the same theme undertaken on German firms.[3]

Level of exports and co-operative practice. Willingness to come to terms with foreign partners is more positively demonstrated by those enterprises already very active on the international markets (see table

Table 4.5 Production organization and co-operation

	Co-operating firms, % (n = 142)	Total of the sample of firms, % (n = 707)
Has the firm decentralized the various stages of the production process?		
Yes	62.7	55.0
No	37.3	45.0
The firm mainly uses		
mass production	52.5	48.5
small-scale production	47.5	51.5
The firm mainly produces		
standard products	57.5	45.0
products adapted to suit each type of customer	42.5	55.0

Source: CESAG, Strasbourg/CESPRI, Milan, 1987.

Table 4.6 Level of exports and co-operations

E = exports/turnover	Co-operating firms, % (n = 142)	Total number of firms in the sample, % (n = 707)
E < 5%	15.5	36.9
5% < E < 50%	19.0	16.5
20% < E < 50%	39.4	27.6
E > 50%	26.1	19.0

Source: CESAG, Strasbourg/CESPRI, Milan, 1987.

4.6). Co-operation emerges as a means of sustaining penetration of foreign markets. In some cases it may also be regarded as the first step in precipitating a process of internationalization, to be subsequently bolstered by complementary measures.

The propensity to enter into co-operative agreements has clearly grown in recent years; 71 per cent of the firms studied confirmed that they had entered into more co-operative agreements in the five years immediately preceding the sample date.

A definite correlation was observed between the size of the foreign market to which the Italian goods were being sent and the tendency to enter into co-operative agreements with firms native to that country. But it must be stressed that in some cases there is no reciprocity. In these cases it is simply a matter of enterprises entering into an agreement specifically to get a foothold in a particular market, taking advantage of the partner's relations, commercial know-how and distribution network.

The content of co-operative agreements

Analysis of co-operative practices reveals a wide diversity in the agreements as regards their content and the type of relationship between the parties. An initial differentiation may be made between two principal categories of agreement: those which mainly relate to products, and those which relate more to know-how. In addition, the type of relationship between the parties is identified: mainly supplier to customer, or mainly partner to partner. If one further looks at the simplicity or complexity of the agreement, eleven types can be distinguished, the first four simple, the other seven more complex.

- Type 1 concerns a supply of technology from an Italian enterprise to a foreign firm.
- Type 2 is a sales agreement in favour of an Italian firm; a foreign enterprise sells the Italian firm's products.
- Type 3 concerns a production agreement; the foreign firm produces on behalf of the Italian firm.
- Type 4 relates to the acquisition of technology on the part of the Italian firm.
- Type 5 is an agreement which combines both a supply of technology and a production agreement in favour of a foreign firm.
- Type 6 is a symmetrical agreement: the acquisition and supply of know-how between an Italian firm and a foreign partner.
- Type 7 combines the acquisition of know-how and a production agreement effected by an Italian enterprise on behalf of a foreign firm.
- Type 8 is a counter-agreement, involving acquisition of technology/ supply of products on the part of the Italian firm.
- Type 9 is a complex agreement in which the Italian firm supplies components to a foreign firm which also assists in the marketing of the finished products from the Italian firm.
- Type 10 is a marketing agreement. The Italian firm sets up a marketing network abroad.
- Type 11 is the counterpart of type 10; the Italian firm becomes the base for a marketing network for foreign products in Italy.

These eleven forms are the essential types of industrial collaboration agreement on the international level practised by Italian enterprises. There is a wide diversity of types but by looking at actual examples one can see that there is a finite number of practicable agreements and that not all the possible combinations of agreement are realistic.

By examining the firms in terms of their belonging to a particular sector within the range of possible types of agreement, a certain number of close correlations are thrown into relief:

- in the case of consumer goods, marketing agreements predominate, but this does not exclude other forms, especially those concerning the provision and acquisition of technology: 34.9 per cent of agreements in this sector dealt with marketing, 25.8 per cent with the provision of technology and 16.3 per cent with the purchase of technology;

- in the case of transport undertakings, production agreements predominate;
- in the case of intermediate goods, technology and production agreements predominate;
- in the case of capital goods, know-how and partnership agreements predominate: the numbers of marketing agreements and those for the supply of know-how are roughly equal.

These findings beg several questions. What are the determining factors in these agreements?

- Are there distinctive elements which typify the enterprises which practise marketing agreements and those which practise the supply of technology?
- What enterprises purchase know-how?
- What enterprises enter into partnerships, and with whom?

These questions are addressed in the following section.

The Main Types of Agreement by Macro-activity

Types of co-operation in the consumer goods sector

The consumer goods sector, largely comprising those industries classified by Pavitt as traditional industries, throws up two peculiarities as regards co-operation; one concerns the forms of co-operation, the other the size of the firms involved.

As we have seen, marketing agreements (34.9 per cent) dominate the consumer goods sector ahead of technological agreements (25.6 per cent concerning the supply of technology and 16.3 per cent the acquisition of technology). The strength of the relationships which are formed around these types of agreement make it possible to postulate two distinct relationships:

- Marketing agreements occur principally in the domain of consumer durables (furniture, clothing, etc.) and are more usually exercised on the initiative of the smaller firms (less than L40 billion turnover in Italy). Marketing agreements are moreover strongly linked to a company philosophy of substantial involvement in exporting, especially to nearby markets.
- Of the technological agreements, 80 per cent involve large

companies. The acquisition of technology relates equally to both consumer durables and to general consumer goods (foodstuffs, etc.). On the other hand, the provision of technology effectively stems only from major companies exercising their international activity, especially in distant markets.

Study of the determining factors which are specific to the type of agreement has shown size to be the main explanatory factor. In the case of large enterprises almost one agreement in two is for the supply of technology (against barely 16 per cent where small firms are concerned); on the other hand, in the small firm context, four agreements in ten are of the marketing type.

Analysis of the data, supplemented by interviews, gives support to the proposition that small firms see co-operation as a means of extending and consolidating their presence in nearby markets. This confirms a thesis postulated by De Woot:

> Many small and medium-sized enterprises manufacture products which have an international application. The creation of a sound European base could be a strategic priority for them. Bearing in mind the size of these firms, European countries are the most interesting because of their geographical and cultural proximity. The SME is not always adequately equipped to Europeanise its activities on its own and it is here that cooperation becomes of interest.[4]

Such co-operation is primarily designed to be aimed at marketing; our research confirms this unambiguously.

This type of marketing agreement is traditionally based on relations with a particular partner who markets and distributes the products on a regular basis. It goes beyond initiatory exporting (blow-by-blow commercial relations) and supported exports via representatives or agents. Here the Italian firm operates under contract with a foreign firm with an undertaking as to volumes, prices and with a long-term economic prospect. Typical examples are to be found in the footwear and clothing industries; for a number of reasons the Italian firm will sign an agreement with a foreign firm for the supply and delivery of a range of products of a clearly specified quality. The foreign firm sees an advantage in this in terms of supplementing its marketing effort. This type of agreement has a very positive satisfaction rate. The timescale for the implementation of the agreements is relatively short – six to twelve months.

In the case of the large firms, co-operation has a different significance. It can be the means of obtaining a monetary return on one of the links in the value chain (supply of technology) or alternatively the means of supplementing the value chain (purchase of technology).

There are usually two constraints associated with the provision of technology:

- The geographical constraint: distant markets are usually involved, appearing to dictate the provision of technology where products of a low unitary value are concerned. This tendency is also noted in the case of foodstuffs (e.g. pasta, biscuits or drinks).
- The technical constraint: the provision of technology is systematic in the case of products for which technical standards are mandatory (e.g. domestic electrical products).

As a general rule, contracts for the supply of technology in respect of consumer goods have a high satisfaction rate and involve a delay in their implementation of the order of eighteen months. They are made at the instigation of Italian firms in two-thirds of the cases.

Technological agreements do not, in fact, imply technological superiority, but rather a kind of pragmatism exercised in order to penetrate and secure more distant markets by overcoming the constraint of distance (in the case of products where the cost of transport is high in relation to their low unitary value) or perhaps those constraints linked to local markets (standards, preference for local products, etc.).

Principal agreements concerning capital goods

Capital goods firms have been classified into two groups: mechanical and electrical engineering. Two factors are significant here:

- a decisive proportion of agreements relate to know-how;
- a very different agreement practice and content are revealed depending on whether mechanical or electrical engineering is concerned.

In the case of capital goods, marketing agreements represent barely one out of five, whereas agreements principally concerning know-how (provision of technology, acquisition of technology or partnership) account for one in two. The relative sector (mechanical or electrical engineering) is decisive. An analysis of the correlation in order to find the main determining factors in these types of agreement illustrates the very strong link between marketing agreements, technological provision and partnership on the one hand and electrical engineering firms on the other hand.

- the mechanical sector favours marketing agreements (principally with EC countries) and agreements for the provision of know-how (with developing countries and East European countries and also with the US and Japan). Partnership agreements are more rare (one agreement in seven) and purchases of know-how play a very minor part (one agreement in eleven).
- The electrical engineering sector displays a technological dependence through its principal agreements (partnership and acquisition of technology). The philosophies of integration and technological up-dating dominate. The preferred partners are German, American or Japanese, provided they have the required expertise.

In the case of mechanical engineering, agreements indicating a certain technological freedom (provision of technology, marketing agreements) dominate.

Marketing agreements are made almost exclusively within the EC. They originate in firms which market certain products (industrial machinery) through a preferential partner, who usually provides the storage and maintenance functions. Marketing agreements thus formalized still exemplify a market reinforcement strategy.

The very important technology provision agreements are of two types:

- The provision of technology, demonstrating a technological superiority. The partners are the developing countries and East European countries. This provision of technology reflects classical thinking with respect to the end of the product life cycle and valorization of the technology in the undeveloped markets.
- A significant proportion of the technology supply agreements relate to the tactical or dictated provision of technology. This practice falls within a strategy for access to new markets. It is used essentially in developed markets of the US or Japanese type in order to embrace the standards applicable to these markets better, to understand better the data coming from these markets, or else to overcome the hurdle of preference given to national products.

The electrical engineering sector – the principal sector of the

Italian economy at the level of international trade – amply illustrates the technological up-dating and integration (networking) philosophies.

Updating through the purchase of know-how is effected by means of access to product diversification through technological short cuts. The main partners are German, then American and Japanese. These agreements are solicited by Italian firms and by foreign firms equally; it is therefore not a question of a strategy which only the Italians have fully mastered. Italian firms are subject here to a real technological domination (especially in industrial electronics), and are compelled to acquire technology from dominant others. Where they acquire a technology they do so clearly in order to reduce the risks, the costs and the time spent on research, but the contracts often appear to them to be one-sided as there is no counterpart.

Networking policy is a procedure which offers much better prospects for Italian firms. The logic of this is perfectly illustrated by partnerships as it is a matter of reciprocal exchanges of know-how, often with joint industrial operations. It is felt that this philosophy enables each of the partners to rationalize its production. The agreements are mostly made with US partners for activities such as robotics, consumer electronics and information science. The agreements often concern projects or products for which no single enterprise possesses the technology or has the full capacity for research and development or for production. The agreements are complex and virtually irreversible in the short term as they dictate the way the firms complement each other in the value chain.

Agreements in intermediate goods activities

In the intermediate goods sector most agreements relate to or incorporate production agreements (see table 4.7). However, within the EC, agreements in this area are mainly of the other kinds, especially marketing, and relate more to intermediate goods linked to materials. In the case of other activities, particularly chemicals, the areas of co-operation generally fall outside the EC.

The most important distinction here is that between the practices of those firms belonging to an industrial group and those which are independent of any group. Enterprises which belong to a group are more involved in an extensive movement relating to technology

Table 4.7 Intermediate goods and co-operation agreements

Types of agreement	%
Production agreements	17.6
Production agreements + provision of technology	29.4
Provision of technology	17.6
Acquisition of technology + production agreement	11.8
Other agreements (including marketing)	23.6
Total	100.0

Source: CESAG, Strasbourg/CESPRI, Milan, 1987.

(provision or acquisition) rather than in production. Furthermore, these technological agreements are transverse: they involve firms engaged in different activities (e.g. chemicals, biotechnology, information science, new materials). Through this type of agreement one can see the formation of new concepts, concepts which demand mastery of two or three discrete technologies. Firms which do not belong to a group tend more towards traditional agreements where intermediate goods are concerned (production and/or technology agreements). These agreements are almost exclusively made within the same system and come within the traditional international division of labour.

Objectives Pursued within the Framework of International Agreements

On the basis of the various international studies carried out by CESAG, it is possible to make, in particular, the two following observations:

- In the case of highly competitive activities, where the products are of similar quality, the cost of inputs is the determining factor because this affects the prices which may be charged and thus the net margin. Under these circumstances, internationalization appears to be a potential mechanism for providing inputs at the best possible price (by opting, at each stage of the production process, to purchase all the components from the least expensive areas of production or marketing), to develop economies of scale and the effects of experience and synergy, to improve the level of utilization of the productive capacity and to reduce seasonal or cyclical variations.

- For the less competitive activities, firms have a tendency to direct their strategy towards the differentiation of those products which offer better profit levels. The diversity of world markets makes it possible for this policy to be amply exploited through reducing the opportunities offered by a heterogeneous demand.

The comparative advantages vary from one country to another because of the existence of institutional and cultural factors which act as formidable barriers, overturning the theoretical hypothesis of market unity and transparency and making it difficult to extend a firm's competitive advantages beyond national frontiers.

In addition, the cost of factors of production and distribution, the tax imposed on fixed assets or profits, industrial or scientific traditions, marketing or financial know-how, the quality of educational and training systems, the state of the infrastructures, the wealth of natural resources, etc. are all factors which accentuate the appeal of certain countries and the unattractiveness of others. It is the nature of each company's activity which will dictate the preferred choice of international geographical area.

A complex analysis of international co-operative agreements ultimately raises a number of questions:

- What information can be drawn from an analysis of the agreements for each country?
- Is it possible to determine routes by means of which one can become involved in international co-operation by considering the various combinations regarding type of agreement/types of macro-activity/size of firm?
- Can one identify efficient agreements by means of a detailed analysis of the effect of these agreements and their associated content?
- What are the main factors which block the implementation of international agreements?

Based on the Italian sample, the first section which follows covers the objectives of the participants in international agreements, identifying preferential areas according to type of agreement and how practices differ according to size of firm.

The second section, by highlighting the conditions associated with successful agreements and exposing the causes of failure, provides a profile of efficient agreements.

The Aims and Objectives of Participants

Agreements by country and by sector: main factors

The agreements examined are here classified by their main objectives (see table 4.8). The breakdown of agreements by country (using the Italian experience of 1987) and by macro-activity offers a wealth of information.

The sale of Italian products is the primary justification for agreements with other industrial countries, especially the EC countries, the USA and Canada. Two exceptions must be stressed: Japan and the Scandinavian countries, where agreements for the exchange of technology predominate, in the sense of sales of Italian technology to Japan and the acquisition of Scandinavian technology by Italy. In the field of technology, it will be seen that Italy sells more technology to France than it acquires, whereas it sells little technology to West Germany but acquires a lot from it.

The sale of Italian technology predominates in agreements with the less-developed countries of Africa and Latin America, as well as China and the other socialist countries. An exception must be made, however, in the case of the new industrial countries of Asia; here marketing agreements take precedence, accounting for 80 per cent of the cases (see table 4.9).

Small and medium-sized enterprises (SMEs), generally characterized by their relative weakness as regards financial and managerial resources, tend to prefer geographically and culturally 'close' markets, that is, within the EC. Distant or complex markets (Latin America, Africa, China, Eastern European countries) are considered to be too risky to be truly attractive (see table 4.10).

The four main policies embodied in international co-operative agreements

By analysing the various data from the Italian survey given above we can identify the four policies which encourage the tendency for firms to co-operate on an international level:

- a product sales policy;

Table 4.8 Countries and types of agreement: the Italian experience

		Aim					
Country	No.	Supply of technology	Acquisition of technology	Exchange of technology	Marketing abroad	Marketing in Italy	Misc.
France	32	21.9	12.5	6.3	31.3	9.3	18.7
Germany	31	3.1	22.6	9.7	25.8	6.5	32.3
UK	18	5.6	11.1	5.6	27.7	27.7	22.3
Benelux/Denmark	14	7.1	21.4	–	42.9	14.3	14.3
Spain	16	56.2	–	6.3	31.2	–	6.3
Greece/Portugal	11	36.3	–	–	36.3	–	27.4
+ an EC partner	4	–	–	75.0	25.0	–	–
EC total	126	18.2	12.7	7.9	30.9	8.8	20.5
Austria/ Switzerland	15	13.4	26.6	13.4	13.4	6.6	26.6
Scandinavia	9	–	33.3	–	11.1	33.3	22.3
US/Canada	43	14.0	11.6	14.0	34.8	11.6	13.0
Japan	18	50.0	5.6	11.1	11.1	5.6	16.6

Other European countries	4	50.0	–	–	50.0	–	–
Total Non-EC OECD countries	89	21.3	14.6	11.2	24.8	11.2	16.9
Yugoslavia and Israel	6	50.0	–	–	16.6	–	633.4
Africa and Middle East	3	66.7	–	–	–	–	33.3
China	6	100.0	–	–	–	–	–
Asia (excl. Japan)	5	20.0	–	–	40.0	20.0	20.0
Other Asian countries	6	50.0	–	–	–	–	50.0
Latin America	7	100.0	–	–	–	–	–
Comecon	6	66.6	16.7	16.7	–	16.7	–
Total developing and socialist countries	39	66.6	–	–	7.7	5.1	18.0
Total	254	26.9	11.8	7.9	25.2	9.4	18.9

Source: CESAG, Strasbourg/CESPRI, Milan, 1987.

Table 4.9 Agreements by type of industry and by country: the Italian experience

Partner country	Sector Total	Advanced technique	Sectors with high economies of scale	Very special-ized sectors	Tradi-tional indus-tries
France	35	1	12	10	12
Germany	34	3	8	12	11
UK	20	2	5	7	6
Benelux/ Denmark	14	–	5	3	6
Spain	16	–	4	6	6
Greece/ Portugal	11	–	3	2	6
Several EC partners	4	1	2	–	1
EC total	134	7	39	40	48
Austria/ Switzerland	17	2	6	4	5
Scandinavia	9	1	3	3	2
US/Canada	43	10	10	11	12
Japan	18	3	4	4	7
Other OECD countries outside EC	4	–	2	2	–
Total non-EC OECD countries	91	16	25	24	26
Yugoslavia and Israel	6	–	2	–	4
Middle East	3	–	3	–	–
China	6	–	–	3	3
Asia (new industrial)	5	–	–	1	4
Other Asian countries	6	2	–	1	3
Latin America	7	–	3	3	1
Socialist countries (oxol. China)	6	–	–	4	2
Total developing, new industrial and socialist countries	39	2	8	12	17
Total	264	25	72	76	91

Source: CESAG, Strasbourg/CESPRI, Milan, 1987.

Table 4.10 Breakdown of agreements signed by small and medium-sized enterprises by country: the Italian experience

Partner country	Total (n = absolute values)	Small and medium-sized firms (as % of n)
France	35	71
Germany	34	65
UK	20	65
Benelux/Denmark	14	79
Spain	16	75
Greece/Portugal	11	91
Several EC partners	4	25
EC total	134	70
Austria/Switzerland	17	65
Scandinavia	9	44
US/Canada	43	53
Japan	18	55
Other OECD countries outside EC	4	100
Total non-EC OECD countries	91	57
Yugoslavia and Israel	6	66
Middle East	3	33
China	6	17
Asia (new industrial)	5	80
Other Asian countries	6	50
Latin America	7	29
Socialist countries (excl. China)	6	17
Total developing, new industrial and socialist countries	39	41
Total	264	62

Source: CESAG, Strasbourg/ CESPRI, Milan, 1987.

- a technological up-dating policy;
- a technological integration policy (*maillage*);
- a technological valorization policy.

The *product sales policy* is generally the dominant one and is expressed in two ways:

- agreements for the marketing of Italian products on the foreign markets;
- agreements for the provision of technology.

These development strategies are representative of the stronger sectors of the Italian industrial fabric, that is, the traditional activities and the very specialized activities (see table 4.11). For these it is therefore a question of extending their penetration of markets already exploited.

Table 4.11 Variety of agreement by type of industry, % (Italy)

Variety of agreement	Type of industry Total	Advanced technique	Sectors with high economies of scale	Very specialized sectors	Traditional industries
Provision of technology (n = 71)	27	13	32	27	28
Acquisition of technology (n = 31)	12	22	12	10	11
Exchange of technology (n = 20)	8	30	8	5	4
Marketing abroad (n = 65)	25	–	18	34	30
Marketing in Italy (n = 24)	9	–	10	14	7
Other marketing agreements (n = 49)	19	35	20	10	20
Total (n = 260)	100	100	100	100	100

Source: CESAG, Strasbourg/CESPRI, Milan, 1987.

Marketing collaboration makes it possible to accelerate growth abroad, the foreign partner placing its own sales network at the other's disposal. It is also one of the factors which make Italian firms flexible, as recourse to a foreign partner's distribution network enables time and money to be saved.

Agreements for the provision of technology facilitate the penetration of new markets at little costs. These are often markets regarded as sensitive and which it is therefore prudent to test without incurring undue risks. This variety of agreement also enables all manner of protectionist barriers to be surmounted and makes it viable to perfect new, original products through the payment of royalties proportional to sales or the payment of a lump sum.

The *technological up-dating policy* is manifested by the decision made by Italian firms to acquire foreign technology. The propensity to acquire foreign technology is greater in the advanced technology sectors and in those sectors which are sensitive to economies of scale (i.e. those dominated by foreign competitors) than in the principal sectors of transalpine industry. In the European Community Germany is the main supplier of technology, but the Benelux countries (particularly the Netherlands with Philips and Unilever) and Denmark are also well placed. Elsewhere Switzerland and Scandinavia play a leading role. France seems to play a more modest role in these agreements.

Technological integration policy or *maillage* is manifested by agreements for the exchange of technology and the development of joint projects. In this area the USA and Germany are given preference by Italian firms. This policy particularly affects high-technology industries. Overall this sector is deficient, that is to say Italy is essentially an importer, but it has proven its competitiveness in two branches where it has an excess and therefore an export capability: telecommunications and air navigation equipment. There is a clear logic dictating international collaboration between firms in those sectors of activity where expenditure on research and development is high, both in pre-competitive research and in applied research. In addition, high-technology products tend to have a relatively short lifespan, technological development being so rapid. These two factors account for the need for considerable investment, often exceeding the capabilities of a single firm. Therefore there is naturally pressure to seek industrial complementarity or proximity. Germany and the USA offer Italy a wider field of activity and complementarity. Japan is aiming to improve its position, following the well-known strategy which consists, initially, of encouraging its partners' imports.

Technological valorization policy concerns in particular the socialist countries and the developing countries, both of which are important acquirers of technology, but it also applies to the Mediterranean countries, with which Italy has a policy of very active economic trading, aided by the Levantine tradition.

Policies for the provision of technology particularly affect traditional industries and highly specialized sectors of activity, the solid launch-pads for Italian industrial development, as well as those industries sensitive to economies of scale. The advanced technology sectors, which are currently of relatively minor importance in Italy (in 1986 Italy's share of the world's exports of advanced technology was only 3.5 per cent against 12.8 per cent for West Germany, 5.9 per cent for France, 20.6 per cent for the United States and 23.3 per cent for Japan), play an even smaller role in these international co-operation strategies.

A Profile of Efficient Agreements

The majority of firms involved in co-operative arrangements, whether SMEs or large firms, are satisfied with them, believing that their aims and objectives have been met. In particular, co-operative agreements have been regarded favourably where the competitiveness of the firm is concerned. They have been accepted as appropriate in a large number of cases (see table 4.12).

Table 4.12 Degree of satisfaction expressed, as % of co-operative agreements signed (n = 272)

Questions	Total sample	SMEs	Large firms
Have the aims and objectives of the Italian firms been met?			
yes	65.1	61.2	71.6
partially	25.7	27.1	21.9
no	5.5	6.5	5.5
unspecified	3.7	5.2	1.0
Have the aims and objectives of the partner firm been met?			
yes	61.4	57.1	68.6
partially	21.6	27.7	23.5
no	4.4	5.3	2.9
unspecified	8.1	9.9	5.0

Source: CESAG, Strasbourg/CESPRI, Milan, 1987.

This section will analyse efficient agreements in more depth, demonstrating both the typical components of successful agreements and the main stumbling blocks, and will also outline European preferences as regards the policies of co-operation.

The typical components of successful agreements and the main stumbling blocks

The agreements which have proved to be the most highly regarded are technological agreements and, in particular, reciprocal exchange undertakings (see table 4.13).

From examination of the relation between the content of agreements, the aims and objectives and the rate of satisfaction obtained, it becomes evident that technological agreements are deemed the most successful for two reasons:

- the strategic aim is perfectly clear: the objectives are well defined, the qualities sought from the partner are specified and accepted ('we co-operate because we respect each other');
- a kind of balance exists: there is no doubt that each partner brings something to the arrangement and each finds it to his advantage.

Marketing agreements, by contrast, are much more asymmetrical.

Industrial collaboration on the international level is practised either defensively (to overcome the competition) or offensively (in order to increase the competitive advantage) but, in any event, this process demonstrates a certain maturity of thought in the matter of strategic adaptation, with awareness of the concept of collaborative management as opposed to traditional management. However, firms come up against a number of obstacles in negotiating and signing these contracts (see table 4.14).

Among the various obstacles to be overcome, it appears that cultural proximity is the decisive one. In relation to co-operative agreements, differing managerial cultures mean one has to take into account two criteria: the risks run because of the agreement and the time-lag before the effects of the agreement are felt. The success of the agreement will virtually depend on the mutual level of confidence between the partners; where this is high, there will be considerable saving of time and reduction in the risks inherent in every shared activity.

Given these conditions of managerial culture, European firms do not appear to offer any specialities or superiority over other areas, particularly the United States (so far as Italian firms are concerned). Table 4.15 shows that the number of impediments encountered through cultural differences is as high (in relation to signed agreements) in the EC as in other OECD areas outside the EC.

Table 4.13 Success of collaboration by type of agreement (%)

	Objectives met:									
	By the Italian firm					By the foreign partner				
Type of agreement (absolute values)	Yes	Partially	No	Unspecified	Total	Yes	Partially	No	Unspecified	Total
Sale of technology (71)	10	25	61	4	100	6	31	58	5	100
Acquisition of technology (31)	–	13	87	–	100	–	19	78	8	100
Exchange of technology (20)	–	15	80	5	100	–	15	80	5	100
Marketing agreements (65)	6	31	58	5	100	8	29	49	14	100
Marketing agreements in Italy (24)	–	46	54	–	100	–	46	54	–	100
Other marketing agreements (49)	8	25	65	2	100	6	18	74	2	100
Total (n = 260)	6	26	65	3	100	5	27	62	6	100

Source: CESAG, Strasbourg/CESPRI, Milan, 1987.

Table 4.14 The main obstacles encountered when signing or managing co-operative agreements, according to type of firm (as %, n = 272, more possible replies)

Obstacles	Total sample	SMEs	Large firms
Adjustment to Italian tax system and currency exchange	11.4	12.4	9.8
Adjustment to foreign tax systems and currency exchange	5.2	5.3	4.9
Technical standards	12.9	13.5	11.8
Differences of management culture compared with the partner company	19.1	16.5	23.5
Language difficulties	9.2	10.6	6.9
Difficulties in implementing the foreign partner's technology	5.2	5.9	3.9
Difficulties for the foreign partner to implement the Italian technology	9.2	10.6	6.9
Opportunist behaviour on the part of the partner	4.4	4.7	3.9

Source: CESAG, Strasbourg/CESPRI, Milan, 1987.

The prospects for international co-operation

The main question to be asked here relates to the place of Europe when defining what is and what is not a privileged area in the field of international co-operation.

Examined from the Italian point of view, this question leads to the following observation: Italy displays great pragmatism in the matter of industrial co-operation on an international level. Marketing agreements will benefit from the advantage of proximity (Europe holds a number of trump cards in this respect). In the case of technological agreements, firms will take advantage of skills. Consequently, Europe will extend over a wider co-operative area.

As a general rule, with the arrival of 1992, intra-EC agreements will be advocated. In Europe, Germany appears to be the preferred partner, well ahead of France, the United Kingdom, Mediterranean Europe and Benelux, in that order. But regardless of any declared policy for the provision of technology, marketing matters continue to dominate.

Table 4.15 The main obstacles encountered when signing or managing co-operative agreements, by partner country concerned (in absolute values)

Partner country	Total number of agreements	Technical standards	Differences in managerial culture	Linguistic difficulties
France	35	2	8	3
Germany	34	4	8	3
UK	20	1	–	–
Benelux/Denmark	14	4	–	1
Spain	16	1	3	–
Greece/Portugal	11	2	1	1
Several EC partners	4	2	2	–
EC total	134	16	22	8
Austria/Switzerland	17	2	4	3
Scandinavia	9	–	3	2
US/Canada	43	8	9	3
Japan	18	3	3	5
Other OECD countries outside EC	4	–	–	–
Total non-EC OECD countries	91	13	19	13
Yugoslavia and Israel	6	–	1	1
Middle East	3	1	1	–
China	6	2	2	3
Asia (new industrial)	5	–	4	–
Other Asian countries	6	1	1	–
Latin America	7	–	–	–
Socialist countries (excl. China)	6	2	1	–
Total developing, new industrial and socialist countries	39	6	10	4
Total	264	35	51	25

Source: CESAG, Strasbourg/CESPRI, Milan, 1987.

The HSD (Ernst and Young Audit et Conseil) survey confirms the ranking of the collaborative alliances sought by Italy, France and Spain (see figure 4.1). Through its reputation for sound industrial know-how and its reputation for impenetrability, Germany will be much sought after. It seems reasonable to assume that the economic might acquired by Germany as a result of its reunification in 1990 can only strengthen this tendency.

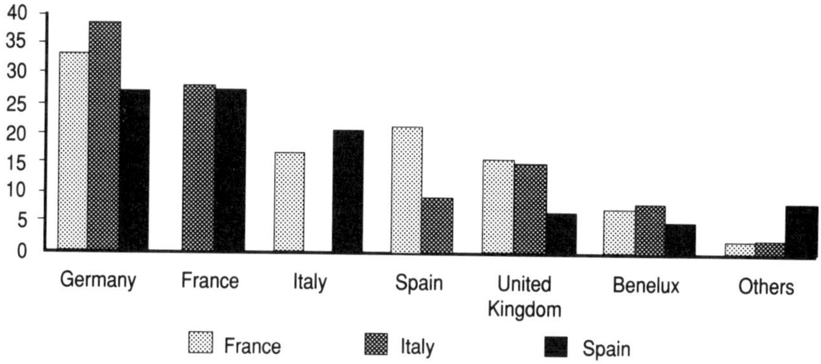

Figure 4.1 The desired nationality of Community partners
Source: Ernst and Young Audit et Conseil.

Conclusion

Chapter 3 demonstrated, on a theoretical level, the need for co-operative practices. In Chapter 4, through a study of existing international collaborative practices and an analysis of the factors of success, extrapolation of the advice concerning the need to co-operate enables one to come down in favour of an increase in inter-company co-operation.

The single European market will speed up the movement towards co-operation, especially international co-operation, as the new competitive environment gives rise to two factors: globalization of the competition and an acceleration in the rate of innovation. Globalization involves a consolidation of the basic conditions for competition and faster diffusion of trends in consumption. The rapid communication of innovations will encourage firms to adopt a policy of international rather than local distribution. In this context, agreements could become a permanent feature as an efficient method of exchange. They would constitute a fresh organizational tool which would enable firms to develop their overall management policy at a lower cost of adaptation.

But a question arises: does not co-operation therefore become a new form of competition? Will not these agreements become the latest competitive barriers? The co-operative networks set up are in fact in danger of colliding with each other. In the context of a highly competitive world, one is tempted to believe that the better organized networks will triumph over the others.

Part III of this book will specify the rules to be followed in order to increase the likelihood of efficiency in co-operative networks.

Notes

1 The German sample (2,000 firms) was drawn up with the help of the RKW and resulted in the processing of the replies to 200 questionnaires and 36 interviews (year of reference 1984). The Italian sample was drawn up with the help of Confindustria in Rome and CESPRI/University L. Bocconi in Milan; aimed at 4,000 industrial firms, it led to the processing of 816 questionnaires and 30 interviews (year of reference 1987).

2 K. Pavitt 'Sectoral Patterns of Technological Change: Towards a Taxonomy and a Theory', *Research Policy*, no. 6, 1984.

3 S. Urban and S. Vendemini, *Entreprises allemandes et coopération industrielle á l'échelle européenne*, Documentation française, Paris, 1986, Série Etudes et Recherches du Commissariat Général du Plan.

4 P. de Woot, *Les entreprises de haute technologie et l'Europe*, Economica, Paris, 1988, p. 123.

PART III

Conditions for the Success of Co-operative Strategies

Introduction to Part III

It now seems clear that international industrial co-operation has become an active reality.[1] Stimulated by the construction of Europe, it has its foundations in a whole series of economic factors as well as in the development of technology.

Whatever weight these explanations may carry, one must not imagine, however, that the process will proceed completely smoothly. Like any kind of change, modifications to management methods will meet with a certain amount of resistance. While, within the economic context of the late twentieth century, this type of strategic alliance undoubtedly represents a chance to be seized, a productive opportunity, it is also felt by certain aggrieved parties to be an unnatural restriction, presenting a danger of losing the specific advantages possessed by a firm.

It is true that there is always the possibility of failure; but this may be reduced provided the participants take precautions and arrange their co-operative procedures carefully.

The effectiveness of an alliance is built up methodically. It is not enough that the partners are responsive to co-operation or sincerely convinced of its necessity; it is also essential that they implement it without selfish ulterior motives and with the organizational firmness which any delicate operation demands (chapter 5). The desire to maximize the effectiveness of the whole body thus formed (rather than to favour just one of its component parts) assumes, of course, that the interests of each of the parties concerned are protected against the risks of running off course or the diverting of resources. The commitment made by the protagonists will be all the more profitable if the balance between the partners has been guaranteed by suitable legal forms of organization, if the know-how garnered or passed on will be protected, and if the institutional environment has demonstrated its support, indeed its capacity, for finding equilibrium (chapter 6).

Note

1 There are no exhaustive statistics which accurately measure the extent of the phenomenon. Our statement is however supported by a whole series of sources, such as the INSEAD data bank analysed in the work by F. M. Contractor and P. Lorance, *Co-operative Strategies in International Business*, Lexington Books, Lexington, Mass., 1988, ch. 6; the research carried out by CESAG (Robert Schuman University, Strasbourg), ISI (Fraunhofer-Gesellschaft zur Förderung der angewandten Forschung eV, Karlsruhe), CESPRI (Universita L. Bocconi de Milan) and LAREA-CEREM (University of Paris-Nanterre); the data bank and publications of the French Ministry for Industry (Industrial Strategy Observatory), together with those of the OECD; the half-yearly list of restructuring operations published by the Institut National de la Statistique et des Etudes Economiques; the catalogue of agreements prepared by COST (Coopération européenne dans la domaine de la recherche scientifique et technique), EC, Brussels; the work carried out by MIT (Cambridge, Mass.) and by the Strategy Research Center at Columbia University, New York; also that presented to the annual conferences of the EIBA (European International Business Association), led by Alexis Jacquemin (University of Louvain).

5

Effective Partnerships

The Pitfalls of Co-operation

Co-operative alliances induce organizations and people to work together with the common aim of increasing benefits and reducing risks. It is well known that finding the balance between maximizing benefits and minimizing risks is *per se* a delicate exercise. Where this balance has to be found between partners of different nationalities, the exercise presents potentially formidable difficulties. Three main problematic areas may be postulated, concerning complexity, structural curbs and strategic egotism.

The Pitfall of Complexity

It is essential that complexity be well managed. If complexity is properly dealt with it becomes a source of competitiveness; if not, it can be the cause of dysfunctions. It is possible to illustrate both these assertions by a study of co-operative alliances because complexity is one of the variables central to the phenomenon.

Complexity factors in co-operative alliances

These factors must first be correctly determined so that in due course they can be properly controlled.

Three variables of complexity should be taken into account: the activity which is the subject of the collaboration; the environment in which it is carried on; and the attributes and particular skills of the co-operating partners (see figure 5.1).

Most strategic alliances are formed around one of a firm's fields of activity (within the three traditional vectors – market, product,

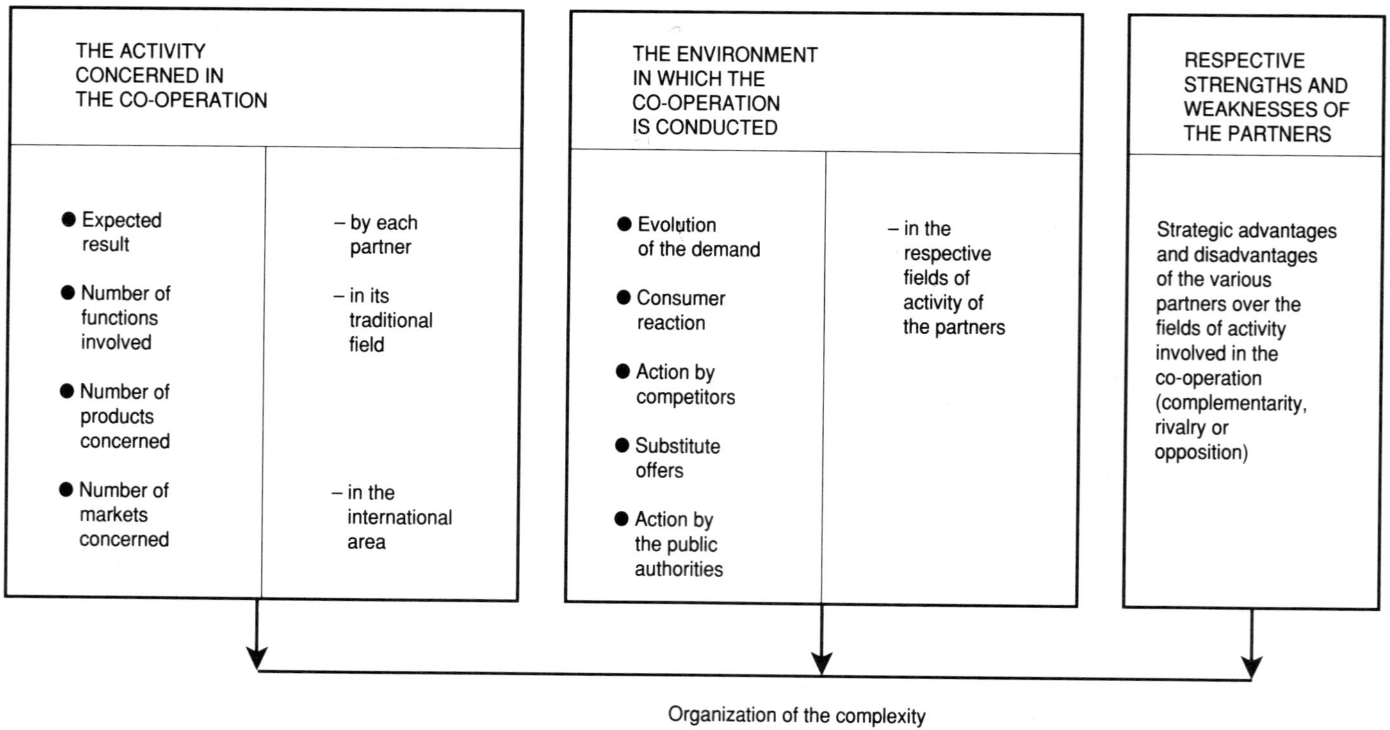

Figure 5.1 The complexity factors in co-operative alliances
Source: Sabine Urban and Serge Vendemini, CESAG, Strasbourg.

technology) and not at the universal level of the firm as a legal entity. The competitive position of the partner firms thus depends on the reciprocal quality of their market/product/technology portfolios, and the pertinence of the combination of these. It therefore becomes a question of co-ordinating the knowledge and know-how and the production and marketing methods in respect of a lesser or greater number of products and ranges, intended to service a variety of market types. In view of the international character of the alliances concerned, a comprehensive economic and technological monitoring system will be needed. As a result there will also be a need (bearing in mind the considerable amount of information to be analysed) for a fairly sophisticated data-processing capability to facilitate the ready comprehension of the problems posed: i.e. one that will simplify without distorting.

We know that throughout the world the socio-economic environment has become uncertain (difficult to forecast) and unstable (constantly evolving). Co-operative alliances entered into between two or more partners must therefore take into account the changes which will affect their respective situations within their distinctive environments. In particular, it is appropriate to monitor:

- the evolution of demand;
- the changes in consumer preferences and reactions in specific markets;
- the actions of the main competitors;
- the actions of the public authorities;
- the alternative products offered.

A significant change in just one of these elements might profoundly disturb the basis of the co-operative alliance concerned, alter its direction or modify the balance within the partnership. If the interests of the alliance are transformed its lifespan and effectiveness may be very quickly called into question and the strategic interplay between the parties thus complicated.

The commitment to partnership, like any other strategic decision, presupposes an evaluation of strengths and weaknesses. In this case the process involves drawing up an inventory of the particular assets and competencies of the partners. This is a delicate operation as there is no completely reliable technique which can be applied; the margin for error is considerable however the inventory is drawn up (whether within the organization or externally by auditors, management or financial consultants etc.). Furthermore, the methods of evaluation and analysis used are not consistent. Practices and references vary widely from one country to another, complicating interpretation of the data.

The task of alliance negotiators is thus highly complex. They have to reduce as far as possible the complexity at the level of the operational organization. The degrees of complexity to be grasped ultimately depend on the type and intensity of the partnership relations. The variants are summarized in figure 5.2. According to the interviews conducted by Killing, it is essential that, in order to guarantee their success, co-operative alliances are organized in the simplest possible manner. The complex nature of the international partnership should be reduced by applying simple operating procedures. The principle is simple; the practice less so!

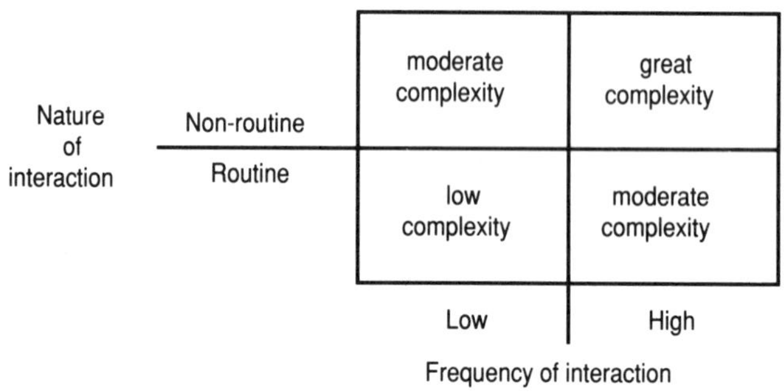

Figure 5.2 Organizational complexity
Source: J. P. Killing, 'Understanding Alliances: The Role of Task and Organisational Complexity', in F. J. Contractor and P. Lorange, *Cooperative Strategies*, Lexington Books, Lexington, Mass., 1988, p. 60.

Complexity threatens deflection of the partnership

The danger here is in fact a double one in the sense that, on the one hand, the alliance may be deflected from its aim of a collaboration whose purpose is to be advantageous for all the partners and, on the other hand, the collaboration agreement is in danger of being destroyed through the breakaway of one or more partners.

In the first place, there is the risk of the uncontrolled disclosure of information. This risk, which manifests itself in various forms of industrial espionage (the unintentional transmission of technology, the watering-down of technical or marketing advantages, the pilfering of innovative ideas, the loss of the acquired edge or the effects of experience and the head-hunting of key personnel) is by no means negligible. It has been the subject of a great deal of attention, especially in the United States (the Americans feel they are being taken advantage of by the Japanese[1] and in Germany (the Germans are very jealous of their technological superiority and their marketing successes). The efficient German firms express their reservations as to industrial co-operation very explicitly because they are afraid that their lead will be diluted over the external markets, whereas their very success has been the result of good adaptation of products to demand, of the quality of the technological and marketing services they supply and of the attention paid to after-sales service. Why then should a German firm want to share its pertinent knowledge and know-how when it has proved itself and ensured its own profitability? Their reluctance is understandable. You do not voluntarily give away something which is productive. Quite naturally you therefore come to believe that you must also be on guard against the danger of unintentional leaks, possibly by reacting in a highly radical manner: refusing to co-operate.[2] It is possible, however, to reduce these risks in a less brutal manner by adopting suitable protective measures, as we shall see in chapter 6.

In Italy, the climate of mistrust towards co-operation is much less pronounced, probably because Italian industrial firms make wide use of technological agreements and of marketing agreements combined with the sale of technology. There are grounds for believing that proper formalization of these agreements reduces the risk of uncontrolled leaks of information.

In the second hypothesis mentioned above, the co-operative alliance concerned is in danger of being destroyed through the partners being diverted. It is clear that in practice co-operations rarely occur purely by chance or through a single act but stem rather from a carefully considered commitment to new forms of management.[3] That is to say, a given firm finds itself involved in a complex network through which it and other firms are interconnected: firm A is a common subsidiary of firms B and C, it has technical agreements with D and E, it places orders with F and is linked by marketing agreements with G, and so on. The network does not remain static; it is formed at a particular time because of the specific attributes of each partner, of its environment and the objectives allocated to the alliance at that time (see figure 5.1). As time goes on the interests evolve and a partner other than the original partner can appear to be more useful. One is therefore dropped in order that a link may be formed with another which better matches the evolving needs of the firm concerned. In other words, the original links are broken in order to form other, more useful associations.

This type of behaviour is possibly efficient in the short term; however, it is not conducive to the creation of a climate of confidence (which is essential) between partners. Efficiency has its price! Continual changes to the network of alliances, justified by an oportunist philosophy on the part of one or other of the partners, could in fact lead to a lack of justification of the co-operative management, the very aim of this management being to reduce the problems created by uncertainty and the continual disturbances caused by the parties. To counter this potential disadvantage, the partners must pay particular attention to their aims and the methods of implementing the alliance, as soon as they join in the game.

The Pitfall of Structural Curbs

In this context 'structure' is taken to mean the socio-economic elements of organization as typified by a certain intractability or relative stability, relating to institutional or cultural factors or to those associated with the background of each firm.

Institutional curbs

These relate especially to R&D co-operation. There is, in fact, in every industrial country (and especially in Europe), a whole series of incentives or sponsorships – local, regional or national – which favour the country's own firms. It is not unusual for government aid to amount to 40–50 per cent of the R&D effort employed, granted in a more or less surreptitious manner. In most cases, such 'aid' (admitted or not) is awarded to 'regional' firms so that the economy of the region will ultimately benefit from the spin-offs from this research. The disbursement of public monies in other national areas is still not, it would seem, a finance-allocation practice which the public authorities will accept.

A commitment on the European level will demand a profound

change in thinking which is currently still permeated by nationalistic self-interest. On the whole, public authorities emerge as the essential defenders of national employment. They therefore have a tendency to favour jingoistic measures in the national interest with which the taxpayer can identify.

Moreover, and this applies particularly to Germany, R&D activities or the spread of new methods of production are conducted with the support of professional organizations (e.g. in textiles and engineering) which also take a somewhat nationalistic view of the problem, because of the nature of their members. In this context, international co-operation procedures are only considered by default (in the absence of a suitable national partner) or taken step by step with great care. It would seem from specific experiences that more positive trends may be forthcoming in the future.

It should be noted that R&D and production techniques are not the only activities which benefit from the attention of public authorities. Tertiary functions are increasingly becoming involved, such as the methods of penetrating foreign markets, making data and consultation networks available, the engineering of complex financial operations and the development of professional skills. All these ties of solidarity between public and private actors operate essentially on the national level and, to a still limited extent, on the European level. The philosophies of the separate nations, each guarding its own interests, its overall financial equilibrium, represented by the balance of payments, will not be swept away at the stroke of a pen, on the pretext that Europe has an interest in so doing.

Cultural curbs

At present, cultural reservations are stronger than one might imagine.[4] They express themelves in various ways.

In Germany, for example, one sees the very profound impact of neo-liberal doctrine, widely diffused following the Second World War to mark a clean break with the Third Reich, with its planned economy and autarkic policies. Since the beginning of the 1950s we have seen the success of a market economy freed from state domination and conceived in accordance with the models of the Fribourg and Cologne schools.[5] This brilliantly dictated 'ordo-liberalism' has moulded thinking, inspired the political economy and forged an image which has impressed the whole world. In the theoretical reasoning invoked, competition stimulates the competitiveness of firms more than collaboration.

Victims of a kind of ideological fog, many bosses in fact foster mistrust towards industrial co-operation, which they see as a brake on competition, as a technocratic stranglehold, a ruinous form of control over company decisions and decentralized initiatives. To those who hold such opinions, European industrial policy is often felt to be confusing the natural and efficient operation of the market. Similarly, the potential efficiency of Community institutions is still not accepted by the majority of firms.

In this context of a liberal culture and decentralized policies within a federal entity, the bureaucratic centralism and nationalism prevalent in France provoke strong suspicions, at the same time curbing any desire to co-operate with French firms overly tainted with Colbertism. On the other hand, in a highly organized country like Germany, the Italian organizational model, subtle, difficult to encompass and exceptionally flexible, seems quite bizarre. At first sight it inspires only a limited degree of confidence.

If we refer back to Italy, we see that 'differences of managerial culture between partners' is the main obstacle encountered when agreements are being signed or operated.[6] This problem is felt more intensely by major enterprises than by small and medium-sized firms (factor quoted in 24 per cent and 16 per cent of cases respectively).

Following the same line of thought, one must remember that the ability to assimilate cultures from different origins varies. In this respect the Japanese seem to be more gifted than others. 'Japan has a key tradition of selective absorption, assimilation and adaptation of foreign cultural characteristics which still makes its companies quite receptive to new technology.'[7] The Japanese tradition of openness to Western technology began in 1867. Subsequently the country has applied entirely systematic methods of learning and integration of external contributions. The thirst for knowledge has been widely stimulated by the system of initial and continuing education. Schematically, the classic Japanese model evolves in two stages: in the first stage, technologies of interest which might be transferable are identified throughout the world. In the second stage steps are taken to adapt and improve existing technologies. It goes without saying that, nowadays, the Japanese have generally got beyond merely producing imitations, often a caricature of the original, and are perfecting their own advanced technologies. It remains true that, the more developed the existing national R&D structures, the more quickly and more productive firms are able to absorb and improve imported technology.

Reciprocally, progress appears more hesitant. Western companies, European and American, are less expert at adopting and applying practices in the Japanese manner.

Uncertainties linked to the history of the firm

A strategic decision taken by a firm at any given time will naturally be conditioned by previous experience. A success story will influence the decision-makers in one direction whereas a series of setbacks or misadventures will lead the management of a firm to make choices of a more defensive nature. This common-sense reflection has been confirmed by the work carried out by CESAG on the conduct of German firms, using a sample of 222 SMEs and major industrial groups.[8]

On this basis it appears that the general idea of European industrial co-operation is positively attractive to only around a third of firms, even though the sample in question was dominated by firms with a strong commitment to exporting, having implemented major internationalization efforts since the first oil crisis and having conducted active policies of adaptation (re-centring of production, investment, R&D). The question, therefore, is how to distinguish those firms favourably disposed towards co-operation from those (the majority) which are wavering.

The questionnaire distributed and the interview chart used in the CESAG study (see note 2) were designed to disclose the pertinent data for the firms over a period of ten years: the destination of exports and industrial sitings abroad, their evolution, the product policy adopted and the arguments used by the firm to counter competition (emphasizing technological trump cards or ability to meet demand, brand image, quality of service, comparative price levels or efficiency of marketing methods), employment policy, tangible and intangible investment, purchasing practices and financial results obtained.

The primary observation to arise from this analysis is that the arguments used by German firms in favour of penetrating the European market (the main one) and other international markets are essentially technological. They testify to the assurance and pride of a country which for more than a century has enjoyed a sound manufacturing tradition. This attitude would not seem to be conducive to a desire to share industrial experience with other European partners, usually seen as being of a lower technological level; possibly equal but never superior. On the other hand, the Germans consider that, in a number of high-tech fields, North American and Japanese firms have made clear advances, enabling them to play a leading role, and it is therefore with them that they must learn to make terms. At all events, competition is more vigorous, on the national market as well as on the international markets. Some reaction is therefore essential. There are two possibilities: either exploit the strengths, the accumulated strategic advantages of German firms in as pertinent and aggressive a manner as possible, or else try to neutralize any weaknesses found by implementing compensatory or updating policies.

This alternative in fact provides the key to the will to co-operate or otherwise.

From the cluster analyses made, the following theory can be postulated and confirmed: that the desire to co-operate in R&D matters applies in particular to those firms which have recently suffered setbacks on the external markets, their policy being centred around such well-tried marketing arguments as proximity of services, brand loyalty tradition, the image of product quality and reliability, or the firm's reputation for honourable dealing. Industrial co-operation on a European or international scale is therefore seen as an escape route for weak firms which have suffered setbacks on the export markets and are seeing their edge over the competition disappearing, or for those firms in a bad competitive position and highly exposed to international pressures. Here, co-operation is perceived as a possible means of securing the rapid renewal of a partially obsolete portfolio of activities, or as a means of holding back the competition.

In the second case, that of a successful past, industrial co-operation on the European scale appears to be rather pointless and inefficient. Reservations as to the idea of co-operation are therefore expressed by strong firms, those which have shown themselves to be effective and which do not wish to dilute their advantages on the European market or modify the competition conditions deemed favourable to them in this market.

In the matter of financial co-operation the investigations carried out lead to the same conclusions. Dynamic firms which have seen a strong increase in outlets since 1975 and confront international competition by good technological adaptation to demand for the product and by judicious specialization, avoid taking the co-operation route. An equally aloof attitude adopted by German firms may also be explained by the fact that the German financial system responds well to the development requirements of the more dynamic firms which, by this very fact, inspire confidence.

The desire to co-operate in the matter of know-how is also influenced by the weight of the past. The sequence of events is as follows: a degree of competition strongly felt on the international markets triggers the idea of co-operation. This is then perceived as a desirable course of action between firms allied in order to ward off troublesome competition. On the other side of the coin, those firms which, not having perceived an increase in the pressures of competition and having gained the assurance which comes from a long-standing presence on the international markets, combined with explicit technological mastery, are frankly impervious to the prospect of co-operation. Why indeed should they wish to alter the rules of the industrial game when they have brought the firm into a winning position?

This question of managerial logic suggests a third form of reticence.

The Pitfall of Strategic Egotism

Basically, co-operative alliances are formed because two or more partners decide to share in the advantages of a joint search for efficiency, an acceleration of the rate of learning or the promotion of research and innovation, and to reduce the impact of external threats which, by their very nature, involve risks and the cost of adaptation. Their intention is easy to justify; how could they fail to subscribe to these promising prospects? In practice, apart from those factors just quoted, reluctance stems from disturbing conduct on the part of certain partners. Firms are in effect autonomous entities, endowed with their own decision-making powers and accustomed to fighting for business, i.e. orders, for themselves. Their corporate responsibilities come second to their personal interests; these are the rules of the game in a market economy in which each must continually prove himself. The principle of partnership disturbs this traditional way of thinking, by questioning the firm's decision-making powers, its power and its future.

The threat to autonomy

Partnership poses a potential threat to the autonomy of power of the legally independent firm.

This statement merely underlines a fact: an effective partnership implies having respect for the partner, taking into account its constraints and objectives. There is therefore no question (in the field of activity affected by the collaboration) of giving priority to the choice of just one of the partners; rather, the common advantages must be maximized, possibly by sacrificing particular privileges on one side or the other. Each of the partners has its freedom of movement partially restricted.

This necessity is more readily accepted where the associated firms have comparable operating structures and where they are of a similar size. Very unequal partnerships introduce latent imbalances, the bigger partner naturally having a tendency to take advantage of its size and consequent socio-political influence, and as a result to neglect the problems of its lighter-weight partner.[9] A certain equality of position at the beginning of the partnership process helps to create the essential climate of confidence.

There is no lack of examples of successful partnerships between firms of a similar size, particularly between medium-sized firms. On the other hand, where the bigger groups are concerned, the clash between the 'captains of industry' is a factor which it is difficult to overcome, the peculiar interests of these groups calling into question sensitive values at regional or national levels (poles of activity, employment). The recent misfortunes of the JESSI (Joint European Submicron Silicon) programme are evidence of this. In addition to a few small firms, the research group included such firms as the French Matra-MHS, the Belgian Mietec, the German Telefunken, the Dutch group Philips, SGS-Thomson and Siemens, the latter three being of comparable size. In September 1990 Philips, faced with severe problems of profitability and management, decided to withdraw from work on developing semiconductor static memory devices, part of the activity of the European research programme Eureka which incorporated JESSI. The remaining alliance, although not unbalanced, was not able to avoid the vicissitudes of short-term difficulties. The 'chips of the future' remain Japanese.

Subsequently, the UNIDATA agreement, signed in January 1974 between CII, Siemens and Philips with a view to close co-operation on the European scale in the field of information technology, has also failed to withstand the pressures, even though it linked industrial groups of the same substantial size. UNIDATA collapsed after the CII entered into an alliance in May 1975 with the American group Honeywell-Bull. Political arguments carried more weight than economic logic in this operation and the German press stated that CII had 'opted for Americanization to avoid a so-called Germanization'.[10] As a result, in September 1975 Philips also withdrew from the project. The European information technology industry had made a brave attempt which failed to overcome national self-interest, shared by the pioneering firms of more than one country.

These reflections are intended simply to add substance to a widely confirmed observation: that liaisons between entities of similar size and culture have a much greater chance of success than others. This does not alter the fact that there is no absolute guarantee of success or failure.

The 'Trojan horse syndrome'

This syndrome has been particularly studied by Kenichi Ohmae of the McKinsey Group.[11] He feels that alliances fail or are prematurely abandoned because of fears on the part of management of introducing a 'Trojan horse' into their firm, that is to say a subterfuge which will enable potential competitors to penetrate their domestic market at little cost.

This risk does indeed exist. Some firms, on the pretext of sharing in the considerably increased costs engendered by technological research and entry into the world's markets, merely aspire to scale national or sectoral barriers to entry and to gain access to still unexploited technological knowledge. The pillaging of latent resources, the intent to ransack the intangible assets of a competitor, constitute unprovable but very real objections to the creation of co-operative alliances.

The question to be addressed is whether the absence of a co-operative agreement would better safeguard the interests of the aggrieved partner. When it is remembered that alliance policies are to be found mainly in certain sectors of activity such as automobiles, aeronautics, information technology, telecommunications and the electrical industries, sectors characterized by major barriers to entry, rapidly evolving technologies, substantial fixed costs and high exploitation risks, the response to the question posed is not obvious. Co-operation is certainly not an easy means of development, but is it an avoidable evil?

Partnership as a pretence

It seems that, in some cases, co-operation between the partners is more simulated than actually practised, depending on how decisive the nature of the stake is.

We stressed earlier that the main areas for co-operative alliances were R&D and production, in that order. The aim is therefore indeed to gain access to technology or know-how which one of the partners lacks or handles poorly, in exchange for a *quid pro quo*. The terms of the exchange are not easy to assess. Is this *quid pro quo* in the same field (i.e. R&D or production) or in another (marketing, for example)? Is it effectively funded by the partner in terms of transferable corporate assets?

As in the matter of patents or manufacturing licences, fraudulent cases do exist. In order to get what it wants, a partner may negotiate illusory reciprocal arrangements.

Even pre-competitive co-operation, aimed at jointly producing a new idea which may subsequently be exploited separately, is not always free from self-seeking ulterior motives. In programmes such as ESPRIT, the firms which co-operate are none the less competitive. There often results a lack of transparency between the firms; the results passed on remain partial or even incomplete.[12]

These subterfuges also apply to the stated aims and objectives. Taking up the distinction made by H. A. Simon regarding the spheres of decision-making within the firm, it might be suggested that the 'programmed decisions' (here the explicit aims) have a tendency to give way to 'unprogrammed decisions' (here the implicit, hidden aims). Gianfranco Viesti uses the term 'objective façade' to indicate situations which are in fact conflicting, where the co-operation agreement is principally aimed at destabilizing a 'rival partner' who holds a better position on the experience curve. It is then a question of dispersing the technological skills of the partner rather than helping it to extend them. Such cases are not rare. 'In the judgement of many observers, this has been and is the clear strategy of many Japanese firms, for example, in the partnerships they conclude with Western firms for commercial purposes. The Japanese pattern is very clear: get an American involved to build the business, then get rid of the American.'[13]

Ultimately, this situation modifies the respective bargaining powers of the partners as it progresses. The one originally well endowed with knowledge and know-how finds itself trapped, partially stripped of its substance and thus weakened. Reciprocally, the firm which benefits covertly from the transfer of technology loses its relative vulnerability and acquires instead a growing influence.

Balance in an alliance is difficult to achieve and will always tend to be unstable.

Managerial Organization for Partnership

The interviews conducted in the context of research carried out by CESAG have revealed several essential conditions for the avoidance of the disappointment which may result from unsuccessful or mismanaged attempts at co-operation and which result in domineering attitudes or a unilateral appropriation of the alliance's advantages.

A successful co-operative effort presupposes, in the first place, that the aims of the operation to be undertaken have been clearly defined and unambiguously formulated. The motives of each of the partners must be known and explicit and these must relate to a philosophy of joint interests. The determination of these aims has the merit of forcing the management to reflect on what is really possible and desirable and, at the same time, specifies the reference points for a later objective assessment of the eventual agreement.

After this aims-determining phase comes the phase during which the necessary co-operative operations are methodically organized. The determination of the ways in which the activities will be co-ordinated assumes a primary importance.

It then becomes advisable to decide on the need for the co-operative alliance to be constant and on the conditions to be observed to ensure its proper development.

Consensus on the Aims of the Agreement

A consensus must be sought on the aims of the agreement. This will enable the true co-operative intentions of all the partners to be verified, it being understood that they are seeking not only to achieve their own aims and objectives but also to obtain mutually advantageous results.

Joint determination of aims

This raises the question of going beyond the traditional approaches of a strategy based on confrontation between competitors. It is a difficult process: conflict can arise between the traditional strategy of the independent firm and this new approach between firms joined by a partnership, in so far as the flow of information and the sharing of resources which the alliance presumes could call into question a key element in one or other of the parties' competitive strategy.

The search for a strategic synergy assumes equilibrium between co-operation and competition, between individual aims and joint aims, as figure 5.3 illustrates. A mutually positive result will not be obtained unless all partners play the alliance game honestly. In this case a 'giver–giver' kind of attitude will put the seal on mutual confidence and will enable a 'winner–winner' combination to be achieved, an indication of the alliance's success and endurance.

The partners must also define what they seek to get out of the alliance, jointly and severally.

Precise specification of aims

The aims of the agreements must be precisely specified. In order to assess results or performances, a reference point must be defined for evaluation purposes. The following aspects must be clarified in this respect.

1 *Immediate or longer-term results?* The quest for short-term advantages can be justified in so far as the overall competitive environment is very aggressive and where the two (or more) partners who decide to co-operate do so with the intention of recovering quickly and jointly the extent to which they lag behind other competitors.

But it is not easy to ensure the success of this operation, as there is a strong possibility that the partners will not be able to pool resources to precisely the same value. The exchange will therefore be mismatched in the initial stages and the alliance's equilibrium could

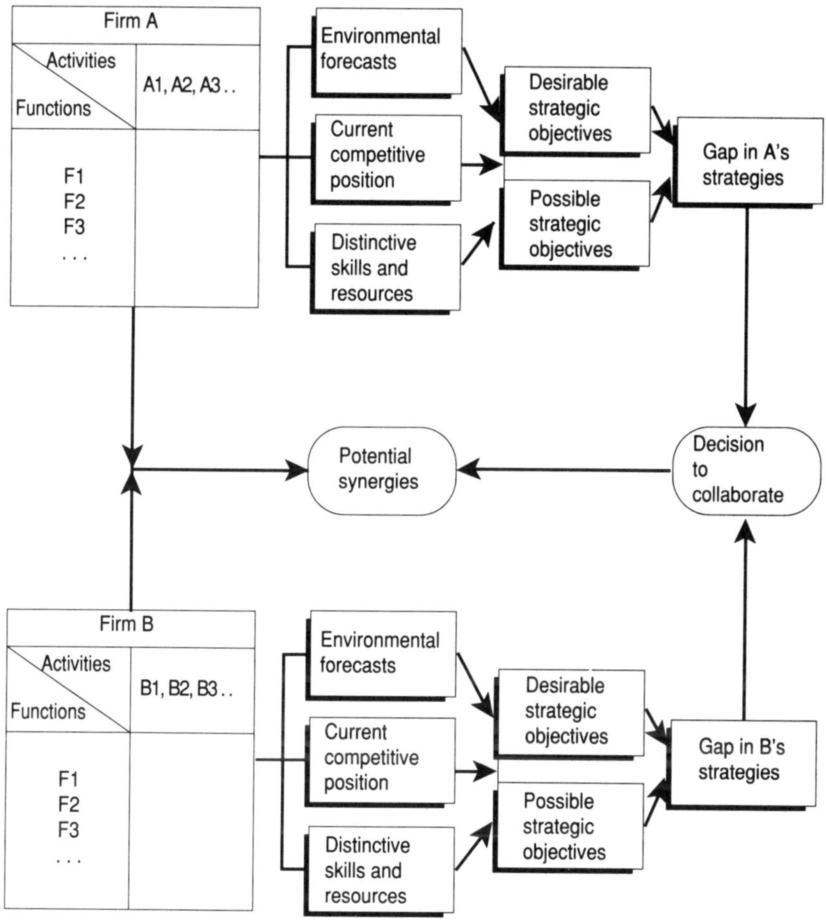

Figure 5.3 The joint quest for aims and objectives
Source: Sabine Urban and Serge Vendemini, CESAG, Strasbourg.

suffer from this, especially as the reciprocal negotiating strengths will change as the alliance progresses.

It is therefore advisable to agree on a balancing system right from the start. A relative advantage for one in the first stages of realization of the agreement must be compensated by a relative advantage for the others in the following stages. This means that medium-term objectives will give the alliance a better chance of success. Such an agreement will be better favoured where the respective contributions made by the partners are complementary and where each has need of the other's contributions to achieve its own objectives. On the other hand, deceitful behaviour on the part of one of the partners will condemn the agreement to failure and collapse. In order to achieve a lasting collaboration there must be a willingness to share, but it must also be recognized that there is no room for naïvety. Not all collaborative agreements bear the seal of sincerity and honesty. One party might be tempted to take out more than it puts in, its partner being seen essentially as a milch cow or as merely another player in the competition game who must be worn down.

2 *Quantitative results or qualitative benefits?* In order to be able to assess the effectiveness of an alliance one must obviously know what one expects from it. Quantifiable aims have the advantage of being less open to dispute than qualitative aims.

As examples of the former, one might quote:

- reduction in the cost of supplies by *x* per cent within a specified period of time;
- reduction in the cost of manufacturing a particular component of the whole product;
- reduction in promotional costs by grouped advertising activities;
- reduction in logistical expenses or administrative costs on the foreign markets;
- easing the cost of R&D;
- increases in sales margins, i.e. a more favourable return on sales;
- increase in shares of the market;
- increase in return on investment.

For all these fields it is possible to put a figure on the objectives, for a given period or moment in time, in respect of each of the partners.

Aims of a qualitative nature are more difficult to specify and to assess. By way of example one might quote:

- certainty of supplies;
- improvements in the quality of manufactured goods or in the reliability of products;
- greater flexibility on the part of all the partner firms;
- a division of the risks inherent in R&D activities;
- ease of access to new technology;

- a more concentrated market exploitation;
- better service to customers;
- improvements to the administrative services through the pooling of computers or the joint writing of software;
- the advantages of reputation or image linked to the pooling of discrete skills.

In any event, each partner must be aware of the existence of these aims and objectives and agree to discuss them with the other partner(s).

Where the objectives of the partners are dissimilar, negotiations are likely to be delicate. How, for example, does one compare the granting of access to a technology by one partner with the access to a market which the other offers through his distribution network? An analysis of Italian co-operative practices confirms that such complex agreements can be perfectly well managed to the mutual satisfaction of the partners; but in this event the factors of size of firm and sector of activity are very important.

3 *Direct or indirect benefits?* Here the evaluation exercise becomes even more delicate, because secondary objectives are not necessarily explicit and consciously perceived at the outset. It may be that the partners are committing themselves to a co-operative alliance based on certain specified (quantified) aims and on mutual confidence in the future. This might prove more fruitful in practice than was anticipated. In other words, one partner may obtain through the other unsuspected development opportunities or an unexpected network of useful contacts. In the same way, it may happen that, thanks to the partnership, one or the other of the firms will benefit from substantial inputs in terms of employee training, the positive aspects of which will have repercussions in areas of activity unaffected by the agreement. The beneficial effect is therefore spread wider.

Appropriate Co-ordination Procedures

By observing a series of specific cases, even if these are insuffıcent to validate a general theory, one is led to believe that many partnership experiments fail not for technical reasons but for organizational reasons.

Given that the aims of the alliance have been determined without ambiguity, the contributions made by the partners and their activities must be organized in accordance with a logical and coherent plan. The convergence of co-operative goals and the decisions taken in the same spirit assume first of all the existence of a climate of confidence between the partners. On an operational level, it must be possible for this mutual confidence to be expressed at the appropriate level of management and monitored very firmly by the application of agreed procedures.

Mutual confidence: an essential element

Collaboration assumes a pooling of resources and thus a co-ordination of the content and timing of the contributions made. This truth is heavily stressed by Peter Buckley and Mark Casson in their essay on the theory of co-operation:

> The definition of co-operation advocated here is co-ordination effected through mutual forbearance. This identifies co-operation as a special type of co-ordination. Co-ordination is defined as effecting a Pareto-improvement in the allocation of resources, such that someone is made better off, and no one worse off, than they would otherwise be. Co-ordination is an appropriate basis upon which to build a concept of co-operation, for it articulates the idea that co-operation is of mutual benefit to the parties directly involved.[14]

If the mutual gains are assessed at the level of the firms or at the level of their activities, this mutual confidence, this willingness to get on with each other and effectively make the co-operation work, will be expressed at the level of the individual and not at the level of the organization. The extent to which individuals are involved and the quality of this involvement will be decisive.

It must be borne in mind that individuals do not always act rationally and that their positive or negative reactions to the idea of co-operation are very often strongly influenced by emotions.[15] This serves to underline that the result of a co-operative agreement depends on a mass of details, or on gentle nudges which, like the enzymes in a chemical process, can produce effects which are disproportionate to the inducing factor. As Godfrey Devlin and Mark Bleakley have noted, it is desirable that the persons designated by the management to organize these strategic alliances are of premier quality, accustomed to working in a multinational environment and fluent in foreign languages.

Being chosen to work for the alliance should be seen as enhancing a person's career prospects within the company and not as a sideways move. It will increase the motivation of the individual towards the alliance and should improve the likelihood of its success. The only attitude which can be adopted by senior management is one of to win (together). Anything else should be considered as unacceptable.[16]

Mutual confidence and loyalty between partners will not just happen all of a sudden; they arise out of *use*. Co-operative activities undertaken over a range of operations, as a package, rather than agreed step by step, therefore show more promise.

In Europe the process of co-operation seems to be gradually getting on to the right road. In practice, there is every chance that industrial co-operation will become better accepted as cultural divisions are broken down. Mutual mistrust has a tendency to disappear with improved knowledge about the partners concerned. School and university programmes, travel, cultural exchanges, the information and images conveyed by the media, international artistic rallies and meetings – all have an essential role to play in this respect.

Establishing operating interfaces at a suitable level

In chapter 3 we showed that co-operation occurs at different levels: at the level of an operational function, at the level of an activity or at the level of a company which is seeking to co-ordinate or restructure its portfolio of activities by diversifying it or, alternatively, by re-centring it on the company's core business. Accordingly, co-operative agreements must be negotiated and executed at the most suitable level in the hierarchy, and this level will vary according to the type of co-operation concerned.

On the other hand, experience has shown that it is helpful if the finalizing and implementation of the agreement is carried out at the same level of authority and interest in all the various firms involved, the level which directly concerns the people involved (works manager, head of the laboratory or chief buyer, for example). These personnel must, of course, be able to count on an international logistical service, properly set up for this purpose.

The delegation of decision-making and organization to the level most closely involved in the co-operation must not, however, overlook the principle of recourse to a higher authority in order to resolve any conflicts or tensions which may arise. These seem to be inevitable, not merely because of the complexity of the operations, which makes it impossible to forecast all the many eventualities which could arise from their application, or because of particular vexatious occurrences, but also because of the incidents involving negligence or human error which are all too easy to imagine in a structure which no longer benefits from the steadying influence of routine.

Methods for co-ordination procedures

We know that co-operative agreements come in many guises, in terms of both the level of activity at which they operate and the objectives sought. They also vary in the legal framework which governs them (see chapter 6 below). Consequently they also vary widely in terms of the procedures applied to make them work. Every agreement, like every contract, creates the 'law of the parties'; in other words, there are as many special cases as there are agreements. As a result, only general observations can be made here.

The first such observation is that the co-ordination of the partners' joint activities assumes a learning effect. This progressive process often starts even before a formal co-operation agreement has been signed between two partners. This applies in the case of indirect co-operations which are set up through suppliers or research institutes, as shown in figure 5.4. An indirect co-operation can also be formed through professional associations or organizations which seek, for example, to harmonize technical standards or tax regulations on the European level. The partners then become associated stage by stage, with limited stakes which consequently do not arouse resistance or provoke manifestations of mistrust.

Once the co-operation agreement has been signed, three types of co-ordination become available:

- co-ordination is achieved within each partner's existing organizational framework;
- the partners decide to form an *ad hoc* task force to be responsible for the administration of the co-operative agreement;
- where the stakes are particularly high and complex, leading to a long-term co-operation, a special legal structure is created: a 'programme management company', consortium, or similar.

The need for a training period is also justified by the fact that some skills are complex and difficult to co-ordinate.

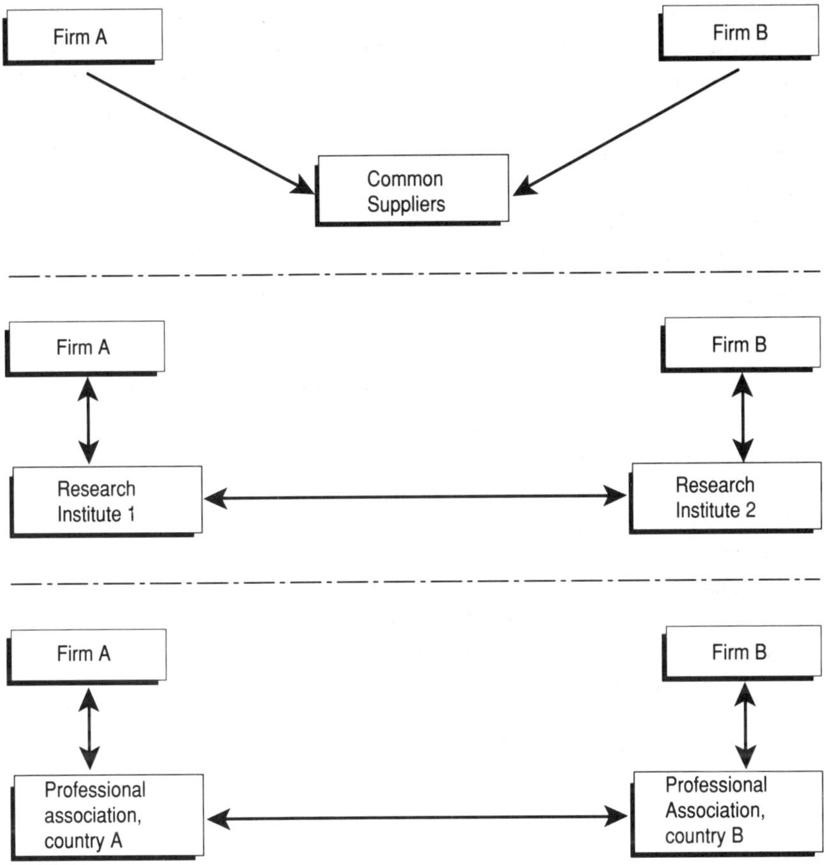

Figure 5.4 Indirect co-operative liaisons
Source: Sabine Urban and Serge Vendemini, CESAG, Strasbourg.

Manufacturing excellence is a complex web of employee training, integration with suppliers, statistical process controls, employee involvement, value engineering and design for manufacture. It is difficult to extract such a subtle competence in any way but a piecemeal fashion.

There is an important distinction between technology and competence. A discrete, stand alone technology (for example, the design of a semiconductor chip) is more easily transformed than a process competence, which is entwined in the social fabric of a company.[17]

Secondly, explicit rules must be laid down, in the matter of contributions, time involved, circulation of information and reporting as well as control.[18] Often the necessary resources for the operation of an alliance are underestimated at the beginning and the harmonious course of the co-operation is later disturbed in consequence. An inequality of contributions does not augur well for the future. 'In a recent alliance between a UK and a Japanese company, for every 20 Japanese employees sent to the United Kingdom for training, the UK company sent one employee to Japan. It is obvious that the potential for learning from the partner is dependent to a large extent on the size and quality of the resources devoted to the alliance.'[19]

Moreover,

> co-ordination can only be achieved where communication exists. To this end, all interdependent members of the organization who need to be co-ordinated must be linked into a communication network. In addition, norms of behaviour and incentives must be used to ensure that this network is actually used. It is particularly necessary to avoid the breaking off of communication as is typical in conflict situations. Starting-points for regulations referring to the communicative aspects of co-ordination are obligations to report, rights to initiate or submit proposals, rights or obligations to consult others and, as an extreme, the rights of participation in decision-making processes. In addition there are regulations for the openness of information and feed-back of information, for the form of information, for the information target groups and sources as well as times and frequency of information exchange.[20]

The evaluation stages must be specified according to a predetermined timetable, so calculated as to avoid premature, impatient action as well as indifference resulting from a too-elastic phasing of operations. In any event, the responsibilities must be clearly defined; they should not be lessened by the adoption of a vague principle of co-responsibility.

Thirdly, the defensive boundaries must be defined. The partners united under the terms of a collaboration are committed to share certain resources, certain liabilities and certain advantages. The terms of an agreement must be respected without any wish to cheat; the items pooled or made available to the other partner(s) must be provided, but an alliance will not legitimate access to resources not covered by the agreement.

From this point of view, the concept of fair play appears to vary according to firm and to country. Hamel et al., for example, quote the case of a failed co-operation:

Consider one technology-sharing alliance between European and Japanese competitors. The European company valued the partnership as a way to acquire a specific technology. The Japanese company considered it a window on its partner's entire range of competencies and interacted with a broad spectrum of its partner's marketing and product-development staff. The company mined each contract for as much information as possible.

For example, every time the European company requested a new feature on a product being sourced from its partner, the Japanese company asked for detailed customer and competitor analyses to justify the request. Over time, it developed a sophisticated picture of the European market that would assist its own entry strategy. The technology acquired by the European partner through the formal agreement had a useful life of three to five years. The competitive insights acquired informally by the Japanese company will probably endure longer.

Limiting unintended transfers at the operating level requires careful attention to the role of gatekeepers, the people who control what information flows to a partner.[21]

Agreement Stability or Development?

How should the progress of co-operative agreements be organized within the participant firms? By placing stress on the necessary stability, or by promoting the idea that the competitiveness of a firm depends essentially on its ability to handle change and that this state of mind must therefore be applied to all aspects of the firm's organization?

This dilemma is not clear-cut in theory and there is no simple answer. The following thoughts are intended merely to underline a few elements of decisional logic in both directions and to present the results of some empirical studies which might clarify the discussions.

Which decisional logic should be adopted?

In so far as the co-operation is intended to reduce uncertainty, it is expected that a certain degree of stability of the agreement be sought. This requires partners of good faith who honestly pool their resources. Adaptation to the other's culture takes time, and there needs to be a period of learning in order for any confusion to passs. In addition, joint strategic measures call for very careful planning and a degree of equanimity, and thus of time – just enough to ensure that the complementarity and mutual patience are justified. Operational interdependence will be built up on the way: this demands stability in the operating structure.[22]

On the other hand, various authors emphasize the strong likelihood of instability in co-operative alliances, owing to the fact that the initial motives of the partners are not in fact very positive. This relates to somewhat dishonest alliances which are especially aimed at weakening or emasculating a rival. It also relates to agreements based on a need to rectify previous errors in strategy, in which event the co-operation appears merely to be a 'second-best alternative to self-development'.[23] Under these circumstances, once one of the partners has obtained what it surreptitiously sought, the agreement will break down without any hope of resurrection.

According to other observers, co-operation agreements have a tendency to fail because of errors of judgement. The partners underestimate the transactional costs (i.e. the costs of monitoring efforts, of investing in ways to bond performance, and of cheating) or were unable to appreciate accurately the clear advantages arising from co-operation. The monitoring of performance is a delicate task and doubt can be a poor counsellor.[24]

To the reluctance within each partner's own organization with its own strategic commitments must be added those external factors which affect the conditions for the realization of co-operative agreements. It is known, for example, that the identity of the British group ICI was fundamentally changed as a result of agreements signed with the Japanese group Fujitsu. What will be the effect of the financial and strategic hold which Fujitsu has over ICI on the forty-odd Community ESPRIT projects in which ICI is involved? The European spirit which presides over these co-operative agreements, financially supported by the European Community, will inevitably be significantly affected.

As a general rule, strategic management must be reviewed wherever major changes occur in the environment of firms; the dynamics of the co-operative agreements may be affected as a result of these.[25]

The lessons of effective practices

The phenomenon of co-operative alliances is a recent development. The lessons to be learned from experience are therefore limited to the extent that empirical studies which analyse the results are still rare. They do, however, enable some interesting observations to be made.

1 *The mortality rate of alliances varies according to age and function.* An analysis of alliance mortality has been made by Bruce Kogut on a particular category of co-operative alliances – joint ventures – covering 148 US experiences.[26] This showed that the instability of alliances made itself felt especially after a lifespan of five to six years. It seems that the anticipated positive effects were exhausted by then and the vitality of the collaboration was inadequate to find a new impetus. The mortality rate appeared to be lower in the case of some alliances (those centred on production, financial co-operation and the development of new products) than in others (particularly those dominated by concentration on marketing or after-sales services). This tendency for interest in co-operation to vary according to the nature of the objectives seems to be a general one.

On the other hand, it has not been possible to verify the variations in mortality rate according to sector of activity or country concerned. The *bonne alliance* does not occur systematically in certain branches, nor is it guaranteed by the nationality of the partners.

2 *The vitality of agreements depends very much on the state of mind which motivates the partners.* The analyses made in Germany have demonstrated the fact that industrial concerns in the Federal Republic were not, in general, particularly attracted to a model of co-operative development.[27] However, those which accepted and tested the idea were much more positively oriented towards enhancing and multiplying their experiments; one experiment provokes another. The proportion of firms favourably disposed towards several forms of co-operation is relatively high. Statistically, certain varieties of co-operative alliance stand out: almost two-thirds of the firms favourably disposed towards co-operation on R&D were also in favour of technical co-operation or collaboration regarding know-how.

On the other hand, certain varieties of co-operation are seen to be explicitly rejected in Germany: combined R&D collaboration and financial co-operation, or R&D collaboration combined with a co-operation which tends to protect the markets, or financial co-operation and collaboration in the field of industrial know-how.

3 *The intensity of the co-operation depends on the degree of maturity of the activity concerned*, as illustrated in table 5.1. The first three columns

Table 5.1 Intensity of forms of co-operation and degree of maturity of the activity

	Activity				
Form of co-operation	Emergent	Mature	Declining	Fragmented market	World-wide cover
Adaptation	+	++	++	+	++
Functional	++	+	+	++	+
Co-ordination	=	++	++	N	+

N = negligible; + = significant; ++ = high
Source: Sabine Urban and Serge Vendemini, CESAG, Strasbourg (Italian survey, 1988).

relate to the classic concept of life cycle, the last two to the geographical distribution of these activities, a 'fragmented' activity being concentrated on a local market, still protected by barriers to entry.

As regards the forms of co-operation, the international agreements analysed have been classified according to the aims and objectives allocated to the co-operation, namely:

- adaptation co-operation, including those agreements which seek essentially (and in descending order of importance):
  - development of market shares;
  - access to new markets;
  - acquisition of technology;
  - product diversification;
- functional co-operation, covering
  - access to economies of scale;
  - reduction in costs, time and risks;
- co-ordination co-operation, covering
  - rationalization of the portfolio of activities;
  - making the firm's technologies profitable;
  - access to new finance.

Two co-operation development schemes appear to stand out. The first mainly applies to the newer, emerging activities, still characterized by fragmented and protected markets. In this case it is the functional type of co-operation which is sought. The competitive edge needs to be sharpened by functional efficiency and the resulting price cuts.

The proliferation of this type of agreement is therefore logical and its stability depends on how efficient the partners are in mastering the functions.

The second scheme concerns those firms whose main activity (or activities) has reached maturity (or has gone over the top and is close to decline). The great unified European market could therefore be a disturbing influence. Here the desire to co-operate comes from the decision-making centres concerned with the aim of accelerating the processes of adaptation and the re-centring of activities. The co-ordination of competitive advantages and the coherence of portfolio distributions dictate the orientation and evolution of these alliances.

Bearing in mind their strategic dimension, there are grounds for believing that these alliances are aimed at achieving a certain degree of stability in order to be fruitful.

4 *European partnerships are taking root in the culture.* Each year ANRT-ANVAR Europe surveys, *inter alia*, occurrences of interest to European firms with regard to the BRITE-EURAM programme on industrial technology and high-tech materials.[28] What does it find? A composition of industrial partners around hard and lasting cores. The custom of collaborating is gaining strength; and the more complex the field, the more the co-operative practices are taking root and stabilizing. Technological requirements make this essential.

The Search for the Right Partner

As has just been shown, the success of a co-operation presupposes that the participants have organized their partnership efficiently after having clearly avoided the pitfalls inherent in these alliances. Furthermore, it is important that each firm involved has succeeded in finding a suitable partner, that is to say, one that meets in a suitable manner the requirements expressed.

This self-evident observation poses the problem of establishing an efficient procedure for bringing the parties together. Sometimes mere chance will suffice but, in the complex world of business, this possibility cannot be recommended as a course of action. It is therefore desirable to set up information systems by means of which potential partners can make known their attributes and locate the complementary ones they seek.

The information required ranges widely over different fields. It has to cover scientific and technical areas as well as economic or political ones (the current rules of the game). In other words, it is advisable to create new 'information products',[29] tailor-made to enable the potential partners to obtain diplomatic information as regards the problems posed. The process implies the setting up of an effective means of bringing the firms together and the provision of efficient tools on which they can rely.

Effective Methods

In the previous section, three main forms of co-operation have been defined and explored:

- co-operative methods aimed at improving the adaptation capacities of a firm at the level of one or other of its activities in order to give it a boost towards a better competitive position:
- functional co-operation, aimed at improving the performance and coherence of operational functions within a given activity;
- co-ordination co-operation, aimed at conferring a certain logic (susceptible to the effects of synergy) on the coherence of the combination of activities within a firm.

Each of these three types of co-operation has its own different information requirements. In the first two cases, it is a matter of facilitating the quest for fairly well targeted partners, aiming at short- or medium-term actions. In the third case it is more a means of monitoring technology which is required, with long-term application.

The search for targeted information

Every firm, no matter what its size, has within its organization a system of information and communication. This usually corresponds to the current internal demands of the production unit. But this in-house system is very probably unsuited to meet the demands imposed by the search for an international partner. It will therefore be necessary to have recourse to an external specialist organization, especially where the domain of the documentation and the scientific, technical and economic information has become industrialized.

The computerization of data and the formation of networks is today undergoing an exponential expansion. There is no question of lack of information; indeed, the volume will soon become a burden and the very amount of information available will result in it being valueless if it is poorly handled (classified, stored, processed). In other words, pertinent information, of the required quality, is scarce. If it is to be retrieved, accurate updating methods must be applied, by means of which the raw material represented by readily available and accessible 'trivial' information will be transformed into a 'personalized information product' which might meet the demand expressed by a firm searching for a partner.

What, therefore, are the procedures to be followed, and towards what kind of content should they be directed?

First, the procedures must be systematic. It must be clearly understood just what the party making the request and the one making the offer of a partnership are actually seeking. This is not always explicitly expressed. In reality, the term 'information' covers a somewhat obscure concept which must be decoded if subsequent lack of satisfaction is to be avoided.

The level of information required to nourish a partnership may vary in intensity (ranging from simply making documentation available to offering personal advice) and represent expectations expressed in varying degrees of precision (see table 5.2). In any event, the circulating agency and information counsellor must be capable, as the interface between the two parties, of understanding the problems facing each of them and of framing these operationally, classified (standardized products and components, materials, processes, markets concerned) so as to be able to respond to the question 'look for information on what?' This 'problem audit' must be supplemented by a 'firm audit' which looks at the firm's potential and its environment, thus enabling suitable solutions to be proposed for each case (see table 5.3).

To the extent that co-operation is intended to achieve gains in productivity or to control the cost and quality of products better, the process of bringing the partners together must incorporate quite detailed data. An ideal co-operation would be one which enabled each of the partners to utilize the other's theoretical and practical knowledge in order to increase their mutual knowledge and thereby to improve the production conditions or to penetrate new fields of activity.

Secondly, the content of the information must be useful. The partnership's aim is to produce a solution to industrial problems:

Table 5.2 The various meanings of the word 'information' in the services offered to firms

	Documentation	Information on an industrial subject	Advice
Objective	Respond to a request for information	Investigate a subject formulated by the firm (little or no connection with the applicant's context)	Analyse and formulate the problem jointly with the industrialist in order to adapt the response according to the potential of the firm and of its environment
Content	Unprocessed data; white matter (documents)	Analysis of what exists bearing on white matter and grey matter (experts)	Risk evaluation
Methods employed	Document analysis summary/ indexing	Multi-disciplinary synthesis	Scenarios
Expected results	Indicate/ stock/retrieve/ distribute a set of documents	Report showing the various possibilites (state of the art)	Recommendations

Source: ARIST, Alsace.

performance, employment conditions, economic factors (selling price, lifespan, cost of exploitation, etc.). The interfacing service must therefore identify (from the point of view of what is to be supplied as well as that demanded by the partnership) certain types of knowledge which might combine together in a positive manner, in particular:

- technical knowledge about production plant and equipment (the state of the art as concerns manufacturing techniques);
- techno-economic knowledge of products (survey of supply);

Table 5.3 The various meanings of the word 'information' within the firm

	Communication information	Operational information	Cognitive information
Objective	Ensure liaison and promotion	Manage/automate	Manage: development/ strategy
Content	The actions concerned are linked to the functioning of the organization: internal communication, external communication	Management of clearly typified operations: production, supplies, customer orders, administrative and financial management	The actions concerned are more vague, less structured, the objectives less well targeted, the means of action less well defined
Methods employed	Internally: electronic mail, meetings, office automation etc. Externally: information incorporated in the products: price, characteristics, origin, instructions for use, etc. promotional messages and associated techniques/advertising.	Each operation has its 'own' information system. Messages sent/received processing procedures, data storage: files and industrial data banks research and indexing systems: nomenclature, scope of operations sequencing of manufacturing following-up prospective customers, etc.	Integration of external sectoral, economic & technical data which has to recognized, acquired, filtered, processed, and which necessitates a network of sources of information.
Expected results	Contribute to making information flow more smoothly: 'information is worthless, unless it is circulated' Contribute towards a better knowledge of the firm and its products Brand image	Good day-to-day management of the firm: be aware of the state of each operation with enough reliability, accuracy and speed in order to react to hazards, control the timing, control machine expenses, control costs	Facilitate decision-making in uncertain environment: orientate the firm's activities: alter the balance of competition to one's advantage, minimize the risks
Parties involved	All	Functional and operational management workshops	General management marketing management R&D management

Source: ARIST, Alsace.

- economic knowledge (survey of demand);
- marketing knowledge (distribution survey);
- knowledge as to how to get things done (study of subcontracting);
- supply-prospecting knowledge (study of suppliers).

Obtaining this sort of relevant data is not just a daydream. In the space of a few days, bodies such as ARIST (Agence Régionale d'Information Scientifique et Technique) can supply reliable operational information about a given industrial activity, concerning

- the main customers, suppliers and competitors;
- patents, standards and regulations currently in force;
- the relevant technical data (materials, processes);
- economic data (market structures).

A specialist business merger consultant would also be able to supply information on the risks (to the technological and commercial plans) and on the legal validity of the industrial property factors declared by the parties, in cases involving an acquisition of new products and/or new skills which arise out of the parties' field of experience.

Finally, the provision of a targeted information service also develops the principles of a partnership culture and helps the firms concerned to follow an ethical code.

The monitoring of technology

The monitoring of technology is not intended to resolve an immediate operational problem but is aimed at detecting in good time the opportunities and threats implicit in the introduction of new technologies. It is also a research tool for the partners. Their particular interest has a strategic dimension and is therefore fundamental, but the field to be monitored is much wider, as it cannot be predicted where something new and interesting will make its appearance. More often than not the more radical ideas come from unexpected quarters and therefore a wide 'horizontal' surveillance must be set up.

By way of example, we could quote the case of the motor industry. Technological progress has paved the way for a new car fitted with innovative artificial intelligence equipment. The whole design of the car is involved in this development, not just this or that function or component part. One problem is how to find out when experimental innovations will be marketed on the commonly used cars, because after-sales and repair services will have to be reorganized as a result. Under these circumstances, it will be seen that 'vertical' monitoring of engineering developments or new alloys is likely to prove incapable of detecting the opportunities or problems posed by plastics, ceramics and electronics.

But it is easy to imagine the problems of cost confronting horizontal monitoring, costs which a lone firm would be unable to bear in the vast majority of cases. A co-operative arrangement aimed at sharing these costs is therefore justified; and this does not just concern the smaller firms. The major German industrial group Daimler-Benz and the Japanese Mitsubishi group have just agreed on a formidable collaboration (without capital ties) aimed *inter alia* at combining their research into the recycling of car bodies and anti-pollution devices. In the aeronautical field, too, these two giants have begun to exchange engineers and information. The same applies to high-speed trains, on which the Germans and Japanese have decided to combine their development work. For these two parties it is indeed a question of gaining mastery of progress before their competitors do, of sharing the fruits of technological monitoring by utilizing an alliance between companies which share the same innovative and conquering spirit.

The actors who are disposed to pool a technological monitoring system may be brought together – outside particular inter-firm links – in various ways, through:

- consultative and scientific, technical and economic information bodies, accustomed to monitoring techniques and markets;
- research or university laboratories;
- professional organizations;
- public (especially Community) bodies.

Co-operation between firms is an indispensable requirement for those wishing to participate in the European research and development programmes such as ESPRIT (European Strategic Programme for Research and Development in Information Technologies), BRITE (Basic Research in Industrial Technologies for Europe), EURAM (European Research in Advanced Material), RACE (Research and Development in Advanced Communication Technologies in Europe) or DRIVE (Dedicated Road Infrastructure for Vehicle Safety in Europe).[30] At least one of the partners to the agreement must come from another Community member state. The procedure known as 'cost-sharing research contract' is applied to 80 per cent of the finance allocated by the European Community. This consists of reimbursing 50 per cent of the cost of the project to the participating enterprises or institutes. Scientific and technological co-operation exercised in certain defined sectors of knowledge on a Community level thus benefits from a not inconsiderable kind of incentive subsidy (see table 5.4). This co-operative research mainly concerns finalized basic research and pre-competitive technological development. (Finalized research is distinguished from pure research by its orientation

Table 5.4 Framework programme 1990–1994

Fields	Total, Ecu million		Proportion of the total budget (%)
I. Circulation technologies			
1. Information and communications technology		2,221	38.9
Information technology	1,352		
Communications technology	489		
Development of general purpose telematic systems	380		
2. Industrial technologies and materials		888	15.6
Industrial technologies and materials	748		
Measurements and tests	140		
II. Management of natural resources			
3. Environment		518	9.1
Environment	414		
Marine technology and science	104		
4. Life sciences and technology		741	13.0
Biotechnology	164		
Agricultural and agro-industrial research[a]	333		
Biomedical and health research	133		
Life sciences and technology for developing countries	111		
5. Energy		814	14.3
Non-nuclear energy	157		
Nuclear fission safety	199		
Controlled thermonuclear fusion	458		
III. Valorization of intellectual resources			
6. Human capital and mobility		518	9.1
Total	5,700[b]		100.0

[a] Including fishing
[b] Including Ecu 57 million for centralized circulation and valorization action under Article 4, taken proportionally from each of these actions, and Ecu 180 million for 1990–2 and Ecu 370 million for 1993–4 intended for the Joint Research Centre.
Source: European Commission (DGXII), 'Les programmes communantires de recherche: un guide pour les participants', Brussels, May 1990, p. 2.

towards possible applications; pre-competitive research lies, in the technological process, at the stage prior to that of commercial development.)

Apart from the financial support, the value of Community programmes in stimulating the spirit of co-operation *per se* must be stressed. Finalized or pre-competitive research often leads to extensions in grouped activities at the level of the application, the multidisciplinary, multinational teams having learned to get to know each other, to appreciate each other and to work in concert. One successful experience brings another in is wake.

Efficient Tools

Three types of tool may be mentioned, it being understood that these are complementary and not mutually exclusive:

- data bases;
- human resources;
- the media.[31]

Data bases

This tool concerns in particular the targeted field of research. It is, of course, illusory (despite the progress made in information technology) to think in terms of an encyclopedic data bank from which the strategist will be able to extract at the appropriate time all the detailed information he or she needs in order to reduce the areas of uncertainty and ignorance or to find the ideal partner.

This is not to say that cleared paths do not exist. In Europe the best-known tool is BC-NET (Business Co-operation Network), set up in 1988 to facilitate the search for business partners within the European Community.

The field of inter-firm co-operation is wide:

- general collaboration: creation of a joint subsidiary;
- financial partnership, which could result in participations in another firm in another EC country, or reciprocally to a foreign European firm participating in one's own firm, or to cross-financing agreements, or to the search for investors for the development of a project;

- commercial partnerships with regard to mutual distribution agreements or joint action in certain markets which call for a high level of involvement, franchising proposals, etc;
- technical partnerships, concerning relations linked to innovation programmes or relations between order-providers and subcontractors.

The BC-NET nomenclature for types of co-operation is shown in table 5.5.

According to the data published in July 1990 in the Euro Info Centres (EICs) and BC-NET magazine, giving an account of this data bank after two years' operation, commercial co-operation tops the list, accounting for 58 per cent of the recorded co-operation profiles). In the case of requests for distributing agents abroad, the demand is four times greater than the supply. In second place came requests for technological collaboration (26 per cent) and third came requests for financial partnerships (10 per cent), 'General co-operation' representing a mere 6 per cent.

The BC-NET network is used by intermediaries (public or private) in the collaboration process and not by the firms themselves. This peculiarity is explained by the fact that the proper use of a tool of this type assumes the acquisition of a quite complex methodological expertise, representing a major intangible investment which cannot be justified at the level of one firm alone. These intermediaries are therefore consultancies, chambers of commerce, world trade centres, banks, regional or sectoral bodies: there were about 260 of them in 1990. Their roles are not necessarily the same; some intermediaries content themselves with putting potential partners in touch with each other, others accompany the parties in their negotiations. But in all cases the BC-NET network ensures the confidentiality of the operations in progress.

The firm seeking a European partner approaches the approved company adviser for its area. The latter prepares a form entitled 'Co-operation Profile' (CP) and forwards it to the central computer centre, usually by direct link. The information retrieval service compares this application (or offer) with the data stored in its data bank. If offer and application match the details are sent immediately to the newcomer and also to former applicants (or offerers). These then judge the appropriateness and the value of the collaborations suggested by the matching. Once the sorting has been done, the

Table 5.5 The BC-NET nomenclature for types of co-operation

Code	Name	Type of co-operation
11	Joint creation of an enterprise, consort	General co-operation
12	Merger	General co-operation
211	Request to buy a complete company or part	Financial co-operation
212	Offer to sell a complete company or part	Financial co-operation
213	Request for equity capital	Financial co-operation
214	Offer to provide equity capital	Financial co-operation
215	Request for a loan	Financial co-operation
216	Offer to provide a credit	Financial co-operation
31	Reciprocal marketing agreement	Commercial co-operation
321	Request for marketing services	Commercial co-operation
322	Offer of marketing services	Commercial co-operation
33	Reciprocal distribution agreement	Commercial co-operation
341	Request for distribution services	Commercial co-operation
342	Offer to provide distribution services	Commercial co-operation
351	Request for agency	Commercial co-operation
352	Offer to provide agency	Commercial co-operation
353	Request for after-sales service rep.	Commercial co-operation
354	Offer to provide after-sales service rep.	Commercial co-operation
361	Request for franchise (franchisee)	Commercial co-operation
362	Offer to provide franchises (franchisor)	Commercial co-operation
371	Request for general commercial assistance	Commercial co-operation
372	Offer to provide general commercial assistance	Commercial co-operation
41	Reciprocal technological co-operation	Technological co-operation
421	Request for technological assistance	Technological co-operation
422	Offer to provide technological assistance	Technological co-operation
423	Request for R&D assistance	Technological co-operation
424	Offer to provide R&D assistance	Technological co-operation
43	Reciprocal production agreement	Technological co-operation
441	Main contractor looks for sub-contractor	Technological co-operation
442	Subcontractor offers his facilities	Technological co-operation
443	Request for engineering capability	Technological co-operation
444	Offer of engineering capability	Technological co-operation
445	Request for manufacturing rights	Technological co-operation
446	Offer of manufacturing rights	Technological co-operation
447	Main producer looks for O.E.M.	Technological co-operation
448	Producer offers capacity to become O.E.M.	Technological co-operation
451	Request for patents or licences	Technological co-operation
452	Offer of patents or licences	Technological co-operation
453	Request for technology transfer	Technological co-operation
454	Offer of technology transfer	Technological co-operation

advisers get in touch directly in order to obtain further details of the content and practical conditions of the proposed co-operation. The request (or offer) for co-operation remains stored in the computer's memory for a period of validity, defined by the company adviser.

The CP has been designed in order to establish a uniform method of communication between company advisers in Europe. It includes three categories of particulars, concerning:

1 the type of co-operation sought: general, financial, commercial or technological (see table 5.5);
2 the activity sought or offered, classified by industrial activity in accordance with a listing specific to the BC-NET network but based on the NACE list;
3 the geographical catchment area, described in accordance with the NTUS (Nomenclature of Territorial Units for Statistical Purposes) geographical coding – country, region, county or equivalent.

In the event that the initial search (introduced by a 'match code' proves fruitless, a variation is suggested to the advisers: the circulation of a 'flash profile' to all the advisers in the network, notifying them of the search. The object of this is to alert anyone interested and to encourage them to examine the possible interest of the offer concerned to their customers.

After two years in operation, it is evident that BC-NET undoubtedly meets a real need. The number of co-operation profiles recorded (more than 20,000 at June 1990) is a good omen. It has been decided to mount a promotion campaign for the tool and its extension beyond the EC to the EFTA countries and to Eastern Europe is on the agenda.

Apart from BC-NET, there are other data bases resulting from private or public initiatives, some receiving support from the European Commission. An example is Proteas (based in St Andrews, Scotland) which proposes to circulate R&D results throughout Europe in order to encourage technological and scientific collaboration between EC member countries as well as the industrial and commercial exploitation of such research. Another is Data-Star Business, a data base held in Heidelberg, Germany, and sponsored by the German government. Among other things, it aims to disseminate information regarding opportunities for co-operation in manufacturing, marketing, joint ventures and investment. Other data bases are more nationally based, such as Vectra (ARIST network) in France, handling offers and requests for international partnership through a chain of foreign contacts, or Transinove, the data bank created by the Institut National de la Propriété Industrielle (INPI) in Paris.

All these tools, very attractive intellectually, do however have some failings, tied to the fact that the processing of data is very costly and the quality of the information often leaves something to be desired in terms of lack of detail, incompleteness or failure to update. Information is a fragile thing, quickly obsolete, but of primary importance for the parties concerned. There is thus a temptation to retain strategic information. The electronic tool, sophisticated though it may be, still needs people of goodwill to demonstrate its effectiveness.

Human resources

Everyone is aware of the importance of interpersonal contacts. The European Community itself acknowledged this a long time ago, creating in 1973 the Business Co-operation Centre (BCC) which, fifteen years later, set up the BC-NET system. The BCC, more familiarly known as the 'marriage bureau', was conceived to promote widely varying forms of co-operation between European firms through advice and contact with potential partners. In this respect it played a guiding role, both technical and policy-formulating, and in organizing meetings.

Given that co-operation between firms is an important instrument in the development of local economies, the BCC decided to combine its efforts with those of the Commission's services responsible for regional policy, in order to organize in the less developed regions of the Community or those in industrial decline action aimed at promoting co-operation agreements – commercial, technical or financial – between the entrepreneurs in these regions and their counterparts in other member states. After a period of project identification and selection and a stage of information dissemination, this type of action, known as 'Europartenariat', consists of organizing contact days, aimed at putting enterprises in the selected region in contact with firms in other member states who have expressed an interest in collaborating with them.

The BCC is also very active in the promotion of transnational subcontracting; and it helps in the drafting of financial formulae suited to transnational projects.

In order to meet the demands for information and co-operation from medium-sized or small firms, the European Commission (DG XXIII) has also created EICs spread over the twelve member states. About 200 EICs (chambers of commerce, regional development associations, industrial or craft associations, financial institutions) are thus available to the European SMEs in order to keep them informed and to assist and advise them.

In parallel with the programme of action in favour of SMEs, in 1983 the Commission launched its first plan centred on aid to innovation and on the transnational transfer of technology between firms, especially between SMEs. More recently revived, this action, which is aimed at promoting all aspects of the innovative process from invention to the financing and successful marketing of new products and services, has been given the name of SPRINT (strategic programme for innovation and technology transfer).

SPRINT comprises three basic aspects. The most important up until now has been the very positive promotion of the transnational transfer of technology between firms. Once again, this concerns the creation of a chain network which links firms with public or private sector consultants with the explicit task of encouraging transnational technological co-operation between client firms. At the present time some sixty micro-networks have been set up under the auspices of SPRINT, directly oriented towards this type of collaboration and each involving two or more consultants from various Community countries. They have obtained Community support, both financial and logistical, for more than 120 positive agreements between firms for co-operation or for the transfer of technology, in such diverse fields as the design of robots, the management of road traffic, the creation of 'intelligent' greenhouses, etc.

The second aspect of the SPRINT programme relates to the setting-up of a transnational innovation support infrastructure, fostering the formation of European networks of specialists in venture capital, technological advice, strategic or marketing guidance, and design or quality experts. These networks provide a supportive basis for firms in their European technological development.

The programme's third aspect relates to the circulation of available technologies throughout the various economic sectors, including the traditional ones. It employs various means (conferences, training courses, data banks, etc.), some of which, such as the active collaboration between joint sectoral research centres, have made it possible to promote original forms of co-operation, such as the transnational dialogue entered into between the manufacturers and the users of equipment for the adaptation of production plant in the ceramics, textiles and footwear sectors.

All these institutional networks have created informational and personal links. Their impact on the motivation of co-operative phenomena depends, in reality, on the effort put in by the people whom they bring together. From this point of view, the network of relations woven by the parties concerned and their intermediaries plays a decisive role. Stage by stage and in unison they succeed in forging new concepts of company management and in promoting elaborated expertise.

The media

This term is used here in its widest sense. These are the props for the actions undertaken by the parties involved. These are innumerable kinds – too numerous rather than insufficient. Suffice it to mention in this respect:

- bulletins of advertisement publications, numbered in thousands;
- opportunity catalogues or 'technological exchanges', of which there are about 500 in Europe;
- special dossiers which appear in professional magazines;
- specialist events in the form of technology transfer shows or conventions on particular themes (for example, new materials) in which participants may display their desire for co-operation and gauge the value of coming to terms with various other participants.

These encounters enable parties which have the same interests and are procured by specialist consultant-agents to gain direct access to the essence of their concerns.

Notes

1 See, for example, Rudi K-F. Bresser, 'Matching Collective and Competitive Strategies', *Strategic Management Journal*, vol. 9, 1988, pp. 375–85; Kenichi Ohmae, 'Pourquoi les alliances échouent-elles?', *Harvard L'Expansion*, Spring 1990, pp. 25–44; Gary Hamel, Yves L. Doz and C. K. Prahalad, 'Collaborate with your Competitors and Win', *Harvard Business Review*, January/February 1989, pp. 133–9.

2 See Commissariat Général du Plan, Collection Etudes et Recherches; *Entreprises allemandes et coopération industrielle à l'échelle européenne*, survey carried out by S. Urban and S. Vendemini, CESAG, La Documentation française, Paris, March 1986, pp. 63–121.

3 See G. B. Richardson, 'The Organization of Industry', *Economic Journal*, September 1972, pp. 883–96; Jacques-L. Ravix, 'L'Emergence de la firme et des coopérations inter-firmes dans la théorie de l'organisation industrielle: Coase and Richardson', *Revue d'Economie industrielle*, no. 51, 1990, pp. 27–51.
4 Cf. the work by CESAG on Germany (1986) and on Italy (1988): S. Urban and S. Vendemini, *Les entreprises industrielles italiennes et la coopération internationale*, CESAG, Strasbourg.
5 See Sabine Urban and Ernst-M. Lipp, *L'Allemagne, une économie gagnante?*, Hatier, Paris, 1988, pp. 98–107.
6 CESAG, Strasbourg/CESPRI, Milan, 1987 survey: n = 272.
7 J-B. Lehmann, *The Roots of Modern Japan*, Macmillan, London, 1986.
8 CESAG, *Etudes et Recherches*, Commissariat Général du Plan, no. 2.
9 See Yves L. Doz, 'Technology Partnerships between Larger and Smaller Firms: Some Critical Issues', in Contractor and Lorange, *Cooperative Strategies*, pp. 317–38.
10 *Die Zeit*, 15 May 1975.
11 K. Ohmae, 'Pourquoi les alliances échouent-elles?', *Harvard L'Expansion*, Spring 1990, pp. 25–44.
12 See G. Koenig, *Management stratégique: vision, manoeuvres et tactiques*, Nathan, Paris, 1990, p. 196.
13 H. A. Simon, *The New Science of Management Decision*, Prentice Hall, Englewood Cliffs, NJ, 1977; G. Viesti, 'International Cooperative Agreements: New Strategies for International Growth and Technological Learning', *EIBA Meeting Proceedings*, Berlin, 1988.
14 P. J. Buckley and M. Casson, 'A Theory of Cooperation in International Business', in Contractor and Lorange, *Cooperative Strategies*, p. 32.
15 See Ruth Endress, *Strategie und Taktik der Kooperation: Grundlagen der zwischen und innerbetrieblichen Zusammenarbeit*, E. Schmidt, Berlin, 1985, pp. 36–61.
16 G. Devlin and M. Bleakley, 'Strategic Alliances – Guidelines for Success', *Long Range Planning*, vol. 21, no. 5, 1988, p. 22. See also L. A. Gyenes, 'Build the Foundation for a Successful Joint Venture', *Journal of Business Strategy*, November/December 1991, pp. 27–32.
17 G. Hamel, Y-L. Doz and C. K. Prahalad, 'Collaborate with Your Competitors and Win', *Harvard Business Review*, January/February 1989, p. 136. See also J. B. Bleeke and D. Ernst, 'The Way to Win in Cross-Border Alliances', *Harvard Business Review*, November/December 1991, pp. 127–35; H. J. Crouse, 'The Power of Partnerships', *Journal of Business Strategy*, November/December 1991, pp. 4–8; M-I. Lyons, 'Joint Ventures as Strategic Choice', *Long Range Planning*, vol. 24, no. 4, 1991, pp. 130–44.
18 See Hans Jürgen Drumm, 'Coordination', *Handbook of German Business Management*, Poeschel, Stuttgart; Springer, Berlin, 1990, pp. 570–80.
19 Devlin and Bleakley, 'Strategic Alliances', p. 22.
20 Drumm, 'Coordination', p. 574.

21 Hamel et al., 'Collaborate with Your Competitors', p. 136.

22 See B. Borys and D-B. Jemison, 'Hybrid Arrangements as Strategic Alliances: Theoretical Issues in Organizational Combinations', *Academy of Management Review*, vol. 14, no. 2, April 1989, pp. 234–49; Bruce Kogut, 'A Study of the Life Cycle of Joint Ventures', in Contractor and Lorange, *Cooperative Strategies*, pp. 169–85, and 'Joint Ventures and the Option to Expand and Acquire', *Management Science*, vol. 37, no. 1, January 1991, pp. 19–33.

23 Y-L. Doz, 'Technical Partnership between Larger and Smaller Firms: Some Critical Issues', in Contractor and Lorange, *Cooperative Strategies*, p. 325.

24 See J-M. Geringer and L. Herbert, 'Control and Performance of International Joint Ventures', *Journal of International Business Studies*, Summer 1988, pp. 235–54.

25 See Andrew Pettigrew, Richard Whipp and Robert Rosenfeld, 'Competitiveness and the Management of Strategic Change Process', in Arthur Francis and P. K. M. Tharakan, *The Competitiveness of European Industry*, Routledge, London, 1989, pp. 110–36.

26 Kogut, 'The Life Cycle of Joint Ventures'.

27 CESAG, Commissariat Général du Plan, no. 2, 1986.

28 Association Nationale de la Recherche Technique/Agence Nationale pour la Valorisation de la Recherche (ANRT-ANVAR Europe), *Lettre européenne du progrès technique* (*Technical Progress Letter*), no. 57–8, 22 August 1990, p. 13.

29 We have borrowed here the expression coined by Paul Degoul, Director of ARIST (Agence Régionale d'Information Scientifique et Technique) in Alsace who, with Thierry Ferrari, was the inspiration for the ideas expressed in this paragraph.

30 See Commission of the European Communities (DG XII): 'Les programmes communautaires de recherche: un guide pour les participants', Brussels, May 1990, 208 pp.; also DG XII, Politique d'entreprise, Commerce, Tourisme et Economie Sociale, Direction B, *European Actions in Favour of Enterprises*, unit 2: *Improvement of Transnational Co-operation and Development*, Brussels, September 1991.

31 There is no question here of making an exhaustive review of all existing tools; we merely underline the interest of a few 'European' tools.

6

Securing the Interests of the Partners

The great internal market of 1993 will only become a reality if firms in the various states of the Community can co-operate with one another and do so under the best possible conditions of efficiency and profitability. However, disparities in national laws are preventing this objective from being reached. This is why one of the primary concerns of the European authorities is to facilitate inter-firm co-operation by making available a number of structures based on a wider legal system than mere national laws. Consequently, two new types of legal instrument are being added to the traditional forms of industrial co-operation (see chapter 3): as regards legal structure, the European Economic Interest Grouping (EEIG) and the European Company are major innovations; and as regards industrial property, the European and Community patents and the Community trade mark are valuable tools. This chapter outlines the legal bases for these international co-operative agreements, founded on three affirmations:

- International co-operation agreements need a stable legal structure. Five bases for this have been outlined in chapter 3, three of which apply internationally: the contractual basis, the group basis and the company basis.
- International co-operation agreements demand proper formalization of the elements of industrial property.
- The interests of the partners are further protected when the other parties, for their part, undertake to guarantee the security of the ties.

Appropriate Forms of Legal Organization

Inter-firm co-operation has two main characteristics. The first is the existence of a common objective which will form the subject of the co-operative agreement. When entering into traditional contracts, each party aims to achieve an objective which remains personal to itself. The situation is quite different where a co-operation agreement is concerned. What prompts the parties to enter into this agreement is essentially the identification of a common industrial or commercial objective which they are going to make the subject of their contract. Secondly, there is a decision to attain this common objective together. This is really a question of the parties co-operating, that is to say, working together, proceeding in concert towards that common objective which has become the subject of the contract. Without prejudging the matter, it is clear that, more often than not, the routes by which this common objective can be reached and, especially, the respective rights and obligations of the parties, cannot be defined in advance as accurately as in a traditional contract.

The presence of these specific factors will involve and justify the privileged nature of the links which are set up between the parties. There is sometimes a certain degree of intimacy in the relationship. The ties will have, moreover, a degree of permanency and should therefore be made on a basis of equality, and repose on mutual confidence. The privileged nature of these ties explains and justifies the specific provisions and stable legal formats.

The Contractual Basis

General principles of international co-operative agreements

Co-operation is based on preferential relations between the partners. Consequently, the degree of co-operation may be more or less intense. This may manifest itself in specific clauses within a contract (co-operative clauses) or it may permeate the whole contract (co-operative contract).

The purpose of co-operative clauses is to institute a new type of rapport based on solidarity, duration and equality between the parties. These clauses are often found in contracts for the transfer of technology; for example, in the case of clauses by means of which the parties decide to carry out joint research in order to develop a patent, the licence for which is granted by a transfer contract. These clauses can also be found in subcontracting agreements. Even where the entire contract is oriented towards co-operation, the intensity of co-operation will vary. In every case, however, its scope and duration will be made explicit. The contractual provisions may vary in complexity from a simple protocol of intention to an outline agreement covering all the details.

There are various general features common to co-operative contracts. In the first place, co-operation is always limited in scope. However wide-ranging it may be, in practice contractual co-operation always covers a precisely defined field. The ultimate limit, almost never attained, will be the business aims of two partner companies. In practice, co-operation agreements usually cover only a variable period of time within which a process of structural convergence (taking of financial interest, subsidiarization, etc.) occurs. Secondly, the co-operation contract is always limited in time: the parties give it a period of validity, which may be renewed, extended or reduced if the parties so wish. In the third place, in a contract, the parties always retain their own identities. This fundamentally distinguishes a co-operation contract from the formation of a company. Of course, the agreement between the parties may result in joint companies being formed; but these are distinct from the contract which provides for their formation. Even where it results in the formation of joint corporate structures, the co-operation agreement will retain a purely contractual aspect.

Finally, the contracts may be simple or complex (see chapter 4). In the simple format, co-operation is effected within the terms of one or more contracts which may form a whole series of interdependent agreements. Co-operative and decision-making structures, liaison committees, supervisory or co-ordinating committees are usually created under such contracts in order to facilitate the proper transaction of the agreement. Some of these structures have no legal personality and their terms of operation are defined within the framework of the agreement.

In the more complex format, co-operation is often more intense. For this reason joint structures are created, the functioning of which is governed by discrete legal instruments. These co-operative structures are not simple co-ordination or liaison committees as in the case of a simple co-operation. Quite the contrary: in the case of a complex co-operation, the partners to the co-operation form these structures under discrete legal documents. Sometimes these structures are without legal personality (as in the simple agreement); in other cases they have a legal personality (as in a *groupement d'intérêt économique*). Usually they have a reduced legal scope, like agreements between shareholders or partners. In this event, two categories of legal instrument will exist: the contract itself and a contract governing the operation of the structure.

The classification of the agreements

The types of agreement may be divided into two categories according to whethet or not the agreements lead to the creation of links with third parties.

The first category, where the agreement is aimed exclusively at the parties themselves, includes a very large number of contracts with varying aims. They comprise agreements listed by the European Commission, mainly agreements for R&D, rationalization, exchange of information, etc.

The second category covers agreements made with a view to cementing relations with third parties. Where the third parties are not identified, the co-operation agreement is designed to sell all or part of the production or to purchase materials. In effect it concerns more the advantage to be gained by grouping purchasing or by the organizing of sales (consortium agreement). In addition to these advantages there is often the possibility of regulating competition between the parties and thus providing against the effect of unlimited, uncontrolled competition. These agreements may have the effect of restricting competition and result in a partitioning of the markets. This is why they are the subject of close attention from the European Court of Justice, especially as regards cartels and syndicates. What essentially typifies these agreements is that they are generally entered into for quite long, and often indeterminate, periods of time.

In other cases, the participating firms may decide to co-operate in order to supply their services to a specified third party. This category includes those agreements under which the parties agree to co-operate with a view to cornering a particular market in a particular country. They are generally of short (in any case, specified) duration. This type of agreement relates particularly to performance agreements, especially in the case of public works or construction contracts.

The Group Basis

Quite often, firms want to have the backing of an explicit legal structure within the provisions of a co-operation process. In this event the formation of a grouping may meet their requirements.

This section will consider three aspects: the factors which might lead to the option for a form of joint venture (GIE); the classification of the various types of groups; and finally, the innovations relating to the European GIE.

The decision to form a group

The decision to form an international group of companies often arises out of the execution of an international contract. Three technical possibilities then exist: the formation of a joint company; subcontracting; and co-contracting.

The formation of a joint company consists of the setting-up of an entity by the firms concerned in which each holds a share of the capital in proportion with its involvement in the performance of the contract. This joint company, which contracts with the customer, may be formed solely for a specific matter or for the discharge of several different objectives.

In a grouping which comprises one or more subcontractors, the main contractor and the subcontractor participate in the execution of the same project, but within the legal framework of at least two contracts, totally independent of each other: the contract with the customer and the agreement between the contractor and the subcontractor.

For the customer, the advantages are of a practical nature: if just one firm signs the contract there is only one entity with which he or she has to deal. For the main contractor, the advantages of subcontracting are of a commercial nature: in practice it does not have to share with any other firm the right to include the execution of the project in its business references. Furthermore, it will usually have exclusive control over the conditions for the performance of the contract. Finally, the subcontractor will be able to mention its participation in its own references; moreover it will be legally responsible only for the proper execution of that part of the job with which it has been entrusted.

The disadvantage is, for the customer, the fact that just one firm will be responsible and this could be a source of considerable risk. For the main contractor, the disadvantages of subcontracting may be considerable because it is tied to two distinct entities (the customer and the subcontractor) within the terms of two independent contracts.

In co-contracting, the firms participating in the operation are jointly responsible for the contract. There are major advantages for the customer, to whom all the contractors are jointly responsible for the proper performance of the contract as a whole. As for the co-contracting firms, they will have the advantage of being able to quote the project in their business references. Among the disadvantages is the fact that, for various reasons, the customer may refuse to accept one or other of the co-contracting firms. The firms may find it a disadvantage to have to assume joint responsibility for the whole project.

As a general rule, firms which opt for co-contracting enter into a joint venture agreement prior to signing the contract in order to determine the details of their collaboration.

Classification of the groupings

The grouping agreement can take several forms, according to the nature of the ties with the customer or the relations between the firms. Statutory groups offer greater guarantees for international operations and therefore are the subject of longer development.

In the first place, groups may be classified on the basis of the existence of contractual relations with the client. Two types of groups may be distinguished here, depending on whether all the firms grouped together have direct legal ties with the customer or whether the existence of such links is limited to one or some of them. In the first case one talks of a horizontal group, in the second case of a vertical group.

Within a horizontal group, each firm forms direct legal links with the customer. Such a group is horizontal because all the co-contracting companies are located on the same horizontal line *vis-à-vis* the client and are all parties to the contract.

On the other hand, in a vertical group, only one or some of the firms have legal ties with the customer. Thus, for example, just one of the grouped firms, usually the main contractor, signs the contract. So far as the customer is concerned, the other firms are merely subcontractors to the main contractor. In point of fact, there is a degree of co-operation since the parties alter the legal nature of their subcontracts by introducing into them provisions which constitute co-operative agreements. They then organize their internal relations as if they were co-signatories to the contract. The object of a vertical group agreement may be described as an integrated subcontracting agreement.

Secondly, groups may be typfied by the legal connections (statutory nature of the group) between the firms. This concerns groups regulated by special legal statutes, where the parties are required to be bound by the rules defined in the statutes governing the group of which they are part.

Company groupings are contracts between firms for the joint preparation and submission of a tender to a customer, or for the joint execution of a contract. It is assumed, moreover, that this contract is of an international nature, that is to say, that it generates the movement and transfer of services beyond national frontiers. (This is not to say that a group formed to execute an international contract must always itself be international. Several firms of the same nationality may in fact get together to execute such a contract.) In the case of international operations, the firms often form a company (see below). But they frequently prefer an entity with a legal personality but which is other than that of a company, such as a *groupement d'intérêt économique* (economic interest group). A GIE constitutes a very flexible framework for the activities of the constituent firms. The objects of a GIE are different from those of a company. It must remain closely associated with the activities of its members and must contribute towards the development and facilitation of these, whereas the aims of a company may be totally distinct. Recently the know-how and desire to provide medium-sized European firms with a legal framework which will facilitate transfrontier co-operation resulted (after twelve years of deliberation and fine-tuning) in a European Economic Interest Grouping (EEIG).

The European Economic Interest Grouping

This grouping is accessible to all firms, regardless of size. It is open to both legal entities and natural persons. The function of such a body is to expand through the activities of its members.

As an instrument for inter-firm co-operation, designed to encourage the development of the participants' economic activities within the European single market, an EEIG cannot be formed without the prior signing of a contract. This must be in writing since it has to be deposited. Certain mandatory headings must be included in the contract: members, title, registered office, objects, duration. In addition to these mandatory headings, reference to the internal administration and to contractual relationships must be included (see figure 6.1).

The aim of the grouping is to develop the economic activities of its members and to increase the profits from these activities. Consequently, the regulations confer on the EEIG the appropriate legal capacity. This legal capacity exists from the time of registration of the grouping. From then on, the grouping may take on staff (not more than 500 persons), draw up contracts of employment, take out leases, etc. On the question of funds, an EEIG is able to make investments, benefit from bank assistance, contract loans, receive subscriptions, etc.

One of the great advantages of the EEIG is the wide freedom its members have to organize their contractual relationships. An extreme flexibility is given to members as regards the grouping's finances. The EEIG is not obliged to have any capital; nevertheless, the creation of a working fund is necessary and implies contributions from the members. These inputs may be made through current account contributions. The counterpart to the contractual freedom which typifies an EEIG and the non-requirement for capital is the joint and indefinite responsibility of the members for the debts of the grouping. Despite this formidable disadvantage, it may be said that European economic players now have a flexible, pragmatic instrument at their disposal.

The Company Basis

The partners may choose to use adapted company statutes as the basis for their co-operation. Two possibilities occur:

- a company having a legal personality (jointly owned company);
- a company without legal personality (a *société en participation* under French law or a contractual partnership under English law).

Mandatory references

- Title of the grouping
  This must be preceded or followed by 'European Economic Interest Grouping' OR 'EEIG'
- Grouping's registered office
- Object
- Each member's
  - name
  - title or denomination
  - legal status
  - residence or registered office
  - registration number (where appropriate)
  - place of registration (where appropriate)
- Duration of the grouping (if specified)

Other references

- Administration of the grouping:
  - management(s)
  - relations with members powers
  - fact of joint management
  - nomination/dismissal
- Members' contributions
- No. of votes per member
- Distribution of profits
- Evaluation of assets
- Controls:
  - accounts (external auditor)
  - management
- Financial year:
  annual accounts
- Members:
  - co-option of new members
  - retirement of any member
- Group decisions:
  - ordinary
  - extraordinary
  - non-competition clause
  - quorum, majority rules
- Insolvency of a member
- Dissolution/liquidation

Figure 6.1 The EEIG: grouping contract
Source: 'Les nouveaux instruments juridiques', *Referentiel*, Dunod, Paris, 1989, p. 10.3.1.2.

Joint companies and partnerships

This is not a survey of all the types of common entity. Most European legislation recognizes forms of company having a legal personality, usually quite similar.

The common entity may be a trading company. As the intention is to carry out commercial operations, the formation of a non-profit-making company or association would be inappropriate. The decision to give a co-operation the status of a company offers certain advantages and disadvantages. So far as the advantages are concerned, a trading company can provide the objectives for the co-operation and ensure distribution of the profits without the drawbacks of a partnership. In addition, the company's liability will be limited to its capital. Among the disadvantages, the company must be provided with capital, otherwise it will be compelled to subcontract the services provided under the contract to its members. In the trading company type of common entity, (especially a joint subsidiary) three ways of organizing the co-operation may be distinguished: the joint company may agree to and carry out the operation alone; it may enter into the contract and entrust its execution to its members; or the firms may sign the contract and subcontract all or part of the services to the joint company.

Alternatively, the common entity may be a company without legal personality – under French law, a *société en participation*. It arises out of a contract under which two or more persons agree to pool their assets or their efforts with a view to sharing in the profits or to benefiting from the resulting economies. Such a company is one which rests on the *intuitus personae*. It stems from a particular context. Thus, if several firms decide to execute jointly a contract to which they are signatories, usually jointly, they must normally agree to form a horizontal or vertical grouping. But quite often the firms must share the profits from the contract and find it impossible to determine precisely just who among them will be responsible for the execution of the various individual services to be provided under the contract. To overcome these problems three solutions may be identified, aimed at regulating their relations with each other, including the distribution of the profits from the contract: the firms may simply form a *société en participation*; they may enter into a subcontracting agreement while forming a *société en participation*; or they may enter into an agreement for a horizontal grouping and create a *société en participation*.

The *Bürgerlichsches Gesetzbuch* under German law offers a suitable structure for firms that wish to co-operate in order to carry out a specific operation. The BGB *Gesellschaft* does not have a legal personality. It is not entered in the commercial register and third parties cannot sue the members.

Partnerships under English law and joint ventures under American law

A partnership is essentially a body formed with the intention of creating profits and sharing them. It may also implicitly result from behaviour manifested by the joint management of a business, the profits from which are shared. A partnership cannot have more than ten members and allows a great deal of freedom to the partners. A partnership agreement demands what English lawyers call *luberrima fides* (utmost good faith). The rights and obligations are freely set out in the agreement. In principle, each partner is entitled to a share in the profits corresponding to the extent of his or her financial interest in the partnership.

The joint venture under American law is similar. Nevertheless, American law defines a joint venture in a careful manner: ‘A joint venture shall have the following indications: a special combination of two or more persons who seek to profit from a specific commercial venture without forming a partnership or a form of company endowed with a legal personality.’ The joint venture has both similarities to a partnership and differences from it. It is similar in that there is no legal personality, there are at least two participants who have a legal capacity, the means or resources are pooled and one or more business transactions are completed. In a joint venture, however, unlike a partnership, the intention to apportion the shares is not presumed. On the other hand, a joint venture must have a limited objective. It will be seen from this that a joint venture is a specific type of grouping developed for American purposes. The term is often used loosely in international practice to refer to any grouping endowed with a legal personality.

The European company in perspective

More than thirty years after the Treaty of Rome, discussions are still taking place on the creation of a single legal framework for European companies. At issue is the creation of transnational bodies capable of rivalling those of competitors throughout the world. The introduction of the EEIG before that of the European company illustrates the difficulties in completing this project. Various proposals have been made with a view to creating a suitable legal instrument, in particular the fifth directive harmonizing the statutes of public limited companies and the tenth directive on possible mergers of companies from different member states. The difficulties to be overcome include:

- differences between national laws (formation, liquidation, dissolution of the company, etc.);
- differences in company laws (co-management or otherwise, etc.);
- diverse considerations in the matter of taxation.

In 1988 the Commission adopted a memorandum on the statutes for a European company.[1] In 1989, the Commission presented to the Council of Ministers two proposals: a proposed regulation covering the statutes of a European company as regards the position of staff. It is therefore possible to hope that the statutes of a European company will soon be adopted.

By way of conclusion, it may be helpful to recall the three main factors regarding the legal bases for international inter-firm co-operation.

- The first aspect concerns the legal framework within which the co-operation will take place. Depending on the duration of the co-operation and the type of relationship sought, the basis may be purely contractual; or it may be achieved through an explicit legal structure (grouping, company).
- The second aspect concerns the type of relations between the parties. A balance must be found between flexibility and constraints, between guarantees and efficiency.
- The third aspect arises out of the need to ensure the security of the partners.

The Protection of Know-how

It has been emphasized that co-operating firms must select a suitable legal basis to ensure the optimum effectiveness of the agreement and the best mutual guarantees for the parties. As regards know-how agreements, good formalization is essential in order to communicate, exchange and co-operate in a useful manner. The official European bodies are providing management tools for this purpose. The European standard contract is aimed at encouraging and co-ordinating research and development activities (joint research). The

Community licence and the Community trade mark are aimed at breaking down the compartmentalization of national markets and objectively disseminating know-how.

The European Standard Contract

A survey carried out by OECD in 1982 on innovation in SMEs concluded in favour of the primacy of the market as the driving force in innovation: 50 per cent of the cases of innovation arose from a dialogue with the customer, 25 per cent from the work of engineers and technicians and 25 per cent from a company's internal research.[2] Although the distinction between radical innovation (profoundly modifying the product) and minor innovation (product improvement) is not clear, there is general agreement on the determining role of research and development measures in the promotion of both radical and minor innovations. A recent study carried out in France has shown that the interest in R&D shown by heads of firms is growing: 51 per cent of firms' heads stated that they take account of the evolution of the European market when redefining their products, and 41 per cent review their R&D policy; but, at the same time, barely 10 per cent knew about Community research programmes.[3] The European standard is a significant development in the promotion of R&D co-operation.

The workings of the standard contract

The European Commission is trying to encourage links between firms or between firms and research centres in the field of research and development. To this end a standard contract was finalized in October 1988 (see table 6.1).[4] The Commission finances part of this research out of Community funds. However, the contract offers not only advantages; there are also contraindications of which the contracting parties need to be aware.

It is anticipated that the results obtained by the body whose research is financed under the contract will be used in the interests of the Community, by the body which carried out the research or by other Community bodies. To this end, the standard contract imposes certain undertakings on the owners of research findings.

All parties to the contract have the opportunity of using the research findings in their entirety. They will be able to make use of

Table 6.1 The European standard contract for joint research and development: the terms

The position covered by the standard contract	Whom does it concern?
Under a single contract	Parties to the contract (within the Community or otherwise)
Under a single Community programme	Parties (within the Community or otherwise) to a contract issued in respect of the same programme (e.g. from one ESPRIT project to another ESPRIT project)
With another Community programme	Community firms parties to a contract relating to another Community programme (e.g. from an ESPRIT project to a BRITE-EURAM project)
For any Community firm	Any firm which is set up in the Community
For any legal entity in the Community	Any legal entity in the Community (including universities and research centres)
Community research body (e.g. Joint Research Centre)	Community research body (e.g. Joint Research Centre)

Source: ANRT, Paris, *Technical Progress Letter*, no. 57/8, August 1990, p. 2.

the technical knowledge owned by each of the partners. The standard contract thus makes a radical distinction between the actual results of the research, i.e. the technical assets which stem from work financed by the Commission under the terms of the contract ('foreground patents and information') and the technology which each of the parties already possesses, the implementation of which is useful and necessary for the execution of the research and for its utilization ('background patents and information'): see table 6.2.

In fact, foreground items are the property of whoever discovers them. They come within his professional know-how and, where patents are concerned, these are taken out in his name and at his own expense. The owner of background information who cannot, because of prior undertakings, communicate it to third parties, may exclude such background from the terms of the contract, provided he has declared this before signing and if his partners are in agreement.

The standard contract is a flexible framework leading to the

Table 6.2 The European standard contract: acquisition of new types of know-how and respect for know-how held prior to the contract

Assignment of the results of research and development		Assignment of the results for their exploitation	
Foreground	Background	Foreground	Background
Free right of user and licence limited and the carrying out of R&D within the terms of their contract (Art. 16.1.1)	Same right of user and licence as for 'foreground' but with non-discriminatory transfer conditions (Art. 16.2.1)	Free, non-exclusive exploitation right and licence without sub-licensing rights. Not free if the holder of the right is not in a position to market it himself (Art. 17.2)	Non-exclusive right of user and licence under preferential trading conditions if this is not necessary for the exploitation of the 'foreground'[a] (Art. 17.5)
As above but subject to invoicing for cost of the transfer (Art. 16.1.2)	As above but under preferential conditions unless the owner declares 'major business interests' to justify refusal (Art. 16.2.2a) Mandatory transfer in the case of Community firms, optional for others	As above but: • under preferential conditions • solely in order to use the results of their contract unless the owner is using them or is about to do so • unless he declares 'major business interests' (Art. 17.3)	No rights

As above (Art. 16.1.2)	As above but the owner no longer has to plead 'major business interests' to refuse. Business interests will suffice (Art. 16.2.2b)	As above	No rights
As above but: • under preferential conditions • use limited to the beneficiary's • own research in the same field • unless the owner is using • unless he declares 'major business interests' in order to refuse	No rights	As above but: • under commercial conditions • to use the results of the beneficiary's own research in the same field • unless the owner is using • unless he declares 'major business interests' in order to refuse (Art. 17.4a)[b]	No rights
No rights	No rights	If the owner has not made use within the time specified in Art. 17.1.1	No rights
Non-exclusive, irrevocable free licence without sub-licensing rights (Art. 19.1)	No rights	No rights	

[a] unless the owner is using or declares his 'major business interests' to justify refusal.
[b] Refusal possible, if the owner is using or is on the point of using; or if the owner pleads 'major business interests' (Art. 17.4.b).
Source: ANRT, Paris, *Technical Progress Letter*, no. 57/8, August 1990, p. 3.

formalization of expertise and aimed at creating profitable relations between partners.

European partnerships

Transnational research partnerships in the Europe of the Twelve at the beginning of 1990, from the French viewpoint, are shown diagrammatically in figure 6.2. Although the partnerships have been identified, the number of partners per member state has not been quantified. In addition, the disproportionate financial values allocated

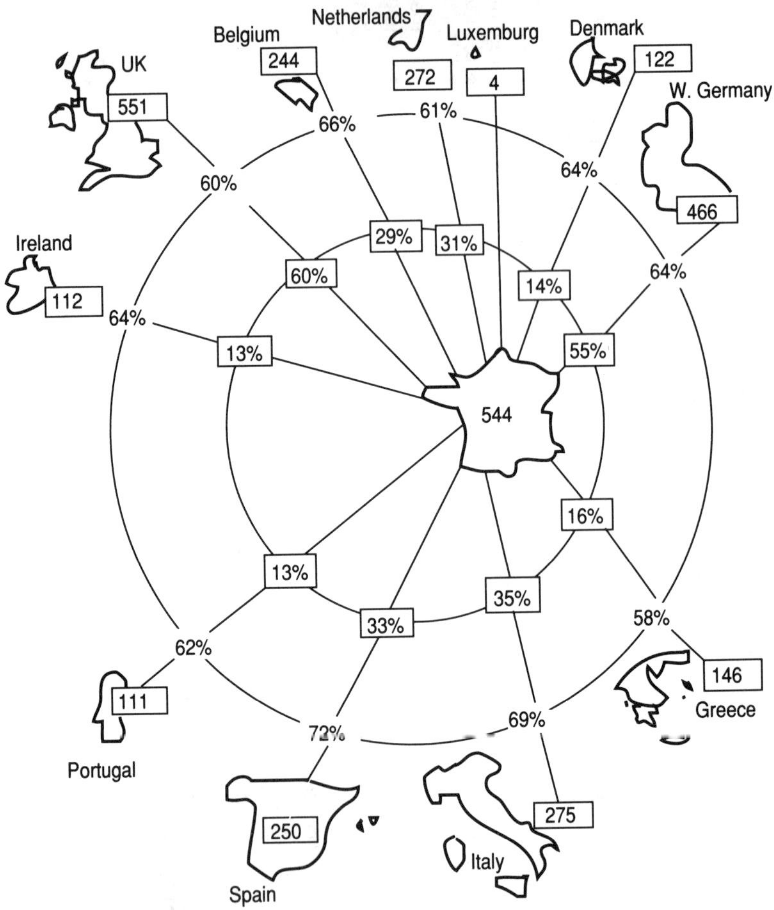

Figure 6.2 European research and development partnerships
Source: ANRT, Paris, *Technical Progress Letter*, no. 57/8, August 1990, p. 3.

to the various projects must be treated with caution because of the mixture of small and large programmes.

The co-ordinated applied programmes (SPRINT for the European service infrastructure, BRIDGE for biotechnology, EUVET for transport, CECA for industrial safety, BRITE-EURAM for industrial technology and advanced materials, etc.), will generate a plethora of international co-operations. Table 6.3 records the level of responses to the last call for tenders two months before the closing date in October 1990.

Table 6.3 BRITE-EURAM Programme

Country[a]	Field[b] 1	2	3	4	Total
Belgium	8	7	8	15	38
Germany	57	31	15	55	158
Denmark	19	5	5	26	55
Spain	36	35	22	19	112
France	55	44	26	47	171
Greece	13	29	17	18	77
Italy	33	22	12	18	85
Ireland	25	23	12	30	90
Netherlands	45	24	11	31	111
Portugal	7	6	7	2	22
United Kingdom	108	105	40	86	339
EC (12 countries)	406	331	174	347	1,258
EFTA (6 countries)[a]	44	17	20	22	103
Total per field	450	348	194	369	1,361

[a] Member countries: Austria, Finland, Iceland, Norway, Sweden, Switzerland
[b] 1: advanced materials technology;
2: design methods and quality assurance for products and processes;
3: application of manufacturing technology;
4: manufacturing process technology.

Two Valuable Tools Promoting Exchanges of Know-how

At present, each member state in the Community grants protected status to the holders of industrial and intellectual property. The patent-holder is granted a national monopoly over his or her right of ownership and use of the patent. A similar monopoly is also granted to the holder of a trade mark, not just to prevent third parties from illicitly making use of the distinctive mark to the holder's detriment, but also so that the consumer can always be sure that the mark will relate to goods or services from the same source and of the same quality. As the rights to industrial and intellectual property are essentially aimed at giving their possessor a monopoly on a product or distinctive trade mark, the contracts covering such rights could be looked upon as a restrictive practice or the abuse of a dominant position. To this end, research has been carried out to draw a better balance between national and Community rights.

The Community trade mark

Included among the legal instruments to be placed at the disposal of firms, the formulation of a Community trade mark will enable firms to identify their products or services in a uniform manner over the whole of the Community's territory. The Treaty of Rome did not foresee such a provision. At present there is no question of substituting a Community trade mark law for national trade mark laws; draft regulations include the following points.

The Community trade mark will have the same effect throughout the whole of the Community's territory. All the factors at stake, in particular the wording, the design, the letters, the figures, the colour combinations, the shape of the product and the packaging which enable a product or service to be identified, may form a Community trade mark. In order to acquire a Community trade mark it will be sufficient to be from one of the Community's member states or a country which is a signatory to the Paris Convention. Therefore a supplier from a country which is a signatory to the Paris Convention may claim protection for its technology under the same terms as a national supplier. Rights to the Community mark will be obtained exclusively by registration with the European Trade Marks Office. The trade mark registration will be effective for ten years but will be renewable. The use of a Community trade mark may be assigned under licence in respect of all or some of the registered products or services. The holder of a Community trade mark must take adequate steps to ensure that the licensee produces goods or provides services which are of the required quality.

The European patent

The European Patent Office is located in Munich. The Munich convention created a true European patent law, applicable to the twelve member states. European patents are issued for new inventions which involve an inventive activity and are suitable for industrial application. They concern inventions which incorporate three characteristics: novelty, the inventive aspect and the industrial application. An invention is regarded as inventive if it does not fall within the state of the art. Inventions which cannot be patented include intellectual works and methods of treatment and diagnosis.

Applications for European patents have to be lodged with the European Office or with the national authorities. By virtue of the Luxembourg Convention, the Community patent confers on its holder the right to prevent any third party from directly or indirectly making use of the invention without his or her consent. The rights conferred by the Community patent do not extend to exploitative acts relating to products manufactured under this patent, once an initial marketing has taken place in one of the member states on the initiative of the patent-holder, or with his consent (*équipement des droits* rule). The patent therefore cannot be used to compartmentalize the common market.

Benefiting from Institution Support

It has been shown that co-operative strategies make it possible to combine two important concepts: that of autonomy and that of solidarity between partners. Up until now the accent has been placed on partnerships between industrial parties which provide, with varying degrees of intensity, more or less all the links in the value chain: R&D, purchasing/logistics, production, marketing, distribution, after sales service, etc. The more the resulting network is encouraged and supported by the socio-economic environment of the firms, whether this concerns the public authorities, social pressures or financial institutions, the more fertile and secure it will be. This assertion can be verified by two different groups of examples drawn from Germany and Italy.

Partnerships in Germany: The Central Role of the Bank

The idea of co-operation was mooted in Germany in the middle of the nineteenth century by the economist Frederic List who, in 1841, was studying not what we now refer to as a 'network economy' but a 'national system of economic policy', highlighting the interactive relations which could exist between the various parts of the system.

To put it another way, in order for an industry with ambitions of world conquest to develop, it must rest on firm foundations: state support, social consensus, efficient intellectual and technical ability (arising out of scientific research and a pragmatic training policy), underpinning foundations, informational and advisory networks and, last but not least, stable financial resources.[5]

The German banks have a special role to play in this respect, going well beyond the traditional functions of savings management and the granting of loans: they mould the business world by 'universal'-type interventions which cover all aspects of a company's life. They are at the core of a partnership network, as demonstrated by a study of the biggest universal German bank, the Deutsche Bank.[6] Its influence on the negotiation of alliances (some of a co-operative nature, others in the form of financial interest) takes three forms:

- the bank is at the centre of a network of industrial complementarity;
- the bank guides the policies of the economic parties;
- the bank circulates management information and advice, providing the means for the declared policy.

The bank at the centre of a network of industrial complementarity

The Deutsche Bank was formed in Berlin in 1870, four years after the Treaty of Prague which resulted in the creation of the north German confederation under the supervision of Prussia and one year before the rallying, in 1871, of the south German states, leading to the foundation of the German empire, dominated until 1890 by Bismarck. The Deutsche Bank was to be one of the instruments in attaining the declared objectives of the authorities: the hegemony of Prussia and the German empire.

The name of the first director of the Deutsche Bank is well known: Georg von Siemens, cousin of Werner von Siemens, founder of the electrical engineering firm, for whom Georg worked in London and in Tehran until the age of thirty-one. Georg von Siemens was to remain at the head of the Deutsche Bank until 1900, by which time the bank had become the empire's principal financial institution. From the time of its inception, the Deutsche Bank was connected with industry and supported by the political authorities, who made no secret of their ambitions: to close the industrial gap between Germany and Great Britain and France. Unlike these two countries,

Germany was not able to rely on financial resources inherited from the mercantile era. In an essentially rural country, the industry-creators were forced to rely on loans and support from the banks. From the end of the nineteenth century, therefore, there evolved an important overlap between bank and industry or, in other words, a co-operative strategy which was to prove profitable.

By taking a financial interest in the various regions of Germany, the Deutsche Bank very soon had a say in the affairs of the leading companies in the more important branches of activity: textiles, metallurgy, engineering, the chemical and electrical industries. In the last field, Germany had two trump cards to play: one was Werner von Siemens, whose historic success is well known, and the other was Erwil Rathenau, a machinery manufacturer who, in 1883, introduced the inventions of the American Thomas A. Edison to Germany by creating in Berlin the Deutsche Edison Gesellschaft für angewante Elektricität, renamed in 1887 the Allgemeine Elektrizitäts-Gesellschaft or AEG, strongly supported by the Deutsche Bank which assumed responsibility for placing an impressive number of the issued shares.

Georg von Siemens cultivated ties of friendship or business relations with Emil Rathenau, AEG and the family group Siemens & Halske. The Deutsche Bank rapidly enabled these two companies to acquire global status, all the time promoting a co-ordinated spread of activities between the two.

It should be noted, however, that these co-operative practices were to deteriorate later on.

Prompted by his industrialist cousin, Werner von Siemens, Georg von Siemens also originated a massive injection of capital by the Deutsche Bank into the Mannesmann company, the two founding brothers of which had invented revolutionary techniques in the field of steel-rolling. The corresponding patents had not been put to the test but the Deutsche Bank, supported by the Siemens family, showed unswerving faith in them over a number of years, without hope of any immediate return on its investment. The subsequent dazzling development of the Mannesmann company proved the bank right. Without the Deutsche Bank there could have been no development of the Mannesmann firm. Through its confidence in the firm, demonstrated from the outset, the bank acquired a decision-making influence which it has never lost.

Over the years, by applying this philosophy of partnership and keeping a watchful eye on promising activities, advantageous links were forged between the Deutsche Bank and the BASF chemicals firm, with oil companies (Deutsche Petroleum AG) and with the burgeoning audio-visual industries (Universum-Film-AG, in 1917). The Deutsche Bank was also present at the union of the Gottlieb Daimler and Karl Benz firms, a corporate marriage which was to become the star of the German economy. The Deutsche Bank and Daimler-Benz continue to this day to maintain astonishingly privileged relations. So much so that, in January 1986, on the occasion of the festivities marking the hundredth anniversary of Daimler-Benz, it was Alfred Herrhausen, head of the Deutsche Bank (and member of the Daimler-Benz supervisory council), and not Werner Breitschwerdt, head of Daimler-Benz, who gave the welcoming address to a host of eminent personalities, including the President of the Republic, Richard von Weizsäcker and the whole Almanac de Gotha of the world's automobile industry: General Motors, Ford, Chrysler, Toyota, Nissan, Mitsubishi, Honda, VW, Fiat, Renault, Peugeot, BMW, etc. Later, the Deutsche Bank was to play a pre-eminent role in the merger between Daimler-Benz and Messerschmidt-Bälkow-Blohm (MBB).

The grasp which the Deutsche Bank has on the German economy does not stop there. It was involved in the formation of Lufthansa in 1926, is a member of the powerful Reemtsma group (cigarettes and agricultural foodstuffs sector), is active in the sugar industry, the construction and civil engineering sector (Philipp Holzmann), the energy sector (Rheinisch-Westfälisches Elektrizitätswerk, RWE), in capital goods, semi-products and international trade (Klöcker-Humbolt-Dentz, Metallgesellschaft, Continental), in retailing with Karstadt – and so on. Furthermore, representatives of the Deutsche Bank sit on the board of directors of many international companies, such as Saint-Gobain, Solvay, Pilkington, Fiat, Avon, Akzo, Unilever, Merck, Coca-Cola and Westinghouse. The bank is fully aware of its great power and knows how to use it with an explicit sense of its responsibility for the wider interest.

The bank directs the policies of the economic actors

The ability to direct the policies of those involved in commerce is obviously not an absolute one, but it is more than merely significant. Through the vastness of the financial resources which it has at its disposal and also through its managerial competence and the interpersonal links which it has formed in various spheres on an international level, the Deutsche Bank is extremely influential. This influence is exerted through the financial institution *per se* and also through the personnel who run it, often exceptionally able people, among whom must be included Emil G. von Stauss, Herrmann Joseph Abs and Alfred Herrhausen as well as Georg von Siemens.

There is no doubt that the Deutsche Bank helps forge Germany's industrial policies. Through the sheer magnitude of the loans it has granted or the financial interests which it holds, and also through its active presence on the boards of some 150 major companies, this bank guides industrial reorganization and investment and development policies. The German magazine *Der Spiegel* has described the Deutsche Bank as a 'parallel government'. No major business deal escapes its attention, be it Volkswagen's alliance policies, the dismantling of the Flick empire in 1986, the restoration of the Krupp and Nixdorf groups to profitability, the reorganization of the aeronautics industry, the largest export contracts, the penetration of the Japanese market or the opening up of Eastern Europe.

The guidance given by the bank carries all the more weight in that all major decisions taken by its board must be unanimous. Although it is not always easy to observe this requirement, it has the effect of ensuring that, without ambiguity or dissent, all the directors of the bank are party to the agreed policy which thus gives it a solid, indestructible appearance.

Influence is also exerted through good relations with other institutions, especially the central bank and the political authorities. Thus Karl Klasen, member of the Deutsche Bank *Vorstand*, affiliated to the Social Democratic Party (SPD) since 1931, was linked by ties of friendship to the Minister of Finance, Karl Schiller and to the Chancellor, Helmut Schmidt, which obviously did not detract from the bank's power. The same Karl Klasen was subsequently taken on by the central bank – the Deutsche Bundesbank – and this too helped the bank, plugged as it was into top-level strategic decisions and information.

Hermann J. Abs, member of the Deutsche Bank's board from 1938 to 1967, was a friend of Chancellor Konrad Adenauer to whom he acted as adviser and interpreter, notably during the delicate negotiations with the American High Commission on the dismantling of the IG Farben group in 1949. The restructuring of the German chemicals industry following the breakdown of IG Farben into

BASF, Hoechst and Bayer was largely conducted by Abs. Abs was also the instigator of the creation of the Kreditanstalt für Wiederaufbau (KfW), negotiated in 1947–8 with one of President Truman's advisers. In the early years, Abs was the brains behind the KfW, a financial institution formed to administer the American money provided under the Marshall Plan for the reconstruction of Germany. He played a key role in directing investment into equipment and the modernization of the Federal Republic of Germany. The 'German economic miracle' did not just happen; it was carefully constructed.

The future is also being constructed by and through research. It was not a mere coincidence that Alfred Herrhausen, President of the Deutsche Bank and valued adviser to Chancellor Helmut Kohl, was, until his assassination in November 1989, a member of the Senate (the decision-making body) of the powerful Max-Planck-Gesellschaft, member of the board of the Stiftverband für die deutsche Wissenschaft, member of the List Gesellschaft and a member of the Senate of various universities – all institutions which play a determining part in pure and applied research.

The bank provides industry with the resources for its declared development policies

It is clear that the Deutsche Bank is not content simply to organize the environment or the framework within which firms operate; it intervenes directly, and in various ways, in their methods of operation.

At the highest level the bank acts as a strategic adviser. It has made an extensive contribution to the perfecting and circulating of analysis grids for industrial activities and financial structures, inspired by American management methods. Its advice is made available in a number of ways; through the bank's qualified staff, through its subsidiary Roland Berger (a Munich company specializing in advising firms), by making human resources available on a temporary basis, by guiding the decisions taken by the management of firms in which the bank has a financial participation, or more simply through friendly advice given to small and medium-sized firms for which the Deutsche Bank is the 'house bank'. The bank is keen to sustain a relationship with firms as long as they continue in business, from their formation to the point where they are taken over, and to help them with partnership alliances, capital restructuring or changes in their portfolio of activities. The bank's declared vocation is not only to advise on development but also to provide assistance during periods of crisis.

Of course, the support given by the Deutsche Bank to a firm is not disinterested. It inspires confidence in the firm's associates: suppliers, customers, co-contractors, subcontractors, insurance companies, trade unions, etc. The presence of the Deutsche Bank is a sign of management stability and competence. The bank also plays a protective role in any stock exchange battles. Because of the power it exercises, hostile takeover bids are difficult to achieve. The shareholders are controlled, the equity capital stable. Alliances are judiciously organized, often under the supervision of the bank. The bank knows how to set up interdependent shareholder networks, to weave all kinds of relations between friendly associates. The experience of one helps the others; useful information is disseminated to all concerned.

In short the bank, with a great deal of pragmatism, attends to the needs of industrial companies. It dedicates itself to meeting their requirements, both financial and intangible; it helps them define their strategy and, at the same time, to find the resources needed to implement this. It is in fact an exemplary partner, whose influence in this role should not be undervalued.

Partnerships in Italy: Co-operation between Firms and Local Authorities

Italy has a distinctive system of partnerships, largely influenced by the long and rich history of this country which has never ceased to demonstrate its commitment to the strong regional and local identities.

If Italian industry has undergone vigorous expansion since 1980, founded on innovation, readiness to adapt (flexibility) and professional competence of a high level, it owes this, in part, to a particular method of organizing production, blending traditional craftsmanship with high technology. This model of partnership-style organization is characterized by three main elements:

- it has been stimulated by the development of technology;
- it has flourished on the fertile soil of local economies;

- it has been nurtured by the public authorities and the regional professional bodies.

Decentralized and interlinked production organization

Since the beginning of the 1970s the Italian economy has been involved in a long process of structural reform, resulting in a revitalization of industry. Tax exemptions have encouraged the modernization of firms which have considerably increased their investment in productivity (through the purchase of machines and precision tools, electrical and electronic equipment; through recourse to automated assembly, etc.), disposed of obsolete plant and carried out a massive substitution of capital for labour. One result of the introduction of these new technologies has been an increase in flexibility of the means of production.

Technological developments have facilitated the extension of the process of decentralizing production, stimulated by the firms' struggle against exploitational inflexibility and their search for an adaptable workforce; in short, the quest for low costs. Innumerable small private companies are therefore emerging and developing under the protective wings of the larger companies. These small firms are usually based on a craft in which they are well skilled, highly specialized technically and able to respond quickly to the signals they get from the markets. Data from the 1982 industrial census confirm that the system of centralized production, based on vertically integrated installations, is being progressively replaced by a networking system in which production is carried out by smaller firms, each specializing in a particular stage in the production process, but able to adapt to the manufacture of various products.

This transformation has also been encouraged on the one hand by the standardization of semi-finished products which contributes towards better co-ordination between the various stages of production and on the other hand by technological innovation (the introduction of numerically controlled machines, expansion of computer links, development of micro-electronics in general), which enables production plans to be quickly redirected and allows for a great variety of manufactured products.

The evolution witnessed in recent years is not yet complete, as confirmed by an official from the Emilia Romagna region, Claudio

Tolomelli in the course of an international seminar organized by the Ministry for Industry in Paris in 1989.

> Just as in the 1980s, technological aspects proved central to ensure the firms' competitive capability, the 1990s seem to point to the centrality of the internal and external organizational arrangements of the firms, with special emphasis on the relation among themselves and between those forms and entities that, at the national and international level, have a primary role in the innovation process.[7]

Small and medium-sized firms may well be in the process of losing their autonomy as far as the workforce is concerned, but in return they have become essential components in a vast integrated productive system on an international scale. 'Along with an integrated approach to the innovative process, the competitive advantages of small and medium-sized firms seem to depend on the extension and quality of the network of relations that they can establish with other firms and with the centres of research and innovation.'[8]

Complementarity of skills, diversity of know-how and speed of adjustment are nowadays the surest proof of an industrial enterprise's competitiveness. The practice of co-operation forms an essential part of this. In this respect, as in most others, experience gained is a positive factor in a firm's efficiency and here again Italy boasts a centuries-old tradition.

Local production systems motivate co-operative practices

There are today around 100 'area-systems' spread over the whole of the national territory with, however, a marked preponderance in the north of the country.[9] A characteristic of these 'localisms' is the concentration of small and medium-sized firms, both industrial and non-industrial, which have emerged: highly specialized, cost-effective and able to benefit from the flexibility of wealth-creating structures and imagination. In some cases their origins are ancient, harking back to the Renaissance or even to the Middle Ages. The following are the more renowned examples, famous in both Italy and abroad: Prato for wool textiles, Brianza for furniture, Como for silk, Pescia for floriculture, Venice for glass, Vicenza and Arezzo for goldsmiths, Modena for the agricultural foodstuffs sector, ceramics and engineering (more recently, biotechnology and graphic arts), the Apuanian area (Carrara) for the production of marble, the Ferenano area for footwear and clothing, the Perousa region for fashion and food industry, the Solofra centre for tanning, leatherwork and currying. Apart from the diversity due to local or historic factors, these local systems of production have a number of features in common:

- A very pronounced product specialization on items fundamental to the economy of the area concerned.
- An industrial development aimed at those sectors, technologies and types of product where the small size of firms is an advantage. The industry will prefer to specialize in those products which maximize the profits to be made from the traditional craft skills already existing there: textiles, clothing, footwear, timber, furniture, metal goods, light engineering. These areas are not, however, limited to the traditional sectors; some of them are acquiring an increasingly high level of specialization in quality products, limited series production or tailor-made goods (manufacture of robots, for example).
- A mass of small and medium-sized firms: there is no market leader.
- The existence of a very close and very complex system of interdependence between local small and medium-sized firms.
- An extremely high spatial concentration of the product, with very many firms located within a limited area. Thus, the town of Carpi concentrates 2,000 clothing textile firms within an area of 30 square kilometres; the Prato system constitutes the greatest textile concentration in the world, with 60,000 people working there.

These local production systems constitute fertile soil for schooling in co-operative techniques, in productive and marketing interrelations between firms.

Apart from the flexibility of the productive system, other advantages may be credited to this type of specific socio-economic organization:

- increased productivity;
- great capacity for technological innovation;
- economies of scale within a field of activity;
- development of dense and complex information networks (the setting-up of inter-firm telematic systems), providing in particular for the transparency of the labour market and the subcontractors' loading schedules;
- a minimum waste of resources;
- high level of job interest, care given to quality.

It is, in fact, a developmental model which has maximized the profitable use of local resources (entrepreneurial ability, professionalism of locally trained workers, finance amassed locally, locally introduced innovative technology), making the best use of local specialities and thus providing routes for self-supporting development.

All this has occurred within a context of progressive integration into the world market, with an increase in the share of the product provided for this purpose. Careful attention is being paid at all levels to the approach of the single market.

The region: supporting and incubating entrepreneurial initiatives

The Italian local authorities, traditionally influential, have not distanced themselves from the growth of the private initiatives referred to above. On the contrary, they have accepted or even instigated it, especially in recent years when the growing complexity of events makes operations more risky, more difficult and thus in need of support.

The regional authorities quickly came to appreciate that a developed network of services is an indispensable complement to a dynamic production system. Regional service centres have therefore been deployed throughout Italy, both 'horizontal' (aimed at meeting needs common to all sectors of activity within a given economic area) and 'vertical' (designed to meet the specific requirements of a particular activity). Included in the first type are export assistance services, help with the financing for investments, and advisory services for company reorganizations; in the second case, branch analysis, product qualification constraints, surveys for the improvement of productive systems, joint research into materials, types of marketing, automation methods, disposal of toxic waste, reduction of harmful effects, vocational training courses (basic or refresher) and efforts aimed at promoting a management culture suited to modern times.

Certain areas, such as Lombardy, Emilia Romagna, Tuscany and Marche, have paid particular attention to the potential which the local economic system offers for the development of opportunities. At the end of the 1970s, Lombardy took the decision to give preference to the transfer of technology to small and medium-sized firms through technical assistance from the CESTEC centre. In Tuscany, the policy adopted has been to encourage and assist the local economic systems to organize themselves by providing the initial capital necessary for the formation of bodies of general interest, such as CESVIT in Florence (1986, for the transfer of new technologies); CESECA in Segromigno (1984, for the footwear industry); LUCENSE in Lucca (research centre for the local economy, formed in 1984); CSM, close to Siena (for the timber industry, formed in 1982); SPRINT in Prato (in 1984, for the textile industry). The Marche region gives preference to direct interventions, especially the setting-up of sectoral or intersectoral centres capable of supplying small firms with technical assistance and aids to innovation. Among these service centres are to be found, for example, ISELQUI (institute of electronics for industrial quality) in Ancona; COSMOB (furniture industry centre) in Pesaro; CEDIM (documentation centre for firms) in Ancona; and CESCAM (centre for the footwear industry) in Civitanova.

In Emilia Romagna, the ERVET regional development agency is particularly active. Located in Bologna, the city which founded the famous Aldini–Valeriani institute for technical education in the nineteenth century, its function is to effect transfers of technology via the school.[10] In Bologna, the regional development finance company has created an impressive network of computerized services, offered to firms at cost price. These vary widely and include data banks, training courses, studies into the dissemination of new technology, market research, surveys of the effect of new production processes, strategy advice, etc. Advice is given through specialist sectoral centres, for ceramics, shoes, agricultural machines, textiles, etc., through multisectoral centres, e.g. for metalworking and organization of subcontracting in this field; and through horizontal centres, for methods of internationalization and financial assistance, for example.

All the other Italian regions have gradually followed the example of the protagonists, encouraging in a multitude of ways the dissemination of modern production techniques, the effects of inter-firm synergy and intra-regional co-operative activities as well as inter-regional and international ones. The European multinationals undoubtedly represent a catalyst for development, a significant driving force. The Italian regions have consequently realized that they cannot limit themselves to the stimulation of local economic vigour but that they also have a mission to encourage the quality of the international research/product/service networks. The 'diaspora' of expatriate Italians scattered throughout the world for more than a century, the footholds they have gained in Europe and, especially, in America, help to direct public policies towards a strong network economy.

Notes

1 European Commission, *Bulletin*, no. 3, 1988.
2 OECD, *Innovation in the SMEs*, OECD, Paris, 1982, p. 26.
3 Institut Français d'Opinion Publique survey (April/May 1990) of 500 company heads, extract in the *Technical Progress Letter*, no. 57/58, August 1990, p. 1.
4 Commission of the European Communities, 'Standard Contracts Applicable to Technological Research and Development Activities in the Community' (DG XII), October 1988.
5 See S. Urban and E. M. Lipp, *L'Allemagne, une économie gagnante?*, Hatier, Paris, 1988.
6 A well-researched analysis has been made by H. O. Eglau, author of a work entitled *Wie Gott in Frankfurt: Die Deutsche Bank und die deutsche Industrie*, ECON Verlag, Düsseldorf, 1990.
7 Claudio Tolomelli, 'Programmes et projets industriels des régions italiennes', in *Politiques et stratégies industrielles en Europe*, Ministère de l'Industrie/OSI, Paris, p. 47.
8 Ibid., p. 49.
9 Instituto Nazionale per il Commercio Estero, *L'Italie et ses économies locales*, Editiones Marsilio, Rome, 1989.
10 See D. Blondel, *L'innovation pour le meilleur et pour let pire*, Hatier, Paris, 1990, pp. 170, 171.

General Conclusions

The setting up of the European single market, the progressive expansion of markets to a worldwide scale, economic developments, reciprocal or compensatory practices – all impose on the majority of firms, regardless of their size, the need to adapt rapidly. The rules of the economic game have been profoundly altered; we have gone beyond marginal adjustments and whole strategies must be reviewed.

The Europe of 1992 is an opportunity to be seized. The integration process could enable the European area to combat a relative decline and experience a new Renaissance, fostered by a solidarity bolstered up by vigorous cross-trading and investment, as well as by fertile innovation. One answer to the challenges which are being issued is to organize new kinds of relations between firms in order to limit the effects of aggravated, unstable and suicidal competition. Inter-firm co-operative agreements are an expression of this essential evolution in the ways of thinking and methods of management.

It has been demonstrated that in this way it is possible to improve the competitiveness of firms at the level of their field of activities, at the level of one of their functional capabilities or at the general level of the coherence of their portfolio of activities. A firm is no longer a homogeneous entity, directed from the centre using line and staff command and control procedures. It has become an organization both more complex and more flexible, in which points of negotiation and decentralized creation meet, a flexible network of discrete skills and aptitudes. Both intra- and inter-firm co-operative relations are moving in the general direction of a separation of the powers of capital and of management. New styles of economic and corporate operation are being introduced, based on new alliances. Competition is taking place between firms, between nations and, more and more, between networks of firms linked by ties of complementarity which do not necessarily take the form of a very costly participation in equity capital. It is more a matter of co-operative alliances uniting associates who pool their diverse resources, and a mutual confidence.

But it is on precisely these points that co-operative alliances are in danger of falling down. A poorly negotiated or badly assessed sharing of advantages and risks will lead to failure and may result in new, subtle and formidable kinds of domination. There are pitfalls in co-operation which one must be aware of in order to avoid them. The effectiveness of the partnership implies a minimum of equilibrium between the protagonists. The mutual interests of the parties must be protected, and they can be, under certain circumstances. A well-planned, well-executed co-operation agreement can be a passport to genuine mutual success.

Index

Compiled by Jackie McDermott